YO-YO DIPLOMACY

TOM PLATE
ON ASIA

AN AMERICAN COLUMNIST TACKLES
THE UPS-AND-DOWNS BETWEEN
CHINA AND THE US

 **Marshall Cavendish** Editions

All columns published in this book originally appeared on an exclusive first-use basis in the South China Morning Post, with the copyright reverting to the author Thomas Gordon Plate.

Cover photo of Tom Plate by Harvey Keys • Illustrations by Craig Stephens

Published by Marshall Cavendish Editions
An imprint of Marshall Cavendish International

A member of the
Times Publishing Group

Other Marshall Cavendish Offices:
Marshall Cavendish Corporation. 99 White Plains Road, Tarrytown NY 10591-9001, USA • Marshall Cavendish International (Thailand) Co Ltd. 253 Asoke, 12th Flr, Sukhumvit 21 Road, Klongtoey Nua, Wattana, Bangkok 10110, Thailand • Marshall Cavendish (Malaysia) Sdn Bhd, Times Subang, Lot 46, Subang Hi-Tech Industrial Park, Batu Tiga, 40000 Shah Alam, Selangor Darul Ehsan, Malaysia

Marshall Cavendish is a registered trademark of Times Publishing Limited

National Library Board, Singapore Cataloguing-in-Publication Data

Name(s): Plate, Tom.
Title: Yo-Yo diplomacy : an American columnist tackles the ups-and-downs between China and the US / Tom Plate.
Other title(s): Tom Plate on Asia.
Description: Singapore : Marshall Cavendish Editions, [2017]
Identifier(s): OCN 987419084 | ISBN 978-981-4751-43-8 (paperback)
Subject(s): LCSH: China—Foreign relations—United States. | United States—Foreign relations—China.
Classification: DDC 327.51073—dc23

Printed in Singapore by Markono Print Media Pte Ltd

To Maximus Pierce Keys,
our first grandchild,
fabulously born July 2017 of
Mr and Mrs Ashley and Sam Keys

CONTENTS

FOREWORD BY GEORGE YEO   9

INTRODUCTION   11

Integrity and Truth • Two Halves Make a Whole •
Yo-Yo Diplomacy • Peace Column • Responsibility to
Protect • The Profession of Rush Hours • No Delayed
Reactions • China Syndromes • Self-Brain Washing
• Binary Baloney • Beijing Consensus • The Tightrope
of Reality • The Quest for Certainty • Theory of the
Two Suns • Make Room for Beijing • World Domination
• The Principle of Hope • A Glint of Evil • A West Coast
Policy Toward China

01   Zhu Rongji's light touch is
sorely missing in today's China   47

02   China and the US must include Japan
in talks on security of East Asia   52

03   Western media's callous delight at China's
stock market crash is totally uncalled for   57

04   China needs to deploy a more silken
touch with its neighbours   62

05   Common sense and patience needed as
US election fever fans Americans' fears about China   67

06   Amid the economic and political storms, China and
the US must realise they are inextricably bound together   72

07   Why should the world fear a powerful Xi Jinping?   77

08   Ruling party's resounding win in Singapore
elections reflects the success of its political model   82

09   Of dinners and deals: the different diplomatic styles of
China and the US make negotiation all the more necessary   87

10   Slow and steady is how China is
liberalising the renminbi – as it should   92

11   Dealing with China's rise: US should learn
from the British the art of the deal   97

12   In deal-making, handshaking Xi Jinping,
China finds a new face of smart diplomacy   102

13   The beauty of restraint in the South China Sea   107

14   US presidential candidates' missteps on China a
worrying reminder of America's international ignorance   112

15   For good Sino-US relations, the Americans must learn
to listen, while the Chinese must learn to talk   117

16   Why Xi Jinping remains an international man
of mystery to most in the US   121

17   Why the case of the Hong Kong booksellers
is more of a worry than China's market woes   126

18   The rich history of mistrust behind China's
warning to George Soros   131

19   When it comes to China, and US foreign policy
in general, Bernie Sanders needs all the help he can get,
including from Henry Kissinger!   136

20 In the end, Pope Francis' 'kowtow diplomacy' towards China will show itself to be smart diplomacy 141

21 If it cares about its global standing, China should allay concerns about Hong Kong's missing booksellers 146

22 Why the Chinese are so territorial about the South China Sea 151

23 Don't be too quick to write off China's future based on a partial view of Xi Jinping's leadership 156

24 How a little-known chapter in Sino-US cooperation may have helped save the planet 161

25 Anyone but Hillary? Why that's not China's best bet in the US presidential election 166

26 Can China lead the world on reducing the threat of nuclear war? 171

27 Why the world needs boring but effective leaders like Hu Jintao, rather than trumpeting swans and political peacocks 178

28 Let's hope the Hong Kong bookseller saga does not mean the end of 'one country, two systems' 180

29 Xi Jinping, the champion of Marxism, may find unlikely comrades in critics of Western capitalism 185

30 Beijing may have lost the court case, but it still rules the South China Sea 190

31 China against the world: A tale of pride and prejudice 195

32   'Blame it all on China' – US and Britain playing a dangerous game with turn to scapegoating   200

33   The Singapore political system may prove a difficult model for China, whatever the West thinks   204

34   Why 'macho' Putin has the lead over Xi when it comes to American minds   209

35   US and China need more soft power, not military hardware, to resolve their differences   213

36   The constant gardener: why the US needs to stick to its time-tested role in Asia   218

37   Duterte's 'pivot' to China offers a reminder that all Asian diplomacy should be guided by subtlety and care   223

38   How China and the US are spooking each other with their politics   228

39   We stick labels on China – or the US – at our own peril   232

40   One phone call won't change US policy on Taiwan – or relations with China   236

41   Underwater drone spat shows why China-US relations are tense – and can only get worse under Trump   241

42   China can lead in 2017, even as a slowing economy tests its grip on domestic stability   246

43   China should beware the trap set by 'dumb Trump'   251

44   Trump comes up short – for better and for worse!   256

45 With hawkish Navarro as US trade tsar,
it's up to China to show diplomatic restraint   261

46 Trump needs to get smart as North Korea
keeps up 'missile diplomacy'   266

47 Why China should reach out to the US
to counter Kim Jong-un   271

48 Think again, Beijing: Carrie Lam is the wrong person
to lead Hong Kong out of the political storm   276

49 How the Xi-Trump summit can rebuild Sino-US trust
and bring stability to the Korean peninsula   281

50 Why the US needs China to succeed, and vice versa   286

BIBLIOGRAPHY   292

INDEX   295

GIVING THANKS   308

ABOUT THE AUTHOR   311

FOREWORD
BY GEORGE YEO

Over the years I've known Tom Plate, he has been constantly reinventing himself. One day, many years ago, he came to my office in Singapore and did a one-man video interview with me using his new Sony video camera. I watched with admiration how he set up the cute little tripod, mounted the palm-sized camera professionally and then proceeded to record the session. On another occasion, he sported a completely different hairstyle with matching eyewear which made me wonder whether he was going through a mid-life crisis.

He developed a keen interest in China very early in his career and took care never simply to follow the crowd. Wisely deciding not to accompany a huge gaggle of American journalists rushing to China to cover a historic US presidential visit, he went to Taipei instead to cover the same story from a refreshingly different perspective.

He affects not to take himself seriously, which is his charm. He disarms you by immediately confessing his ignorance. In this way, he skilfully gathers information from a wide range of sources. His style is perhaps particularly well-suited to an Asian environment. He rarely puts on the show of scepticism which many Western journalists display with furrowed brows as part of their craft. When he thinks something is justified, he is prepared to show enthusiasm and shower praise. He is critical without being nasty.

Tom Plate's columns in the South China Morning Post have been well-received. In Hong Kong, I often hear comments that he is an atypical American commentator of Asian affairs. He is less wont to judge China and other Asian countries as if they were all falling short of Western standards. He was politically incorrect before political incorrectness became fashionable, and remains so. He is neither a China watcher nor a China scholar, but he has a sense of China. More importantly, he has what is not in common supply — common sense. He also has one admirable persistent motivation, which is to encourage diverse communities around the Pacific Lake to live together in harmony.

All this makes Tom Plate worth reading even when we don't agree with him, which is not often. He presents to the Western reader a view of China and Asia that is in short supply.

George Yeo is the former foreign minister of Singapore (2004–2011). Previously, he served in various ministries, including the Ministry of Finance, Ministry of Health and Ministry of Trade and Industry. He is now chairman of Kerry Logistics Network and a member of the Foundation Board of the World Economic Forum.

INTRODUCTION

INTEGRITY AND TRUTH

Analytically, this is what the book is about: a practising American journalist aiming to make the case that war with China is anything but inevitable, and that the unthinkable might happen unless the good people on both sides of the Pacific lock arms in peace and into coherent public-arena intellectual combat against insanity.

A central fact of our times is that China (a superpower trying to get its act together) and America (a superpower trying to keep it together) are baked into emotional and historical angst and substantive contemporary tension. But at the same time they are also totally baked into desperate mutual economic and strategic needs.

So what is the best way to unwrap this twirled-together fortune cookie, see what is inside, and put it back together in a way that adds to, rather than negates, a new world order?

Oh yes, there are good recent books about China ... you could probably spend a slice of your lifetime reading them all. In fact I have, and some of them are great efforts. In the back, a partial list of my campus office collection is recommended to you as to my university students. So it's not as if we don't have enough information or enough perspectives.

But maybe what we face is a measure of information overload — combined with a measure of wisdom under-load as well? As many of these valuable works are by distinguished historians, political scientists and even lawyers, impressive as they are, it is sometimes difficult to see where you and I – the individual – fit in.

It always feels as if history is under the control of forces and people far above our heads. We seem irrelevant to the sometimes frightening, sometimes gripping China-US strategic drama.

In important respects, this can be said to apply to Chinese people on the mainland and in their diasporas around the world, as with Americans.

This book, written by a practicing journalist/newspaper columnist who is also a Prof at a university in Los Angeles, will try to bring it all down to earth. Forget what the leaders of China and America (or their respective foreign-affairs advisers) think of the relationship, what do we (you and I) think? What should we think? What is our moral obligation to think, even if we're not so-called "leaders"?

Or maybe we are leaders.

See if this slightly complicated thought by a true deep thinker on my university campus works as well for you as well as it does for me:

"We are all leaders when we choose to live according to the values of integrity and truth. These values bind us up together in mission and enable us to overcome fear-causing ideas that are projected upon us. In our good-willed attempts to move beyond the anxiety or confusion that arises from what we hear and read as 'news', each of us can ask ourselves: 'Who – or what grounds me – in my personal desire to uphold my values?' The answers to our reflections empower us to act with and for others."

This fine thinking comes from the mind of Fr. Randy Roche, S.J., Director, Centre for Ignatian Spirituality at Loyola Marymount, the US West Coast university where I teach, and it begins this book because it is so insightful and moving and – really – different. His thought is meant for all of us (you – whoever you are, in whatever country – and, in the case of this book, for me, the journalist still careering while teaching and trying to work through the gnarled and gnarly China-US relationship).

The suggestion here is that we look inside ourselves first, well before looking outside ourselves in a search for answers or for certainty, or for good and evil.

This thought was sent to our faculty by Fr. Roche for a number of reasons, none particularly related to China-US; but with the lack of reverence for which I am known, I stole and privatised the Jesuit's message to purpose this book as a personal guide to an individual's thinking about America and China, rather than as some tendentious tablet of policy prescriptions with which you must agree.

It is more for you – the intelligent, caring citizen – than for the genuine specialist, not to mention the all-knowing and perhaps somewhat dogmatic expert. It is a set of thoughts, not an ideological platform. It is a book for peace, not a book for war. It respects China, and will not demonise it. It respects the US, but will not canonise it.

TWO HALVES MAKE A WHOLE

The book was written over a span of two years and comes to you in halves that are quite different.

Further on, the second half (the columns) presents my fortnightly thoughts, over a two-year span, on the bilateral relationship, such as I had been able to sculpt into "Insight" essays every other Tuesday in an English-language newspaper in East Asia. Since June 2015, there have been 50 such columns in that very good newspaper, and they comprise this book's latter half, with substantive post-publication observations to update intent and add retrospective.

That publication is the South China Morning Post, out of pivotal Hong Kong.

Founded in 1903, headquartered in Hong Kong, and now owned by the giant Alibaba Group after a succession of owners, including the Kuok Group and at one time the Rupert Murdoch empire, this newspaper has served history decade after decade as an essential and unbreakable bridge between East and West, offering timely reports and observations not only about one of the greatest cities in the world, but also about its perspectives given its unique proximity to the world's most populous, historically riven and psychologically driven nation: China.

Despite the general opening of the modernizing mainland to the outside world after the Mao era, Hong Kong still offers a perch of special perspective. Now formally a special administrative region of China, its sovereign since 1997 after long British rule, Hong Kong's media nonetheless operate under the territory's local law rather than the national law of Beijing. And so the South China Morning Post, Hong Kong's leading English-language newspaper, owner after new owner, rolls along, doing its greatly admired thing, remaining a rightly respected newspaper and one of the world's best-known media brands.

Criticisms of changes on the paper's ideological tonality and allegations of the loss of total journalistic objectivity (which exists nowhere) are neither surprising nor upsetting. But they may be misconceived. Newspapers that do not change will surely die. I agree with an observation by Joseph Tsau, executive vice-chairman of Alibaba Group: "We think the world needs a plurality of views when it comes to China coverage. China's rise as an economic power and its importance to world stability is too important for there to be a singular thesis."

How can this be wrong? By US standards, my own columns tend

to be rated as "Beijing-friendly". But by Asian standards, they tend to be viewed as balanced. What you see depends on where you sit, right?

As for the editing of my columns, you need to know this: every one has been published in whole by the SCMP, all with a calibre of collegial overview that has proven at least the quality-equal to what my columns received when appearing in the Los Angeles Times, their birthplace, or in any other newspaper anywhere afterwards.

The first half of this book – again, where you are now – will offer a collection of interrelated thoughts that have percolated over the past two years, in the wake of decades of newspaper journalism about Asia and America in various newspapers. The aim is to help us "… move beyond the anxiety or confusion that arises from what we hear and read as 'news'." As journalists, professors and citizens, "we are all leaders when we choose to live according to the values of integrity and truth."

Not a bad way to start, don't you think? We need to be guided by integrity and truth, not only if we happen to be journalists but, as importantly, as citizens of this planet.

YO-YO DIPLOMACY

One day it seems warm, civilised; the next week it's anything but. One month the feel of the bilateral relationship is akin to the long-gone Cold War with the Soviet Union; two months later, clouds darken and it feels as if a big black ugly gathering storm is coming down on your head; and then – something positive happens and you have the feeling of No War, Ever – we love China and Chinese people and they love us too.

This is yo-yo syndrome in the US-China relationship. Up and down, down and up, around and around, and nobody knows where and when the yo-yo will stop.

This became the book's title. Up and down go our emotions,

deepest worries waxing and waning, tension ever present but hope mysteriously hanging around as well.

Some China experts will tut-tut, perhaps partly rightly, about the yo-yo metaphor. It is indeed a rank simplification. It might be read to depict China and the US as two coherent bodies, gym-toned prize fighters in the championship ring going at it; or, going the other way, as two love birds longingly cooing from touchingly adjacent cages; or even – my fear – as a pair of idiot yo-yos edging us toward the apocalypse.

The whole reality of China and the US is an odd-couple relationship. As my colleague and fellow Pacific Century Institute board member Donald Gregg properly notes, the very words "China" and the "US" are huge umbrella terms for a maze of different, competing or cooperating – or both – sectors and forces and various interests of government or vested economic interests. Think not of a pair of slender and gym-toughened prize fighters but two complex and sometimes unfathomable celestial universes hovering in uneasy but geopolitically fixed positions.

Yo-yo suggests two for the tango or for the tangle – no more.

But the bilateral relationship is no simple yo-yo, further explains Don Gregg, who, among other achievements in his illustrious life, was deputy national security adviser under former George W. H. Bush Sr. In reality, it is a constantly roiling ocean beneath which powerful and sometimes dark forces of great power push and heave, churning up potential violence … but also sometimes leaving us with a placid surface no more violent than a great lake, if deep of depth in periodic repose.

Yet, for the cover of this book, the title is *Yo-Yo Diplomacy*, a surface moniker for sure and without apology – but serving the purpose of introducing the theme. Which is to say: sometimes it seems as if China-US relations are absolutely in a yo-yo state, endless up and down pistons, as if in a bad marriage into which both sides are stuck – ready for yet another post-quarrel reconciliation with the unspoken understanding that life without one another is unimaginable.

This is the yo-yo of our times.

Oh, one more aspect of yo-yo terminology: sometimes it seems as if the bilateral relationship is in the hands of officials and generals and politicians and influential journalists who are ... I hate to say it ... absolute *yo-yos*.

PEACE COLUMN

Call me an idealist or even a wild-eyed optimist or whatever you want, but realistically, neither China nor the US will ever invade the sovereign territory of the other.

Let us begin with that. Let both sides keep this in mind. It is bottom-line important.

It is never going to happen. Such atavistic adventurism would be, by far, more nonsensical than China's forays into Vietnam or America's into Iraq.

And yet some stubbornly insist that war with China is in effect inevitable. Why? There is a no valid moral reason, of any ideological or geopolitical gravity, to justify war – or any broadly significant military clash – between China and the US.

War would be an immoral maelstrom and a deep stupidity. The plunge into blackness would allow room for no side to be able to say its reasoning was more legitimate than the other's. There could be no just war at all as both would be morally guilty of endangering the world, not to mention their own existences.

Both governments would have shown as incompetent their military and foreign policies. And both proud militaries would end up substantially decimated, if not worse, even if the tragic and foolish conflict somehow stayed non-nuclear.

This book's hope is to make a small contribution to convince the Chinese and Americans alike to lean in the opposite direction, to think of peace not war, and to distrust fiercely the ideologues and warmongers, on both sides of the Pacific – the "inevitable" crowd.

Stupidity and its twin pal war are not inevitable. Enduring peace and plus a high level of cooperation between the two superpowers is the only intelligent option if the species itself is not to be endangered by the highest known level of insane international non-cooperation conceivable: nuclear war.

RESPONSIBILITY TO PROTECT

When it comes to China, journalists as well as government and military officials have a responsibility to exercise the utmost care and responsible judgment. To my mind, even blithe predictions of a war-conflict are nearly as morally reprehensible as arguments justifying war, as if such could be in either's true national interest.

The fate of the earth depends on these two gigantic powers, with their nuclear arsenals, operating at the highest exposition of best global practices. Scare literature – out of whatever misguided inspiration, ideological idealism or sheer malignity – is not the proper business of journalism or of the press. It is deplorable and must be condemned – always – as well as bravely fought.

The high calling of the journalist is to help foster, by her or his own good work, the most intelligent reportage so as to illuminate common interests and visionary co-responsibilities – not to fire up anew the embers of over-heated and over-reported differences.

This is not to pretend to sainthood, but surly there is humanitarian value in trying to avoid doing the evil of the devil. Make no mistake about it: war, except in purely existential circumstances, is evil. Ask anyone who has been involved in war.

Sure, absolutely – the views of warmongers need to be evaluated with a cool and level head; but conflict conspirators need to be deprived of credibility to the extent possible through the powerful forces of reasonable scorn and immaculate scholarship. In part – small or large, who knows? – the fate of the earth may depend on peace journalism out-weighing war journalism. This is what is at stake.

Public opinion is often minimised as at best soft power. It can be much more. United, it can be a epochal force to slow the warmongers, even push them back, helping to keep war from coming together in fusion. Conversely, united in a passion for war, feral public opinion can push our over-nuclearised planet over the edge and down like a falling planet into the abyss of doomsday.

Journalists are a key driver of public opinion. In a sense their collective finger is on the nuclear trigger too. So the responsibility to protect the public – and our future – is in the hands of the media as much, perhaps, as any other single driver.

THE PROFESSION OF RUSH HOURS

By its very nature journalism is imperfect, even if some journalists believe they are all but perfect.

The sheer speed of journalism can be the enemy of balance and perspective. The conditions of journalism can be as exasperating as they are thrilling. It sometimes breaks my heart that the journalist is rarely permitted by the definitional nature of his work to slow down, to measure the event or development or personality with an almost religious ritual of detail and precision.

But that is the life – and the profession of the rush hour. We have to do it *now*.

We try to get it right but – little surprise – we can sometimes get it wrong. China is easily one of the most difficult of substantive challenges and "current-events" issues to get right. I know – I have tried and I am still trying and I won't ever give up. You can't give up. (*You may well have been wrong with that last column, Tom – so try harder next time.*)

Any prediction or even general sense of direction about what will happen in the future that has to be announced in the immediacy of the moment is inherently a hazardous way of making a living. But this is what journalism does and is.

My university history-department colleagues say they cannot possibly imagine what it must be like to be a journalist, where edgy timeliness is of the essence. I agree and tell them that the pressure of time can be almost unimaginably repressive (but also, frankly, thrilling in the intellectual pressure of the challenge). They shake their head – and walk away and continue with their discussions of the origins of … the First World War … or of the Hundred Years … or the Peloponnesian. What bliss – *for them.*

Still, professional academics, especially my history and social science colleagues, might also tell you that even their work is somewhat time-tentative, in a sense. They too struggle with realities not entirely settled. New data surface to undermine old assumptions. A forgotten trove falls off the top of an archive shelf and shatters a paradigm. A new and more accurate translation of a revered canonical document raises serious doubts about long-assumed narratives.

But yet, the comparison is not wholly right either: academic work is to journalism as Beethoven is to Beyonce. The latter is for now; the former is for eternity. (But maybe in 100 years more humans will be entranced by Beyonce than Beethoven? Hmm… probably not.)

Haste can indeed make waste. Government work itself offers

ample examples. Like journalists, officials sometimes must make quick decisions based on the available (and less than complete) evidence. And, like journalists, they sometimes get it wrong. The only logical procedural alternative would be to delay making decisions; but then in many instances you might have lost timeliness beyond the point of efficacy. This too is a mistake common to the profession of government, as journalism.

The need for speed can become an addiction, of course. Psychologists might tell you that journalists as a class of "patients" tend to require almost pathological instant gratification, reflecting a kind of infantile narcissism – as if a version of candy in mouth along with thumb! And the diagnosis may be correct. I, for one, admit it.

NO DELAYED REACTIONS

No journalist can ever be "right" with a story if the article misses the deadline and is "late", or is in any way substantially dated or lacks currency. Time is – yes – of the essence.

If last week's newspaper on the coffee table appears terribly "old", that perhaps is a sign that it is a very good and timely newspaper indeed. Take a look at the LIFE magazines of the 1930s and 1940s in a library archive. They seem older than rare wine, but at the time of their publication they were as fresh and lively as the latest Beaujolais.

Is anything older than yesterday's tweets?

The true journalist constantly worries – because speed does kill, as well as win races. Surface ships do move more rapidly than submarines, but they lack depth. Does anyone really care? The best editors and news people do. One of my greatest mentors was the late David Laventhol, the founder of modern Newsday, the Long Island and New York newspaper; and at the end of his career the publisher of the Los Angeles Times. In his time he was easily one of the world's most thoughtful of American media leaders.

David tried to impress on his young charges that journalism needed to prove itself not only "quick" but "deep". Without a measure of depth, it would prove too transient and thin to matter; without the quality of timeliness, it would prove irrelevant – not be noticed in proper time.

Like some other notable figures in the world of letters and publishing – but perhaps too few in US newspapers – Dave studied at a great university, Yale. Unlike for a doctor or a social worker, there are no minimum educational requirements, much less continuing-education requirements, for the American journalist. Many top journalists are well aware of this and do go to great lengths to acquire, on top of their basic undergraduate education, a professional degree or even a PhD, or a new language.

Only the well-prepared journalist, he felt, would possess the ken and the zen to interpret the historical moment with efficacy – and so arose the mantra of "quick but deep".

This is not by any means easy to pull off, but in political and international journalism, there is no Plan B. Consider the riveting ruminations of Chinese author Yang Jisheng, in acknowledging an award from the august Neiman Foundation at Harvard University. Acceding to the need for modesty when entering the twilight zone of issues that seem impossible to solve, Yang said: "[Ours] is an unfathomable profession; while journalists are not scholars, they're required to study and gain a comprehensive grasp of society. Any journalist, no matter how erudite and insightful, will feel unequal to the task of decoding this complex and ever-changing society."

I always have, I always do. But we have to keep trying. Sometimes it is really important – as with the case of China. Surely no one needs an advanced degree to know that.

CHINA SYNDROMES

There are serious differences of opinion among observers of contemporary China as to whether this amazing geopolitical phenomenon is *sui generis* ("something entirely unlike anything else") – or simply a vaster but still mundane glandular nation ("no, we've seen it all before").

The "special view" insists that, with something of the order of 5,000 years of history, and a beehive of 1.4 billion people within its borders buzzing around as busy workers, China cannot rationally be viewed as Just Another (If Very Large) Nation.

That would be characterising China as little more than a lumped-together totality of 240 Singapores (a snugly compact and successful nation of 5 million-plus people). One shudders in mild shock and no awe over the lack of insight.

Almost any rounded, reasoned view of China will risk criticism for perceived moral laxity in its propensity to plea-bargain down this gigantic nation's serious sins (as adjudged by the West, always entirely virtuous, of course, and indeed by critics on the mainland itself) from murderous felonies to mere misdemeanours.

There may be some validity to the exculpation charge of excessive empathy, but it is a relatively small transgression or risk if you compare it to the opposite tendency, which is to blame the Chinese government in as many ways as possible for things that go wrong (US trade problems, etc. etc.); to condemn its ruling Communist Party as if it were the second coming of the Devil, when without its centralising and networking force China would come apart like a hundred Yugoslavias; and to tend to interpret China's every thought as ill-intentioned and its every other external move as propelled by a premeditated malevolence for global domination.

Understanding China properly and fairly will take more than

defaulting to intellectually flabby binary moralism and knee-jerk worst-case hypotheses.

Yes, China is "saddled" with Communism – certainly in the sense that its political system garners scant overall respect in Western circles outside of a few cafés on a few boulevards on Paris' Left Bank, and perhaps in a handful of Western university faculty reading rooms.

In the US especially, China's political system remains a reviled one, even though by any measure its performance in economic-development leadership probably rivals the growth achievement of any political system known to history. Yet it is deemed so deficient in its human-rights observance, its respect for religions and many other kinds of fair-playing norms that it gets no respect at all.

Where is the balance in that?

By comparison liberal capitalism, until recently anyway, gets higher marks in all categories, almost by default or ideology, rather than by comprehensive and non-parochial evaluation.

If the infantile black-and-white view above were fair and balanced, when in fact it is absurd and parochial, it might do as the roughest of guidebooks to Communist China. But instead of serving to help us understand this giant nation, it creates a fog of ideology that impedes an understanding of its motives, psychology and strategy.

Every 10 years or so we should all go for a healthy ideology wash and re-read our J. William Fulbright, particularly his 1966 book *The Arrogance of Power*. The then chairman of the Senate Foreign Relations Committee shows that the fierce and heroic Vietnam pushback against first France – and then the United States – was not the backlash so much of militant communism as of nationalism in a communist wrapper.

And so today, understanding China makes it urgent that we understand China on its own terms, across the extraordinary sweep of millennia, without obsessing on the relatively recent European ideological overlay that is formally called communism. We must not wind up making the same mistake as we did in Vietnam: to misapprehend what we are dealing with, and thus to give hasty, inappropriate, irrational and self-corroding responses.

SELF-BRAIN WASHING

Ideology works like those trendy, easy-to-use virtual-reality goggles. You slip them on not to take in what is Out There, but rather what you have purposely programmed to orbit round-and-round inside your head. Why not? Escapism is fun.

But while the selected entertainment can be comforting, virtual reality, for all its techno-wow-and-know-how, cannot tell you about true reality. Worse yet, it may somehow lead you to believe that what you are seeing is the truth, and what your brain may come to believe is the truth, if you re-play the same programme over and over, searing into your head embedded brain-muscle memories that trigger cycles of self-brain washing that spares us the need to see and think for ourselves.

At its worst, our news media in its total impact tends to work in virtual-reality mode. Rather than emphasise the presentation of the new – in the sense of fresh information or new perspectives – it will tend to recycle re-runs, re-heat slightly different versions of previously presented "realities" and interpretations thereof that have been programmed before. Often enough, the so-called "news cycle" is not much more than a process of recycling old or warmed-over news.

Blind anti-communism is one obvious political ideology used to colourise the goggles with which some "view" China. Ethnic hatred against Chinese people is another. They are not the only filters. Others are subtle, and perhaps even less conscious or intentional; but they infect the perception of what is Out There. The path to reality that we seek to understand "passes inevitably through the dense and dark forest of the assumptions and desires that the researcher carries with him", the legendary historian Eric Hobsbawn has written. "We approach our work not as pure minds but as men and women educated in a particular context, in such and such a society, in a specific part of the globe, at a given point in history."

Like fly paper, our minds may wind up embedded with more bugs than truths.

BINARY BALONEY

Beijing Consensus versus Washington Consensus.
Asian Values versus Western Values.
Absolute Good versus Absolute Evil.

If we were to substitute the People's Republic of China for the late Union of Soviet Socialist Republics, with the understanding that the USSR was the ultimate "evil empire" incarnate, then the logical inference is that the PRC is the new big evil.

This example reflects one of two tendencies that blur or confuse perception.

One is the obvious inclination to demonise "the other" – people, political systems or religions that are different from the observer's. This syndrome is familiar and you have heard of this and observed it many times over. Others think this way about us; and we think such-and-such about "them". No sensible middle ground or cultural overlap is conceivable.

What is less obvious is the epidemic of all sorts of hidden biases, even in our best professional efforts to make "objective" comparisons and assessments.

A study by RAND once examined 27 different forecasts of the

economic growth of China as compared to India. The resulting predictions were varied, in part because of the difficulty in making such complex forecasts, but also because one methodological bias or another tainted every one of the forecasts – each bias driven by the nature of the professional discipline making the forecast, not by intended evil.

Forecasts by business groups, for example, factored in heavily the comparative regulatory climates and property-right protections. Forecasts by academic institutions or groups were influenced by a favourable view of government intervention and central planning – factors that other studies ignored. Studies by international institutions were prone to give great weight to improvements (or lack thereof) in the nation's educational system and social reforms.

There is absolutely nothing wrong – and there is a great deal of merit – in including all of these factors, as well as any others of value. But not one study managed to factor all of them into the equation in an objectively balanced and clear-headed way. Each and every conclusion was the product of a model that may been sophisticated but was not all-inclusive. No wonder at the end of all these studies, the conclusions of the China versus India prognoses varied widely.

This is the case with almost all such projections – the outcome is determined not just by the data that is inputted but also by the formula that processes and weighs that data.

This is true of even the best thought-out social science studies at our best universities and think tanks. Our minds are invariably coloured by those factors that weigh most heavily on them and/or by the sheer absence of factors that should be weighing more heavily. Any sort of formulaic or algorithmic approach cannot be unbiased because of all the factors that could be included, including the human factor.

Imagining China today as if it were a Soviet Union Redux (as many Americans do) is perilous for many reasons, not least because of the pat presumption that the past is much like the present. Yes it is; but then again, it isn't. This is a tough issue even for our greatest historians, and reminds me of the reflection by Eric Hobsbawn about reconstructing something as singular as our own life: "Finding one's earlier self is to reconstruct a buried stranger... even one's own past is a foreign country."

Consistently capturing in some objective way a phenomenon as complex and dynamic as the China of 1.4 billion people – and their million problems – is impossible. Our judgments about the Chinese – and indeed theirs about us – need to be arrived at with great care and consummate mutual humility. We would be utterly irresponsible to operate otherwise.

Simplistic binary thinking is the product of a lack of respect for the complexity of others and their world.

One nagging problem, of course, is we are all guilty of the binary conceit, to one degree or other – including, and perhaps especially, the American journalist. I, for one, am hardly sinless. But more than ever these days, I am trying to see the world as it is (complex), rather than as we might like it to be (simple).

BEIJING CONSENSUS?

To me, it is foolish to imagine that the "Chinese model" of development is coherent and transportable enough to serve as a roadmap for other countries in their struggle to develop. But paranoid pessimists in the West believe exactly that.

They worry that the once triumphant "Washington Consensus" – which crashed like the Wall Street stock market in the winter of 2008–2009, triggering what Anatole Kaletsky described as "the intellectual equivalent of a nervous breakdown" – will be superseded by the so-called "Beijing Consensus". In other words, the return of binary thinking: If *we* are not the model, then *they* must be the model.

What exactly might that be?

It's not entirely clear but a key element would include a firm authoritarianism, certainly a system far from anything as remotely mushy as our messy American democracy (a reservation not so hard to understand, actually).

However, for the purpose of both clarity and subtlety, it is the case that not all authoritarianisms are equal.

One example of a kind of authoritarianism to which the West accords increasing credibility is that of the successful Republic of Singapore. Its system is often labelled "soft authoritarianism". International assessments often favour this small city-state, especially for its economic achievements, low level of corruption, professionalised government and educational excellence.

By contrast, an example of an unacceptable authoritarianism would be that of the Russian Federation.

So, where does Beijing fit into the political-export picture? In my view: nowhere.

The extraordinary Chinese experience is anything but a globally applicable, consensus-building phenomenon. Their history is unique, their culture is Confucian, and centralised rule is no stranger to China's history, whatever -ism it is called.

Every nation evolves from its own special background. Some start fast and morph into an empire. Some take their time. Others take forever – and some are still struggling to get it together and may never get anywhere.

Any nation that looks for secrets of success – or some developmental model – from the experience and track record of China, with its many admirable accomplishments but with more than a billion people and (still) a million problems, needs to have its head examined.

Even if Nation X were to wake up one morning and say – wow! Beijing's way is exactly the way for us – it would find the Beijing model very difficult to emulate. China itself struggles with its own Beijing "model" and is well aware of its deficiencies. After all … the Chinese "invented" it!

China's leaders, for whom growing inequality appears to be one extremely worrisome outcome of the Beijing blueprint, themselves often refer to an old Chinese proverb that "inequality, rather than want, is the cause of trouble".

One of America's great political economists, the late Charles Wolf Jr., once wrote of China: "Many an oligarch has lost his head after ignoring this point. With its vast geography, enormous population, rapid growth, and an increasing impossibility of [completely] limiting access to outside information, some observers believe China may be or may become a political tinderbox."

China's leaders have more than enough on their hands ensuring that the so-called Beijing Consensus remains the steady consensus even within Beijing before they'd dream of packaging it for prime-time export. Unlike some semi-hysterical Western commentators, its leaders sensibly try to keep their heads about them. Fear clouds thinking and creates nightmares in the mind that scramble reality, sometimes beyond reason.

Reason is our only hope for the future – and non-binary observing and thinking.

THE TIGHTROPE OF REALITY

Many Chinese believe their nation is the new big thing and the United States is the old big thing.

For their part, some, though not all, Americans tend to agree –

that the US is declining while China is rising. Paradoxically, both sides are only half-right, and that's the paradox of the current world order.

As Oscar Wilde puts it in *The Picture of Dorian Gray*: "The way of paradoxes is the way of truth. To test Reality we must see it on the tight-rope."

The tightrope is the Sino-US balance. China is rising, obviously, but a serious loss in overall economic ground speed could cause the giant superliner to stall. The impact of a crash will be devastating not just in surrounding Asia.

America is not declining (in my opinion) but surely is in a holding pattern; it appears to be falling only in contrast to China's obvious rise. The US flight path gets bumpier but overall manages to hover on a more or less level altitude.

But now when it flies it sees, for the first time since the 1980s, another superliner on a similar altitude.

Experts disagree when, if ever, China will "overtake" the US. That will not be tomorrow, surely: China's population is ageing while America's is constantly freshened by immigration. The two political systems are deeply flawed: the former often moves too rigidly under central command, and the latter often freezes up due to partisan and vested-interest fragmentation. In their own way, each system is both dysfunctional and at the same time inefficiently effective.

The consequences of China's "stall" and America's "stasis" would suck much of the life out of the global economic bloodstream. Neither Africa nor Latin American, even rising together, could pick up the slack and set right the bilateral collapse. It is thus in the interests of both China and the US to help each other survive so as many as possible can thrive, especially themselves.

This geopolitical idea for the future is not that widely shared in either country. The opposite view is more common. This means that both sides are in effect rooting for each to fail. This would amount to a doomsday machine – triggering world collapse, maybe even world war.

The truth of the Sino-US relationship is that it is on the tightrope of a tightly wound paradox. To prevent slipping off the tightrope, each is in desperate need for the other to succeed in maintaining their own balance. Instead of leading to war, the challenge of keeping their equipoise on the tense tightrope of mutual need can only deepen the peace.

It would help if both sides were to put their guns away and lock them in a cabinet. But, alas, it appears that we humans are not hard-wired to always choose the best option.

THE QUEST FOR CERTAINTY

In one of my university courses – "An Introduction to the Media and Politics of Asia" – in front of a classroom of undergraduates with little knowledge of Asia, when the giant subject of China comes up, I always try to simplify. Try to throw a dozen arcane geopolitical complexities at young-adult Americans, and you wind up turning them off and tuning them out faster than you can say Martin Heidegger.

The urge to explain the complex with the attractive qualities of clarity and simplicity is a risky business, of course. Often it fails. Nothing has failed as embarrassingly as economics, for example.

For centuries, economic theory has surpassed in mathematical refinement and reasoned rigour any of the social sciences, and yet has singularly failed us in vital ways. Chief among them has been its ineptitude in predicting serious economic crises so that we can minimise pain and suffering.

This, really, is both a moral as well as intellectual failure. It is as if modern medicine, for all that it costs, could not predict the probability of a disease in the presence of defining symptoms.

In his 2017 book *The End of Theory*, risk-manager guru/author Richard Bookstaber writes knowingly: "Economic theory asserts a level of consistency and rationality that not only leaves the cascades and propagation over the course of a crisis unexplained but also asserts they are unexplainable. Everything's rational, until it isn't; economics works, until it doesn't."

The disease of economic scientism is like a god that repeatedly fails us. Nonetheless, economists will evangelically seek to propagate the faith with formulaic gospels that would seem to make sense, except that in real life they do not.

One such believer in the possibility of pluperfect precise prediction was the otherwise modern-epoch economist, William Stanley Jevons. Though far superior in every sense to most of his contemporaries, the English mathematician fell in love with a pet theory that was to severely take a bite out of his overall credibility.

He believed that severe downturns or stomach-churning economic crisis were related to sunspot cycles, because of his conviction that economic science was a true sister/brother to natural science. Sunspot storm cycles had been pegged to last 11.11 years. If commercial downturns could be shown to similarly correlate, a true science of economic prediction would be established.

Jevons' problem was that, try as he and his researchers might, no data could be found to support the sunspot theorem. It was very frustrating, because no matter how the data was sliced or diced, or put into the theoretical mixmaster in hopes of a different outcome, the conceptual recipe never worked. He should have given up long before he did; but true believers are not known for a gracious acceptance of reality.

This tale of the errant sunspots is of course cautionary, and it is told not only to offer you a sense that economists will sometimes go to insane lengths to prove they are not in fact insane; but also to remind myself – a putative social scientist as well as practicing journalist – that all theories are at best metaphors, or conceptual outlines and frameworks – at best a sort of thought experiment designed to enlighten and deepen our understanding but not to boldly and precisely predict the future, which will relentlessly and eternally escape comic-book pre-capture.

China is no comic-book character. No one should presume to predict the path of its future. Including the smartest Chinese Communist brainiacs.

THEORY OF THE TWO SUNS

So, in view of all of the above, here is my metaphor about China. But it is not a grand theory. And we'll see why.

For my students, I sometimes refer to this metaphor as the "Theory of the Two Suns". This is to get their respectful attention. But it is far less a theory than a mild metaphor – but an insightful and helpful one nonetheless.

It arises out of the rich minds of two Singaporean brains – George Yeo, a rightly praised former foreign minister, and Kishore Mahbubani, currently dean of the celebrated Lee Kuan Yew School of Public Policy. They are serious thinkers about our current world who offer wisdom and perspective.

Their metaphor of the two suns is simple enough.

After the Soviet Empire's collapse, there only one sun remaining to pull everything together in the geopolitical solar system. That was the United States, and as it was the sole magnetic centre of the universe, all the big planets and all the little planets had to revolve around it, seeking to avoid running up against one another or getting too close to the one big sun and maybe even burning up in fiery denouement. Most wisely revolved closely; others kept their orbits at a distance but not so far away. During this time period, basically, world politics was relatively monotonic.

But that was then, and this is now.

These days, we see clearly that a second sun has arrived on the scene, edging closer to the first sun and starting to challenge its visual prominence and palpable heat, thus upsetting the unipolar gravitational system that was once so simple to understand and even to sketch out on a classroom blackboard.

But with the re-entrance of the China sun into the political solar system – for centuries lost in some dizzying black hole of history – the magnetic fields are starting to work at cross purposes.

Many planets/nations want to edge closer to the second sun but they don't want to get too far removed from the first. But others think it might be in their interest to do just that – make a new break for the second sun and settle itself there. Others want to orbit as they have been, at least for the time being, as if nothing is happening. The rest are unsure and nervous.

With this new second superstar pushing closer, everyone feels new pulls of gravity, and one way or the other adjusts their orbits – in the process taking great care not to smash into one another, or allow their new orbit to bring them too close to either sun and risk being marginalised, or even getting burned.

This is a marvellous metaphor for the psychotic geopolitical rumbling of our time. Until we are sure of the finalised positions of the two suns in relation to one another, no one is entirely sure of where they stand, or how they are to move. And, last but not least, the two suns themselves are not sure of where they will stand in relation to each other as events are so much in motion.

This is now the world in which we live.

MAKE ROOM FOR BEIJING

Suzerainty is a word not often used.

In your own life, assuming (as I hope for you) that yours is more healthily normal than that of the political journalist or political scientist, you may never hear of it.

Surely the world's most famous literary spider, the ultra-literate Charlotte, created by the real writer E.B. White, would never spin a word of such obscurity and pretention across her web. After all, if no one seeing it knew what it meant, there would be no way it could have an effect on anyone – whether farmers or their hands.

Every word in language has a purpose, or at least once had a reason for its origination. Otherwise it would not exist. And sometimes there is only one word for the precise description of a situation, where no synonym will do the matter justice.

This is exactly the case in describing what China desires in the South China Sea. There is only one word that captures it best. Suzerainty.

To simplify, suzerainty is sort of like … sovereignty *lite*. Sovereignty means, in effect, that you own it; but *suzerainty* means that, while you're not the owner and maybe wouldn't really want to own it, you want a great deal of sway over it.

The Chinese want to suzerain the South China Sea. I know, suzerain is a noun, and here it is being used as a verb. So let us inaugurate a new verbal usage: to *suzerain*.

Beijing aims to suzerain over the seas and nearby territories the way Washington has always levied a measure of *suzeraination* over the Caribbean and the territories thereof.

Make no mistake about it: China wants to be boss of its backyard. It believes this outcome to be embedded in its destiny. It believes it has been held back for too long by others, outsiders, mainly European.

And it is in a rush to make up for lost time.

Years ago, the late Richard Dennis Baum, an esteemed political scientist at UCLA, a universally respected "China watcher" and a friend and colleague, was trying to describe the return of China to centre stage.

I recall him saying that any short description would run the risk of worst-case analysis if the threat were overstated (my preferred word was warmongering) or, to go the other way, of risk-denial if the threat were underplayed (my word would be panda-hugging). A proper, honest, careful explanation required a delicate balance, he said, but it would be a grave intellectual dishonesty to downplay the significance of China's fierce build-up of its navy.

They mean to dominate East Asia.

You mean, I ask, to invade as opportunities arise?

Probably not, Baum replies, not if you mean the vacuuming up of others' sovereignty. More like they are aiming to achieve, overall … yes, then he used the world … suzerainty. That exact word.

Then, when Richard was asked whether that obscure word of art might be too soft for a hard problem, he thought for a moment and said: "No, I think that's the exactly the right word for it."

WORLD DOMINATION

Probably is not the word for certainty, of course.

What "everyone knows" is not always known to everyone as undeniable fact.

Everyone knows that China's long-range objective is total world domination; yet how that will be achieved or when it will become our collective global destiny is not at all known to everyone. But a lot of people think they *know*. Period.

Perhaps the "certainty" arises from the simple equation of equating

Communist China with the former Soviet Union, the Communist superpower whose existence as an empire was in fact an indisputable fact until it came to collapse in 1989.

Certainty by analogy: While Beijing is not yet a superpower, its political system is still classically communist – certainly more than its mix-and-match economic system. So if the USSR was expansionist, so too must be the People's Republic of China.

It's that simple.

Actually it is not.

If anyone inside the government or the party of the People's Republic of China is seriously thinking of world domination, they should think again. It is difficult to achieve, and perhaps even more difficult to maintain.

Ask the British; ask any surviving Soviet Communist. World domination is a tough assignment. Throughout history empires have risen and fallen on the conceit that they did not have enough and needed more – territory, space, lebensraum, religious converts, whatever.

But with 1.4 billion people to house, feed, educate and otherwise keep content and loyal, the government and party might be best advised to succeed first at the many onerous tasks at home still undone, before venturing out to "dominate the world". On that standard, the People's Republic of China has a very great deal of work to do indeed before it can set sail for world domination.

Common sense might suggest that the Chinese elite could come to that conclusion on its own. Although the post-Mao governments and the post-Mao party can correctly claim to preside over a China that lifted probably a half billion people out of dirt-poor poverty between 1981 and 2012, something like one in 10 Chinese have been left behind in the dust. So we see that there remains plenty of work to do inside the borders of China before the People's Liberation Army makes plans to force-march into Montenegro, Monaco and Minneapolis on its domination tour.

No question, China will indeed aim to dominate transnational economic sectors that it views as central to its survival (energy, commodities), as well as beg, borrow, steal – and if absolutely necessary invent – every last piece of needed technology. Perhaps it is in this sense that we can agree that it plans to probe and stride across the globe as a new colossus. And it may be that the only force that will prove capable of slowing this march toward a more civilised and economically stable survival would be its own unforced errors, whether self-inflicted wounds, breakdowns in concentration, errors of governance and residual excesses of ideology, such as the return of Maoist fundamentalism.

All nations make blunders but with China the penalty for the last blunder would be gigantically tragic. Mao had his day. Let history move on.

The word "certainty" and "China" are not joined at the hip, though there is certainty that China will be with us for another 5,000 years unless we somehow manage to blow the world up. But there are uncertainties of note.

"There has always been some doubt as to whether … the Chinese ever believed that equality ever really existed in international relations," famously wrote the Singaporean scholar Wang Gungwu back in 1968. "This doubt partly explains the current fear that, when given the chance, the Chinese may wish to go back to their long-hallowed tradition of treating foreign countries as all alike but unequal and inferior to China."

Fortunately or not for the Chinese, the world has changed greatly since the dizzying days of the Middle Kingdom at its greatest width and length. There may be many more good days for China. But the good days of old are long past and they won't be like the good days ahead.

Suzerainty, probably.

Global sovereignty for China would take a very great deal longer. Like forever. Which is another way of saying: never.

THE PRINCIPLE OF HOPE

The self-deception of some public intellectuals – whether academic expert or media "expert" – is a phenomenon of our time.

Merely writing about a problem hardly solves it. Newspapers everywhere expose corruption in government and then move on to expose other "problems" as if the corruption is no more and the issue had shrunk to moot.

Similarly, simply developing a new intellectual and philosophical framework, even if from the greatest centres of learning, won't easily or rapidly change public opinion or public perception.

In one sense, of course, I wish otherwise. If the best and wisest ideas were to rise to the surface and the worst were to sink to the bottom, how would we not be better off? How can China and the US reach an optimal relationship that will add to the vigour and depth of world order if the dialogue is constantly degraded by misconceptions and lies? Bad ideas only help us to the extent that, as part of a dialectical public process, they rouse our best minds to fight them with better ideas.

The value of insisting on best ideas and best practices must never be abandoned. Intellectual despair will lead to moral erosion. By contrast, hope raises our spirits and promotes the possibility of progress by insisting that we do our best, not slide back into darkness from nihilism and exhaustion, if we want to better our world.

As the utopian German philosopher Ernest Bloch put it, we

absolutely must live by "the principle of hope". Without it, where are we? What future is there? Why go on?

A GLINT OF EVIL

I have put below four direct unaltered quotations.

Each comes from the work of a different writer, well respected. If you don't mind, though, the authors' names are not included; I find that political debate can become much less reasonable when it becomes much too personal. What's more, my concern is not with the integrity of their views but with the sanity of their views. Consider each perspective, and see if you don't hear some echo of unreason, though not (one hopes) the glint of evil.

1. "… Sooner or later, if present trends continue, war is probable in Asia…. China today is actively seeking to scare the United States away from East Asia, rather as Germany sought to frighten Britain before the First World War."

2. "… The Chinese leadership views the world in much the same way Kaiser Wilhelm II did a century ago …."

3. "To put it bluntly, China cannot rise peacefully."

4. "… The United States is much more likely to go to war with China than it is with any other major power."

War is not inevitable anywhere if there is the political will to block it. If there is war, then somehow that political will has been undermined. The question is, how did it weaken and who weakened it? Was it by design or was it by happenstance?

Many factors will be at play (ideology, national interests, domestic politics, etc.). But no one can quarrel with the proposition that what writers write and say about the world can affect our view of the world, perhaps even change its direction.

The writer Rachel Carlson helped give birth to the ecology movement with *Silent Spring*, her 1962 masterpiece. George Orwell's *1984*, first published in 1949, created images of centralised mind control that remains indelible to this day. Jonathan Schell's 1982 *The Fate of the Earth* made subtle linkage between the inherent evil anarchy of sovereign-nation world order and the odds of an earth-threatening nuclear war.

These were not writers who underestimated the impact of their words. For them, their prose had to be the pathway to truth. Precisely because we, the readers, might actually believe in what we were reading, they had to believe absolutely in what they were writing.

The greatest writing may not be recognised in its time, while lesser writing may well be. It is clear in my mind that this short book – just like my first-ever book *Understanding Doomsday* (1971) – will not likely be commercially mistaken for *50 Shades of Gray*. So the task of the ambitious writer is to seek to imagine how the thought and the writing might be read fifty years from its origination, not simply for the instant reaction on opening night.

A book titled *50 Shades of China* might well market more forcefully while lacking any gradations of gray whatsoever. This, to me, is any book that predicts, much less recommends, war with China.

It is hard to imagine that God (she or he) would have a positive view of using his-or-her God-given writing talent for such a purpose. Like that of the rich man having about the same chance of "entering heaven as a camel fitting through the eye of a needle", that writer would presumably have a long wait in a notably hot place behind a long line of saint wannabes before receiving her or his eternal reward, which should be an eternity in a hellish queue.

Ethical political journalism needs to increase love and cut down on hate. There are no shades of gray of any colour coordination to mitigate that deeply moral responsibility. The fate of the earth, the fate of mankind (and all its other animals) in part depends on it.

Call it the "Silent Earth". It is crying out for peace and respect.

A WEST COAST POLICY TOWARD CHINA

Is there such a thing as a "West Coast" mentality?

If there is, is it a factor in the bilateral relationship?

There is not the slightest doubt that the emotional mentality of the West Coast versus the East Coast of the US on a vital East-West issue such as the China relationship is different.

Let us start with the obvious fact that the West Coast is different from the East Coast. The latter represents fraying, unhappy cities propped up against the washed-up Atlantic Ocean, seaway to the past (Europe). By contrast, consider West Coast cities – Santa Barbara, San Francisco and San Diego, not to mention Seattle, Vancouver and Los Angeles … sprightly and pleasant… all set against the Pacific Ocean, super sea-lane to the future (Asia).

Geography may not be destiny but it sets a tone.

One is outlook. Ours is generally sunny; the East Coast's is generally gloomy. We here tend to believe; they tend to despair. Consider the weather factor on the human psyche: It's happy-go-lucky California Hawaiian versus Kierkgaardian Scandinavian.

On the USA West Coast, there are more Asians than anywhere else outside of Asia. More and more, from all over Asia – and nowadays especially from the mainland – they come and settle. In Southern California there are more people of Korean heritage than anywhere outside of Seoul. There are so many Vietnamese-Americans that a freeway exit-sign on our monster-405 reads "Little Saigon". Asian student musicians overwhelm our high school orchestras.

There are so many Asian college students around here that one of our universities is sometimes dubbed the "**U**niversity of **C**aucasians **L**ost among **A**sians" and another the "**U**niversity of **S**poiled **C**hinese" (which before that was known locally – and affectionately – as "University of Spoiled Children"!). In Los Angeles city, Caucasians now officially number a minority.

There is much optimism in the air, from the ongoing Silicon Valley to up-and-coming Silicon Beach, just south of Los Angeles (and nearby my dynamic Loyola Marymount University). Hollywood executives get up in the morning and after a non-fat latte or two ask themselves: how well will my film market in China? The last one hit the jackpot. And they hear the whisper that the Chinese have become so movie-crazy 10 new modern theatres are being opened every ... day!

New-age non-profits – especially the Pacific Council on International Policy (a think tank) and the Pacific Century Institute (a good-works tank) – add fresh wind to old policy storms. The effect of this demography in our geography is to nurture and sustain a sunny politics of possibility regarding China and Asia, rather than a dreary politics of impossibility.

Perhaps this summary of West versus East coasts is somewhat over-drawn – but not out of all proportion! The attitude is not the same in Washington.

Let me say this about Washington, understating it a little: It is a horrible place – maybe the meanest political town in a First World country, fully in the feral class of a Seoul or a Paris or other notably mean-spirited capital cities. Many from the West Coast when in Washington on business stay no longer than they have to.

So this book arises out of a West Coast mentality. It honours the optimistic, persistently doubts the worst-case scenario, believes in our common humanity, Chinese or Caucasian. By psychology if not by mileage, we are equidistant between Beijing and Washington. Instead of searching for *cause belli*, we search for the equipoise of balance, mutual respect, understanding and common purpose – a Pax Sino-America.

Yo-yo diplomacy, in the age of the Two Suns, won't do the job. Too many chances of collisions, even of a devastating strategic one. It's too risky, too amateurish, too yesterday. The 21st century needs better, the Chinese and Americans together deserve better, the rest of the world has got to have better.

The good professional diplomats on both sides have done a yeoman's job of keeping all the many planets and the two suns from colliding. This book is no criticism of their hard, grinding work and in fact admires them greatly. But evil forces as well as good are in this mix and a profound struggle is underway.

I find this yo-yo hidden war extremely disturbing and dispiriting. Here we have two great nations and peoples – the American and the Chinese. If nothing else, they each deserve respect. Their relationship should be one of mutual respect. That, along with common sense and mutual trust, will save the day. Our best diplomats need our best efforts and help. This book means to be a part of that – to make the case that the warmongers are not only certainly wrong-thinking but probably evil-minded.

The part *Yo-Yo Diplomacy* seeks to play is to suggest to you, with conviction and convincingly, the need for a transformation in attitudes and trust between the two great peoples of China and America. Nothing of significance will move forward without this; and without it something of a monstrous evil lurks ahead. I, for one, can see no other way long-term to get a higher, safer state of global order.

01

Zhu Rongji's light touch is sorely missing in today's China

South China Morning Post, Monday, 15 June 2015

*Tom Plate says China today could do with the foresight
and calm self-confidence of a Zhu Rongji*

RETROSPECTIVE:

And a very appropriate headline it was. To start a fortnightly series of essays on China and America off on a negative note perhaps might not seem like the most optimistic of beginnings. But the fact of the matter is that the answer to China's leadership problems rests mainly within the vast talent pool of China itself. The only question is whether the system permits the very ablest to rise to the top – or only the most conforming and risk-adverse. Of course, that same question can fairly be asked of our own system in the United States, most people would agree. No political system has a monopoly on excellence. Chance and confusion can rain on any day. Inspired leadership can arise at any moment, in an unexpected way. Former premier Zhu Rongji seemed to me to be about the best that you could want or hope for, for China; many Americans might say the same about former president Barack Obama. But one quality that great leaders invariably display is the ability to communicate, to build the consensus, to take their people along with them and to get important things done. This was Zhu in a nutshell.

Because we're human, we sometimes imagine nations as human beings – and babble on about their personality failures as if indulging in serious psycho-political analysis. We envision them as human-like, and declaim their boldness or weakness, or whatever, as if they were a singular personality.

Take the United States, for example – it's an ongoing, semi-functional jumble of competing forces, interests and partisanships that roil above and below constitutionally entrenched layers of competing government authorities. And yet we will depict the America of today as no more complex than – say – Barack Obama without the Harry Truman.

Even though China has four times America's population, it draws comparable anthropomorphic caricature as well. And yet it is such an endlessly sprawling kaleidoscope of the rural and the urban, Confucian/capitalist, central-party/deeply engrained native culture that it's folly to try to sum it up in fewer than a few billion words and a thousand metaphors.

But that doesn't stop us, because when thinking of Beijing, the anthropomorphic feeling is especially pressing: you feel in your heart that some important dimension in its current political personality is missing.

It is just a feeling, not a Princeton PhD thesis. Yes, China is not just emerging, it is emergent; it is no longer weak, and its diplomacy is starting to flex as muscularly as the well-photographed exercises of the People's Liberation Army. And, no question, even with the economy cooling, it is already a powerhouse. We all get this.

But, at the same time, we have the sense of an absent dimension and we glance back in time for something, or someone, to fill in the blank. No, it's not Mao Zedong; the last thing we'd long for is a neo-Maoist figure; Deng Xiaoping was fine, but that's not it. And the current president, Xi Jinping, has been providing strong direction and making tough decisions – generally getting good marks from many international as well as domestic observers.

Still, something is missing – a top-level political personality who listens carefully, with a sense of subtlety and nuance, with placid self-confidence; even the ability to take a blow or two and not get instantly psyched up for war; some supreme serenity, with a brain born for geopolitics.

Here's a hint: Who on the mainland recently has said anything like this – and obviously meant it? "What we want to do is to work for the people's welfare and build China into a strong and prosperous country with democracy and the rule of law. We absolutely won't engage in hegemony or power politics as some other countries do, as we've suffered enough from these. What good can come from bullying and oppressing others? We can become rich and strong through our own efforts, and we won't bully others."

Yes, this was said in June 2001 by the same man who in 1989 refused to unleash troops onto Shanghai's streets to smash demonstrations, as had been done in that other metropolis up north; who wasn't afraid to meet students; who guided China into the great globalised unknown of the World Trade Organization, despite a million honest doubts back home; and who managed to settle down his fellow Politburo colleagues after the "accidental" US bombing of the Chinese embassy in Belgrade in 1999 – just one month after his White House humiliation by Bill Clinton, who cravenly back-pedalled and reneged over his promises on the WTO.

Through all this, Zhu Rongji, then the fifth premier of China, now in retirement, kept China cool simply by keeping his own; by averting his eyes from the inevitable setback, no matter how bitter, and affixing them to where China needed to be 10, 20, 30 years down the road. He was then – and now – exactly what was – and is – needed: a visionary with foresight.

It is no doubt an extreme case of anthropomorphic romanticizing to want to believe that a Zhu-type figure would handle "bratty" Hong Kong with the same tactical deftness and insight as Zhu himself did with those 1989 demonstrators in Shanghai. The strength of the light touch reflects the core of self-confidence that breeds flexibility.

So when, as many expect, Hong Kong's legislature later this week fails to pass the electoral overhaul package for the chief executive election of 2017, many also expect Beijing to turn predictably cold – and sullen – and somewhat forbidding. Or will it shock the world and offer an unexpected but utterly self-confident turn of warm understanding?

Some countries are grand but not great, others are great but not grand; the rare ones are both great and grand.

The late Noel Annan, a Cambridge don, was famously insistent that the legendary thinker Isaiah Berlin's relentless emphasis on the impact of leaders on history was tragically underappreciated, particularly by academics. He once lampooned them this way: "Social scientists have depersonalised acres of human experience so that history resembles a ranch on which herds move, driven they know not why by impersonal forces, munching their way across the prairie."

Real life takes place on no such barren ranch but on vast windy steppes of difficult historical realities. The exceptional leader can prove a huge value-added force. As authors Orville Schell and John Delury put it in their deeply illuminating book Wealth and Power, "Zhu ensured that China would enter the 21st century poised to advance ever more rapidly ..."

China faces great historic challenges and decision-crossroads now. If only its complex political personality contained a visible dimension of the Zhu Rongji touch.

P.S. It is difficult to be sure whether the current president Xi Jinping has a touch of the Zhu in him. The strong-willed leader of China is obviously struggling to keep it altogether. Perhaps the stylistic calculation that worked 15 years ago – the orchestra leader cajoling the brass section to behave itself – had to give way to the Strong Daddy threatening to cut off the children's allowance.

AND THEN THERE'S…

"As we often say in China, a single flower does not make spring, while one hundred flowers in full blossom bring spring to the garden. [...] We should, under the guidance of Deng Xiaoping Theory, the important thought of the Three Represents and the Scientific Outlook on Development, enhance our strategic thinking and confidence, and better balance China's overall domestic and international interests."

– *The Governance of China*, by Xi Jinping, Foreign Languages Press, 2014

02

CHINA AND THE US MUST INCLUDE JAPAN IN TALKS ON SECURITY OF EAST ASIA

SOUTH CHINA MORNING POST, MONDAY, 29 JUNE 2015

Tom Plate says Beijing needs to rethink its policy
towards Japan for the good of the region

RETROSPECTIVE:

Perhaps because Asians allegedly tend to have famously long memories (certainly longer than Americans'), they sometimes tend to have short tempers. Case in point is the Chinese versus the Japanese. Mutual hatred is too often over the top, from two of our most profound and developed cultures: there must be something deeply wrong. But young Chinese university students who travel to visit Japan return home so impressed with that country and culture. Japanese university students, among the sharpest in the world, are smart enough to know that a nation of 127 million has got to work things out with a nation of 1.4 billion. When will both sides come to their senses? I pray that it is sooner rather than later.

Let us divide tense East Asia, Caesarean fashion, into three geopolitical parts.

One is Chinese, the other is Japanese, and the third is – yes – American (even though, as the Chinese are inclined to point out,

America is not exactly native to East Asia, right?).

By the way, no disrespect intended towards the Koreans, but they cannot compose a fourth because of their own division into two parts – a peculiar Korean-style Caesarean sectioning.

Last week, representatives of two-thirds of geopolitical East Asia met to calm tensions. The occasion was the worthy US-China Strategic and Economic Dialogue, with both sides in Washington hoping to talk through bilateral differences and potential confrontations. An excellent idea: the world doesn't need any more wars, and East Asia doesn't need any. But the issues are tough, complicated and the Sino-US relationship continues to need immense work. It is to the credit of the two governments that this urgent task is not lost on them.

But it is also fair to ask how betterment of the East Asian neighbourhood can be achieved if a third of it is excluded from the management committee. No doubt, if East Asia's remaining third had been sitting at the table as well, Beijing wouldn't have shown up at all; or if it had, the talks would have been nightmarish. Even so, it might also be speculated that sectioning Japan off to the side might well prove a serious miscalculation.

Japan, after all, is not remotely Greece, right now the world's saddest modern economy. On the contrary, its per capita income dwarfs China's, and for a population of a mere 127 million, the fact is that its overall economy probably ranks No. 3 worldwide, even above powerhouse Germany. What's more, the Japanese people, according to opinion polls, while remaining pacifist and anti-nuclear, have begun to worry about the soundness of their China tack: go with the prevailing winds, just sell and buy, don't argue, and everything will be A-OK.

China is now Japan's No. 1 foreign preoccupation, and the US second. The political impact is titanic. "To be successful, Japanese leaders must persuade their public that cooperation with China will reduce

Japan's vulnerabilities rather than exacerbate them," advises Japan expert Sheila Smith, senior fellow on the US Council on Foreign Relations, via her surpassingly comprehensive book *Intimate Rivals*: "The old ways of managing its relationship with China are no longer effective."

Japan has begun viewing China more as an existential challenge than as just a jolly-good super-big-time importer and exporter. The causes of this sea change are many, but of course the various claims and counter-claims – and bumps – in the East China Sea have scarcely bolstered bilateral comity. Another is that China's advocacy of a worldwide policy of non-interference in a country's internal affairs (especially its own) tends not to apply to Japan's internal affairs.

Japan is certainly vulnerable to criticism, as is any country. China and others often complain about its "bulimic" memory, especially regarding war atrocities. But as Smith points out, the unintended result of all the nagging is to harden domestic sentiment against China. It is no coincidence that the two most politically significant Japanese prime ministers in recent times have been the showy war-shrine-visiting Junichiro Koizumi and the overtly nationalistic Shinzo Abe. Note, too, that indignant right-wing pressure groups and lobbies that do wish China serious ill have juicy new leases on political life and the Japanese are now debating whether to revise their constitution to expand their military space and, presumably, jump into an East Asian arms race with that good old fighting spirit.

There is immense irony here, and it is truly heartbreaking. Smith points out with poignant perspective that support from the Japanese public for grandstanding PM visits to war shrines and the like actually has been undergoing structural erosion due to generational turnover. And, she reports, the nation's nationalistic right wing is actually less unified than fragmented: all Japanese conservatives are not cut from the same grumpy cloth. But harrowing sea confrontations between fishing vessels and military ships serve to narrow differences; loud rhetoric from Beijing plays into the wrong political hands. Instead of winning over public opinion, Chinese policy would appear to be making the Japanese wonder about their military readiness. Wasn't it Sun Tzu who wrote: "The supreme art of war is to subdue the enemy without fighting"?

Beijing's policy towards Japan needs to be rethought. Smith's definitive book nails the point that Japanese foreign policy in general (and towards China in particular) is almost entirely driven by domestic politics, pressures and lobbies. There is no overall conceptual framework; the national emotion is becoming increasingly existential.

The problem for Chinese as well as Japanese diplomacy is daunting. Both nations field diplomats of exceptional talent and cosmopolitan subtlety; they understand each other's domestic problems; and, when the two sides do talk, they come away believing that deft diplomacy can somehow heal all wounds. That might be true if the bilateral relationship were being left entirely to the diplomats. But it's not. Pugnacious groups on both sides are gaining leverage, and mutually respectful diplomacy loses out to petty pugnacity, especially over stupid territorial issues. As Smith concludes: "The potential for heightened tension – and perhaps even conflict – will make it increasingly difficult to go back to Deng Xiaoping's approach to leaving the problem to future generations to resolve."

And so to recycle Caesar yet again: all of East Asia will remain in three unhappy parts until and unless all three parts get their acts together. Without that, there surely will be conflict. Trilateral issues require triangular diplomacy. No one should be excluded. It is very dangerous. China's Japan policy is in a box that Beijing has got to begin thinking itself out of. That won't be easy, but it is mandatory for East Asian peace and security.

P.S. At this writing, military conflict had not broken out between the two. But there is every reason to have believed it would, could and in a sense should. The problem with representational politics, whether of the voting democratic kind or the non-voting communist kind, is that what is represented sometimes is lunacy.

AND THEN THERE'S...

"As I just said, the main trend in Sino-Japanese relations is good at the moment, but there are indeed some comments that are highly offensive to the Chinese. We hope that Japanese popular opinion will keep the big picture of Sino-Japanese friendship in mind and not do anything that would provoke or offend the Chinese people. This is the only way for our friendly and cooperative partnership to continue to develop."

— *Zhu Rongji Meets the Press*, by Zhu Rongji, Oxford University Press, 2011

03 WESTERN MEDIA'S CALLOUS DELIGHT AT CHINA'S STOCK MARKET CRASH IS TOTALLY UNCALLED FOR

SOUTH CHINA MORNING POST, MONDAY, 13 JULY 2015

Tom Plate criticizes unfair Western reporting on China's market troubles, not least its almost gleeful tone

RETROSPECTIVE:

It's morally a losing bet to wager against China unless your financial strategy is to short the human race. Shorting the Thai baht might be cruel treatment of the Thai people, and trigger a regional financial crisis, as happened in effect in 1997–1999. But the consequences of a collapse of the Chinese stock market would be nothing to cheer about either – to say the least. However, the Western cheering only stopped when the Chinese market was righted anew by aggressive government intervention. I think we all need to pause before rooting for China to fail. For after the fall, the West would be picking itself up, too. China is too big to fail all alone. Many economies would go down with it. So be careful what you wish for.

If you were greatly annoyed or disappointed by the largely cold and unsympathetic Western media commentary about China's stock market plunge, this didn't mean you had to be a member of the State Council or an uncritical panda-hugger. All you'd have to have been was a fair-minded person.

Even quality Western newspapers were dispensing dismissive decrees with unseemly glee. Press punsters could not resist the cheap headline ("The great fall of China"). Instant-analysis types were practically dancing in the pubs watching the "prestige of the party" allegedly shrink along with the Shanghai and Shenzhen composites. Even respected press portals were positively entertained by "the government's frenzied attempts", "dodgy intervention" and "helplessness".

Let us leave aside for the moment whether we Western journalists are capable, in the face of a rough patch for China and its people, of summoning our empathy. The other question is whether Western journalists were being journalistic: it was as if the media had never before seen a stock market bubble burst, or ever witnessed a scary gigantic sell-off.

It was as if something this messy could only have occurred on the watch of a primitive Communist government failing to fit into the fancy pants of sophisticated Western free-marketers.

Waves of low-grade ideological journalism kept coming at you. Beijing's counter-measures were "desperate", and only the country's "compliant press" would find them credible, as the authorities were "in danger of losing credibility" and China's market began to look "more like the Wild West". And of course there was near unanimity on this core point: "the collapse in confidence … is a sharp indictment of the party's prestige", "a grave economic blemish on Xi Jinping and Li Keqiang, China's leaders".

Precious few helpful or positive suggestions were offered – why care about 1.4 billion people assembled in the world's most populous country, which happens also to include a most glamorous and fascinating special administrative region? Let them melt on their margins! Even well-meaning recommendations reeked of an absolutely extraordinary deficit of self-awareness. "The [Chinese] government should … be trying to strengthen the foundations of its economy and financial system," scolded a famous US newspaper, as if such measures were appropriate solely for China. "It could do so by better regulating and policing its securities market to root out fraud and speculation." Hmm … can we think of any other major economy that has suffered through similar traumas for which such a remedy would be appropriate?

The Western news media has always proposed that the world get down on its hands and knees and offer fundamentalist worship to the "free market". But even if the god of an absolutely free market existed, which of course it doesn't, is this imaginary god not the same one that has failed us again and again? It takes no Marxist to point to the lack of the market's magic in 2007–2008, when US avarice, incompetence and deregulation helped seed a global crisis – widely viewed in retrospect as the worst since the Great Depression of the 1930s.

This god that continually fails was surely less than magical in 1997–1999, when relatively open stock and equity markets in Asia had the life wrung out of them by avaricious Western funds viciously shorting even otherwise well-regulated markets.

The famous example was Hong Kong itself, which rebounded when the alert local government of then chief executive Tung Chee-hwa counter-attacked with equities purchases, an astute ploy personally approved by then premier Zhu Rongji. Western financial media were so quick to denounce the SAR government's bold intervention as a betrayal of "free-market" ideals. But the effort worked wonders to bee-sting the short sellers, scaring them off to go buzzing for easy honey elsewhere.

And the West was so very quick to denounce then Malaysian prime minister Mahathir Mohamad, when he erected overnight capital controls to push back on Western speculation against the country. But history was to rate that pragmatic ploy well: the definitive 2001 Harvard Kennedy School study praised the intervention for yielding a faster economic recovery, smaller declines in employment and wages, and a more rapid turnaround in the market.

In a serious financial or market crisis, positive government intervention is a moral necessity. Leaving everything to the magic of the "free market" is like banning quarantines and vaccines in an epidemic. No doubt the efforts of the Chinese government, so very new to the game, lacked the discipline and coherence of – say – a municipal fire department with vast experience in conflagration containment. So the Western media was not wrong to note that the central government's thrown-together fire drill lacked the seamlessness of a Balanchine ballet. What was so troubling was the evident delight scarcely hidden in the reportage. It was as if the media were almost rooting for China to fail.

It might have been hoped that we in the US had moved beyond crowing over the problems of others, whether to psychologically distance the pain of our own problems, or out of absolute malice towards China simply because of its global upsurge, or because it has a Communist government.

As a general observation, what (little) the American public knows about China comes largely from media attitudes and assumptions. This endless cycle of stale air and superior attitudes is malicious and pernicious – a perpetual process that is not in anyone's national interest.

If China were somehow utterly to collapse (as improbable as that scenario would seem by all reckoning), it would not just be the Chinese people who would suffer. The fallout would cause pain for the people of every country in Asia, and in every country in North America, especially in the US, itself having been so buoyed by China's economic surge.

Why anyone would root for China to keel over is beyond understanding. It is not only dumb, from the standpoint of economic self-interest; it is a moral wrong. Where was our decency and cosmopolitanism?

At the very least, Western reports of China's market crash suggested a disturbing callousness and unmerited cultural superiority.

P.S. As this is written, the new US presidential administration of Donald J. Trump is still finding its footing. But its "blame game" mentality is a juvenile approach to the reality of world economics today. You can envision China as an enemy in the international trade game; but is that the best vision for America and the world? The better way is to say: we will win some and lose some with China, our equal – but we will work together to work it out. Why not go smart rather than animal?

AND THEN THERE'S…

"The question is how to be professional, how to be fair to your interviewees, how to make balanced reports, how to convey different voices and different sides." (Lin Gu)
— *China Ink: The Changing Face of Chinese Journalism,*
  by Judy Polumbaum with Xiong Lei, Rowman & Littlefield
  Publishers, 2008

04

CHINA NEEDS TO DEPLOY MORE A SILKEN TOUCH WITH ITS NEIGHBOURS

SOUTH CHINA MORNING POST, MONDAY, 27 JULY 2015

Tom Plate says China cannot escape the blame for regional tensions, given its clumsy diplomacy so far

RETROSPECTIVE:

A new way is needed for Chinese diplomacy – a silken roadway. Instead of insisting that it is always right and flashing its growing might as the US Navy has done for years, the government needs to fan out across Asia with cool and sincere breezes of calm diplomatic reason. I, for one, loved its past-reiterated "peaceful rising" diplomacy: sincere or not, it gave off regional vibes of neighborliness and cooperation. Alas, other nations perhaps thought it showed a glint of weakness, and foolishly tried to take advantage. China picked up quickly on the opportunism and thus decided not to play so nice with neighbours that weren't playing so fair themselves. Too bad. The cycle of action and reaction needs to be broken by visionary leadership, and this will have to come from Beijing – the regional leader. No one else is capable of displaying it, except the Japanese, whom no one will follow.

Let's play the blame game. Let's bash the Japanese government for ratcheting up tension. Bad, bad Japanese, right? Isn't it just that simple?

Since May 3, 1947, Japanese people have lived (and on the whole lived graciously and productively) under the embrace of an American-concocted constitution that with determination tied its defence forces up in restrictive Article 9. But look how well it worked out: Japan became one of the world's greatest economies – until very recently, the No. 1 economy in Asia.

But now Shinzo Abe, working to realise his dream of dumping this iconic and ironic legacy of the second world war in history's dustbin, looks to be on the verge of ... triumph! The prime minister has his party and party allies just a legislative click or two away from expanding the leeway (and budget) of the Self-Defence Forces when they have a need to "defend Japan", or help out allies, or whatever.

Of course, Japan-bashers are quick with the mean-genes argument: isn't it telling that Abe's mother was the daughter of Nobusuke Kishi, who, before becoming the 37th prime minister, distinguished himself as a member of the Tojo cabinet. No escaping those genes, eh?

Maybe, but here is what is far more interesting to me: that in his moment of political triumph, Abe's move elicited such a tepid response from the Japanese people – seemingly far from a gung-ho one in which they pull their samurai swords from the attic. One can imagine that colossally losing a world war – including a pair of atomic bombs dropped on two of their cities, leaving survivors and their children with a grim genetic legacy – might just take the fizz out of the champagne.

So how in the world did Abe carry the day against the admirably noble (and smartly pragmatic) pacifism of the Japanese people? What was the secret behind his mini-coup? Someone must have stepped up big time to help him peddle the idea of military renewal to a populace that on the whole had been saying: "No, we've been down that road before – never again."

What in the world happened? Part of the answer is to be found in the government's recent defence white paper, its message as obvious as the Great Wall of China. At its centre is general obsession, and in the text are many particulars. There's the well-documented Chinese naval build-up, the potent policy influence of a possibly semi-sovereign People's Liberation Army (reflected in Chinese president Xi Jinping's campaign to tame it), and China's fast and furious land reclamation and sandbar resurrection projects, which Beijing says are more like open-to-all neighbourhood recreation centres, but which most normal people say surely look like burgeoning military bases.

Japan's white paper concludes: Beijing is "poised to fulfil its unilateral demands without compromise" by the blunt instrumentality of "coercive attempts to change the status quo".

Is it just Orwellian-style propaganda, hyped-up fodder to justify a major Japanese arms build-up? Or is it the plausible worry of a concerned government responsibly warning its people? If your inclination is to go Orwellian, fine, but half of non-Chinese Asia agrees with the idea that the challenge of China is no joke. Most of the other half doesn't know what to think but is nonetheless unnerved. (What's left is a few countries quietly pocketing aid from Beijing and remaining dutifully silent.)

So whatever Abe is up to, he is not the only guy in Asia who's got China on his mind. The Philippines, not exactly in the forefront of diplomatic pugnacity, has its bright lawyers at The Hague bringing questions before the UN-backed Permanent Court of Arbitration. Other governments are siding with Manila. Arms-buying binges are in progress. Governments are snapping up surveillance planes and naval equipment, as if to ensure no more lonely reefs or sandbars are sand-castled up overnight into landing strips without anyone knowing about it.

And then you have the senior head of the Communist Party of the Socialist Republic of Vietnam, obviously rattled and trying for all the world to seem sincere and contrite, showing up at the White House the other day, looking for a little love.

There you have it: the changing geopolitical landscape of Asia.

To be fair, China does have plausible cases for much of what it's doing in the East and South China seas, along with the gut belief that it is its historical right to take whatever it can before anyone stops them, which is exactly what some neighbours had been doing decades before.

One thing is certain: all these moves have started to make Abe look less like a menace than a responsible leader. And who should get credit if that remarkable image transformation comes into full focus? It does take two to tango. In the last year or so, China has presented to the world not the "peaceful rising" image but the "we're rising and you're not" image.

China's new Asia-wide infrastructure investment programme and its hope to take the lead in forging a modern Silk Road and all the rest might someday add up to a kind of Central Asian Marshall Plan. If so, this will be applauded by all and greatly honoured by history. But in the meantime, Beijing might consider that it would be in its best national interest to treat its neighbours with a more tender touch. Abe could be made to look like a political moderate if China proceeds apace on its current course. Yes, China has such power. But that's not diplomacy. And it is not smart. Its diplomacy needs to be woven of much finer Chinese silk.

P.S. "China on their mind" – not so bad of a phrase, actually – as it's still on everyone's mind, and polls in America suggest the American mind is not really made up. China probably doesn't care one way or the other. Perhaps it should.

AND THEN THERE'S...

"Asia is one of the most dynamic and most promising regions in the world, and its development is closely connected with that of other continents. Asian countries have energetically explored development paths suited to their national conditions and greatly boosted global development through their own. Working side by side with the rest of the world in a time of difficulty to tackle the international financial crisis, Asia has emerged as a major engine driving world economic recovery and growth. In recent years, Asia has contributed more than 50 per cent of global growth, instilling much-needed confidence into the rest of the world."

– *The Governance of China*, by Xi Jinping, Foreign Languages Press, 2014

05

COMMON SENSE AND PATIENCE NEEDED AS US ELECTION FEVER FANS AMERICANS' FEARS ABOUT CHINA

SOUTH CHINA MORNING POST, MONDAY, 10 AUGUST 2015

Tom Plate warns against believing all the tough talk about China as the US presidential race heats up

RETROSPECTIVE:

Every elected American president in recent memory has taken campaign shots at China, that convenient distant punching bag for politicians. Even Bill Clinton had a merry "go" at Beijing – also known as "the butchers of Beijing" in the frenzied and insincere rhetoric of his 1991 run against incumbent George W. H. Bush. Even at the outset of his first term, the man from Hope, Arkansas, had his administration preaching from the human-rights pulpit. His first-term secretary of state Warren Christopher once was even shown the door to Beijing airport in lack of gratitude by Beijing for a human-rights lecture ordered by his boss Clinton. Eventually presidents calm down and start to worry about how to best run their own country, not tell others how to run theirs. Whether Trump's fiery "China is beating us" mantra will make way for more productive language and policy – this remains to be seen. The new and controversial president may learn the limits of his powers over China the hard way, however – as the hard pedagogy appears to be the only way he learns.

The US presidential election circus is getting started, and so is the China debate. The first stop of many on the presidential debate trail produced smashing TV ratings. Like much of the world, Americans are worried about where the US is headed and what quality of person should lead it. In 15 months' time, our decision will be foisted on the world, and everyone will have to live with it.

One direction to which our debate has not yet turned is the China-relations question. The only candidate who seemed to make much of it last week was bombastic billionaire businessman Donald Trump. He muttered about how "we lose to China ... we don't beat China in trade", whatever that might mean. (What, should the US manufacture more cheap toys?)

But what is sure to surface over the long campaign is that many Americans worry about the Sino-US relationship, are either puzzled or troubled about China, or are convinced that they know all the answers.

The know-it-all constituency believes it has China all figured out: it claims that, despite Beijing's charm offensives and rollicking pandas, Beijing is up to no good. This paranoid perspective permits the imagining of a destructive Red conspiracy behind every move China makes, and everything it says and might dream of.

Are the paranoids for real? Many make you worry and want to find a bomb shelter; but one exception is veteran defence official and analyst Michael Pillsbury, who is very smart, knows his China stuff and worked for years at the think tank Rand Corporation. His new book, *The Hundred-Year Marathon: China's Secret Strategy to Replace America as the Global Superpower*, offers ominous views on "evil" China that cannot be ignored, and out-thumps Trump and others in the "we're losing to China" department.

Pillsbury is absolutely sold on the idea that America is naive to believe China is aiming for anything other than to emerge as the biggest elephant in the jungle: the globe's sole superpower. Economic espionage and deceptive diplomacy will be constant. While deferring actual military confrontation for the time being, China's hawks flutter and strut behind the takeover strategy.

What should be the response of the American *ba* (a multi-layered Chinese term that Pillsbury believes captures the Chinese view of America, and which he takes to mean "tyrant")? Start by creating a credible and cohesive anti-China coalition of those unwilling to kowtow, and at every step confront Beijing, it being one canny competitor and no cuddly panda. Pillsbury warns: "Western elites and opinion shapers provide the public with rose-coloured glasses when it comes to looking at China. That, of course, is just as the Chinese have planned it."

If there is any comfort in the Pillsbury perspective, it's that China's new unipolar world order could well take 100 years to realise. That's a long stretch of tick-tock even by a Chinese clock. Our best multinational corporations are lucky to keep even five-year plans in one piece.

Pillsbury and others like him are entitled to their conspiracy view, but common sense suggests that China's policy, like America's, is more a patchwork of daily challenges to ever-changing pressures than some master plan hatched in some secret basement room of the Central Party School.

So the rest of us compose our minds from the hard work of more patient China evaluators. One is Dr Charles Wolf Jnr [*author's note: who was to die little more than a year later in Los Angeles at the age of 92*], who for many decades has starred as Rand's senior economist. He views China much like the US: as a mixed bag of the smart and the dumb, the good and the bad, the old and the new. But, rather than a conspiracy theory, he promotes social-science methodology.

Wolf's most recent book, *Puzzles, Paradoxes and Controversies, and the Global Economy*, offers sane deductions and reasoned correctives for geopolitical emotional insecurity. At the outset, he wearily reminds us that presidential candidates will "talk tough" about China but "toughness is not a policy". For panicky types, he counsels patience, sometimes inspirationally abandoning the temptation to PowerPoint a point by welcoming in the warming glow of historical perspective.

Cleverly, Mao's droll reservation about the limitations of anti-corruption campaigns – "it's hard to squeeze out all the toothpaste from the tube" – enlivens his view that too much anti-corruption activity can cause as much trouble as too much corruption. Anti-China nagging about the "undervalued renminbi" lacks intellectual fairness by ignoring the severe structural asymmetry between the world's two biggest economies.

As for Beijing's blustery plunge into the foreign aid game (a favourite subject of alarmist Western media), Wolf predicts for China considerable frustration. Foreign aid recipients, Beijing will find, tend to have amazingly short memories about what they promised in return for the aid, as the US has found to its melancholy.

The Rand Corporation, often dubbed little more than a paid-in-full policy-scout team for the money-bags Pentagon, is increasingly working the peace side of the all-important Sino-US relationship. But it takes two to play this good and noble game.

For starters, Beijing could embrace a carefully framed Rand proposal, recently tendered confidentially to high-level Chinese, of methodologies for the serial expanding of overlapping mutual national interests. This might read like a mouthful, but the idea is clear enough – and might even prove a game changer. Who knows unless it is tried?

P.S. The laudable RAND effort reportedly ran into political interference at high levels and lost steam. China seems to yo-yo from wanting warmth and cooperation with the US to fearing intimacy of any kind, as if it might catch a bad cold for which there is no remedy. To be sure, the yo-yo tendencies of the various US postures toward China can hardly be discounted for their collective contribution to confusion. Dr. Wolf once told me that he agreed with the view than the Good-Guy/Bad-Guy script didn't fit this scene; and in fact he substantially agreed with a column like this (and, in fact, almost all the others here). I was happy about that. Reason, rather than ideology, much less racism, must guide our relationship and our policies.

AND THEN THERE'S…

"A final take away from the period is a quest for combining foreign technology with Chinese — not foreign — values. The correlation assumed by Westerners between the free market economics, democracy, and scientific progress is inconsistent with the views of the Chinese leadership (who obviously has a vested interest in the continuation of the present order) but also with those of some other powerful segments, including many of the newly rich for whom the existing system may represent the best of both worlds: capitalist wealth united with Communist protection and subsidies."
– *The Chinese Century: The Rising Chinese Economy and Its Impact on the Global Economy, the Balance of Power, and Your Job,*
by Oded Shenkar, Wharton School Publishing, 2006

06

Amid the economic and political storms, China and the US must realise they are inextricably bound together

South China Morning Post, Monday, 24 August 2015

Tom Plate says the pair will have to learn to better manage their differences, to keep the peace

RETROSPECTIVE:

I know, the theme here seems all too obvious. I don't quarrel with your cavil – but will simply counter that the obvious is not always so apparent when a quarrelling couple is eyeball-to-eyeball. How any nation can imagine a stable world order without the Chinese nation adding to the stability seems an impossible intellectual exercise. All the reaching-out, some done openly and others secretly, by the Bush Sr. and Clinton administrations were the right moves for America. There is no coherent Plan B.

China, it seems, cannot win for losing. Exports-predator China is always "beating us", bombastic billionaire businessman Donald Trump declaimed yet again on the campaign trail. But his timing on this point could have been better as last week was not exactly the best possible moment to hold up China's economy as any world-beater. What with the mainland's growth rate slowing and its stock markets roiling, the panda seems to be heading in a direction more lumbering bearish than takeover bullish.

It would have been more far perversely astute to point out that, even when the panda is hurting, the US somehow still takes a "beating". By the end of last week's China slide, the Dow Jones followed in step, falling to its lowest level since 2011. (This was not due to Greece!) Suddenly, the US Federal Reserve has to rethink its plan to push abnormally low interest rates onto a higher shelf. So we conclude that, no matter what China does (shine or slump), its "beating" of America proceeds apace.

Let us not replace irrational exuberance with irrational pessimism. How to foment a historic Sino-US partnership that could save us all a lot of grief? For that, we reach back through history for a consultation with Niccolo Machiavelli, historically cunning adviser, who always tells leaders to look at the world as it is, not as they might like it to be. Sure, some Americans would only be comfortable in a world dominated, as it were, by one huge Trump Tower, looking down on the globe's minions, including all 1.4 billion Chinese and a billion-plus Indians. But this is not the world as it is, or as it will be — ever.

The world as it is, and as it will remain for the foreseeable future, is one vast network of co-dependencies (environmental, economic, health) plugged into a common fate. But, judging from the warrior-like roars wafting up from the pit stops of the US presidential trail, adjustments may prove even harder for America than China in the attitude department. "We are now all in the soup together," muttered one of my smartest friends, an international barrister, reacting to the latest Sino-US market mash-ups.

China is not going to vanish, no matter how much its markets stumble or its yuan tumbles. Its economic downdrafts will be felt as tornado-like downpours in places as far away as Oklahoma, just as its cheap exports have put smiles on the faces of children under Oklahoma's Christmas trees for years. Ill winds of all kinds travel in both directions: What our Fed does next will be felt in Shanghai.

So, what do we mean when we talk about a better Sino-US relationship, especially in the middle of this uncertain economic turn? Almost no one offers clearer thinking than George Yeo, the former Singapore foreign minister, who in his just published book, *Bonsai, Banyan and the Tao*, writes: "The two countries are now bound together at so many points, a serious rupture is almost unthinkable. But it is going to be a very difficult relationship; it will be the single most important relationship for both countries in this century. If it's badly managed there could be war; if it's properly managed there will be another generation of peace."

Without hysteria, we need to accept that this "shotgun" geopolitical marriage (forced, rather than loving) will be an inconvenient affair, at times stormy, but at all times so desperately necessary. Both parties will need to make adjustments in attitude as well as policy, and they will have to do it on their own, together. For, where will they find a "couples counsellor" with experience of this extraordinary kind to mediate competently?

Might there be some silver linings in the current economic clouds? Here's one possible sliver: maybe both sides tamp down grandiose plans for endless defence spending. Competing choices have to be made, tough priorities set. The US must accept that if it tries to do too much globally, it may accomplish little anywhere. Beijing must accept that if it bets half the Bank of China on a dumb fleet of aircraft carriers, it will sink the ideal of lifting up all its people, not just the elite's yachts.

A keen observer of our oddest couple is Hugh White, of Australian National University, whose provocative 2013 book *The*

China Choice, made the case for a US resizing of its Asia profile. The professor still holds this view, as he told me last week: "As the seriousness of China's challenge to US primacy in Asia becomes clearer to Washington officials, the choice in how to respond becomes starker. The more they understand the huge costs and risks of containing China, and the better they see the scale of concessions needed to accommodate its ambitions, the more likely they will find themselves drifting towards an option of accepting a much reduced strategic role in Asia. Yet each continues to assume that the other will give way so they can get what they want without having to confront the other militarily. Each is almost certainly wrong."

Politicians on either side of the Pacific who propose to "beat" the other offer an unrealistic option, a potentially tragic vision and a loser's game plan. America must accept the validity of China's strength, as it overcomes setbacks and grows, and not foolishly imagine its rise to be little more than the product of an American decline. Beijing must kept its silliest generals quiet and contain its naval build-up that's eating away at its future. Both sides need to accept their limits so as to expand their possibilities. When push comes to shove, real trouble will always (pardon the verb) trump imagined trouble; and of real trouble there will be plenty. Threat invention, on the campaign trail or inside governments, is quite unnecessary.

P.S. The columnist needs to try to avoid becoming the Boring Lecturer. Enrollment will drop dramatically – who would want to listen? But imperial pugnacity on either side will knock all common sense of out the ring. Sino-US relations are a serious business, potentially lethal. I know, once again … obvious!

AND THEN THERE'S...

"Fearful that economic failure could soon lead to political disarray, Chinese leaders have become preoccupied with resolving their economic problems at home and with building foreign relationships that will make that task easier. New York Times Beijing bureau chief Patrick E. Tyler, who has lived in China for five years, observed: "If any generalization is to be made about 1.3 billion people, it would be that the Chinese want nothing more than to have a long period of peace and stability in which to develop their economy. Prosperity at home and military expansionism abroad are fundamentally incompatible in China today."

— *China's Future: Constructive Partner or Emerging Threat?*, edited by Ted Galen Carpenter and James A. Dorn, CATO Institute, 2000

07 | WHY SHOULD THE WORLD FEAR A POWERFUL XI JINPING?

SOUTH CHINA MORNING POST, MONDAY, 7 SEPTEMBER 2015

*Tom Plate says critics of Xi Jinping's apparent moves
to strengthen his rule should also see the positive*

RETROSPECTIVE:

Anyone who believes with confidence that it is simple to get inside the head of a leader such as Xi Jinping is out of his mind. Whether the head of a state as vast as China or as compact as Singapore, the leader (assuming he or she is actually prone to lead) has to process a complex calculus on the way to a decision. Nor is it so obvious that the leader at the top can simply snap a finger and see his will done promptly. Totalitarianism as an intellectual concept is endlessly fascinating but in the practice of real life difficult to maintain. The concept is over-rated as a guide precisely because of the daunting complexity of implementation. In this column, Xi Jinping's rise to paramount power is offered as a paradigm-alternative to systemic indecision, in a vast nation of 1.4 billion souls.

As Hongkongers can certainly testify, political parades in the public square or citizen protests occupying a thoroughfare can hide as much as they reveal. Last week, Beijing put together for all the world to see a titanic military show, the first such lavish one in years, designed to knock people's eyes out – perhaps especially on the mainland. Yet just before that, in central Tokyo, worried citizens ginned up a vastly smaller but still potent peace appeal that caught the eye of a world more familiar with Japan's former militarism than widespread pacifism.

The Beijing celebration was an official government showing; the Tokyo protest was anything but. Both events raise pressing questions for East Asia and the West.

Japan, once Asia's leading military power, held the region in fear until the cataclysmic end of the Second World War. Its abject surrender was what the Beijing display was cheering; but the Japanese need no help from anyone to recall that the end of their military era was punctuated with the atomic levelling of two cities.

Surely the collective conscience of the Japanese people (though not of posturing politicians) can honestly say to the world: what is war for? The Abe government's aim to remilitarise by eviscerating its anti-war constitution strikes many Japanese as brutish arrogance, if not psychological denial.

The Chinese who claim or brag they loathe all Japanese may not fully appreciate that their closest archipelago neighbour in fact looks, in an anti-war respect, to be further along the evolutionary tunnel than China is. "War is the sword of Damocles that still hangs over the head of mankind," said President Xi Jinping at the parade. He hit the nail on the head. The question now is whether his government will steer a wise course that makes the militarism of the Abe government look primitive and retro, or goad Japan into tragic but seemingly justifiable action.

Indisputably, China was well within its rights to organise a showboat parade on the 70th anniversary of the war's end. After all, UN Secretary General Ban Ki-moon himself, no noted warmonger, took his spot on the reviewing stand; and that was a good decision. But no high-ranking US official from Washington was to be found; and that was a bad decision.

What's more, let me argue that a truly far-thinking Japanese prime minister would be up there, too. At some point, East Asia needs to come together, if it's not to come apart.

What is Beijing's game? On the exact occasion of President Barack Obama's well-publicised environmental fact-finding visit to Alaska, five Chinese navy ships were bobbing off that state's coast. Yes, the naval quintet was totally within its rights to be in international waters; and we all know the US Pacific Command floats its own boats around China like gamblers around a Macao craps table. But this ill-timed if harmless exercise invited ominous speculation. The Pentagon announced that Chinese ships had never been spotted in the Bering Sea before; others asserted China was "getting tougher in maritime space", as one US analyst put it.

Xi's seemingly dramatic announcement of a 13 per cent cutback in People's Liberation Army manpower did not elicit swoons of gratitude in the US. One senior policy insider, who nonetheless urges efforts to tone down tensions with Beijing, said: "His cuts suggest only a greater and continuing emphasis on PLA modernisation, with a focus on advanced technology, including anti-access, area-denial and other dimensions of security. These are more threatening and hazardous for the US than the 300,000 manpower cut."

Maybe so, but Xi's cut was not slight, and underscored his determined campaign to plant the military snugly under the umbrella of the Communist Party.

Predictably, the West is sounding the alarm that Xi may turn into a Stalin. But it would be simplistic to assume that a stronger Xi is automatically a bad thing. A seamlessly unified Beijing command would have the ability to unplug hot-headed sectors of the military spoiling for a good dust-up with the US. A stronger Xi can take a broader national-interest view in a serious crisis and communicate authoritatively to Washington – not to mention to the PLA – a decision to negotiate, not escalate.

Keeping the military under control during a crisis is not always the easiest part of a leader's job, as revealed in President John F. Kennedy's struggle to contain the feral testosterone of his Joint Chiefs of Staff during the 1962 Cuban missile crisis. Today, it may be that it is China that has the control-of-escalation problem, not Washington.

So if the main point of the hardware show in Tiananmen Square was to spotlight Xi as a man not to mess with, don't assume the worst. As defence analyst Michael Swaine, of the Carnegie Endowment for International Peace and one of the most prominent American analysts of Chinese security issues, has put it: "During the Mao and Deng eras, the power and prestige of the paramount leader were generally sufficient to permit him to compromise on principle when necessary without admitting he was doing so."

The historic example, of course, was when Mao Zedong and Zhou Enlai executed that famous turn to Richard Nixon and Henry Kissinger as if suddenly among dear friends. It is hard to imagine a Politburo committee coming to a timely decision of that magnitude and imagination. So perhaps we need to observe Xi with more careful attentiveness – and less ideology.

We might even struggle to imagine that he understands his China at least as well as we do.

P.S. I added that very last "kicker line" (really, at the last minute when finishing up this piece) out of appreciation for the late Lee Kuan Yew, who gifted me a lot of his time for my books and

columns between 1996 and 2009. Why give Plate so much time
as compared to what was offered to other Western journalists? Lee
was said to reply that, for one thing, I was the first American
journalist he'd met who did not offer to tell him how he could run
Singapore better. I cannot be 100% sure the modern founder of
this amazing city-state ever actually said this; all I can tell you
is that I know for sure I never told him how to run Singapore. It
seemed to me he was doing a rather excellent job, even if he was
not the absolute darling of Western human rights circles.

AND THEN THERE'S...

"Today it is the People's Republic of China that attracts admiration, an admiration that again has survived adversity: the brutality of Maoist dictatorship and its catastrophic consequences, the failure at the junction after Mao to choose the route of political opening up, the resort to political murder in 1989. Philosophers praise China as a civilization state. Business people around the world, and academics, are falling over each other to get in on the China act. [...] When Xi Jinping came to power in 2012, the man that the world again thought would be a reformer instead lurched to the Maoist left, tightened all of the screws of dictatorship, and turned to an ideology of aggressive nationalism."
– *The Perfect Dictatorship: China in the 21st century*, by Stein Ringen, Hong Kong University Press, 2016

08

Ruling party's resounding win in Singapore elections reflects the success of its political model

South China Morning Post, Monday, 14 September 2015

Tom Plate finds reasons in Singapore's latest election results for taking its governance model seriously

RETROSPECTIVE:

Not all successful governments are alike. Happily, they can vary from a sturdy Scandinavian parliamentary democracy to a more controlling and centralised Southeast Asian one. What's the right way to govern, and what is the wrong way? And is there only one way (i.e. the American way)? The answer will depend on whether your criteria emanate from ideology or utility. Many people will say that the government that governs the best is the one that delivers the most. Freedom from want surely comes before freedom to speak; only if the two freedoms can be shown to be inextricably linked can it be said that democracy is best.

You don't automatically think of "elections" when thinking of Singapore; many will come to a stop at "authoritarian". Blame the latter perception, if you want, on the first prime minister, Lee Kuan Yew, for whom dissenting views were an obstacle which a state on a fast-track course of economic development could ill afford, especially if the ruling party had all the right answers, or at least enough of them to justify its rule.

But after the iron-willed Lee died, at 91 in March, if you thought that was the beginning of the end of his People's Action Party (PAP), you thought wrong. Last week, the government, led by his son Prime Minister Lee Hsien Loong, surprised the world (and maybe even himself) with a landslide election win that has to be viewed as a vindication of father, son, party and policies – all bound together.

Being bound together is not necessarily so terrible of a political thing. Outsiders ridiculed the "nanny state", as the Lees' Singapore has been dubbed. But when it turns out that the "nannies" sport high IQs and aren't stashing the people's money in foreign bank accounts but are on the whole producing positive public policy, such "binding" feels more like the special social glue (or social capital) that is the essence of a successful society.

You know all about the sparkling statistics – a high per capita income, low crime rate, highly rated health system, solid schools and almost a cultural fever for higher education. Problems? There are plenty, including the rich-poor gap, immigrant workers, high-cost housing and so on; but none are remotely unique in the region, much less worldwide; and the Lee government had "street cred" in pushing to solve them.

To quote a former cabinet member: "The world is changing fast. Governance can't stop changing." To that end, the new government to be formed should, in this post-Lee-Kuan-Yew era, dial up a little more tolerance for dissent and media latitude.

Another anti-Singapore sling has been that it is so tiny, its success is no big deal at all. Wrong again. Half the world's countries – the UN recognises 193 – have populations fewer than 10 million, and many have fewer than Singapore's, including Ireland, Uruguay,

Norway, Kuwait and New Zealand. So instead of criticising it for electoral impurity, why not take an open-minded look at its overall governance philosophy?

Policies are to be hatched not in the bowels of multinational corporations or in conference rooms of musty parliaments and half-bought congresses, where the sun rarely shines; but in venues that honor intellect and aim to hatch best practices (such as the Lee Kuan Yew School of Public Policy); and with bright and honest government officials who are paid well.

Yet, despite the 50-year streak of achievement, the PAP had feared the worst. The party was still shaking in self-doubt from the 2011 elections, in which a handful of parliamentary seats were lost (a big, big deal in Singapore), the PAP lost some of its halo and Lee Kuan Yew, among other grandees, retired from the government.

Suddenly, the party that had been running things for so long feared voters would tilt for opposition candidates just for the sake of change.

Note that a meaner, incompetent kind of government – think, oh, of Thailand's – might have pushed panic buttons of delay. Or have risked the system's integrity by sanctioning only well-vetted, like-minded candidates with near-identical perspectives (see Hong Kong's rejection of the 2017 election proposal).

Rather, the Lee government, staying on the high ground, won big, despite a tremendous opposition effort. But, as a noted Singapore journalist put it: "People were so rattled by all the rallies and extensive use of social media, they took flight to safety, fearing big gains by opposition and a weakened government. Shrewd electorate." That journalist was the enduringly perceptive Cheong Yip Seng (author of the book *OB Makers: My Straits Times Story*, one of the best insider accounts of government-media relations ever).

One candidate from the losing Reform Party compared the result to those in China and North Korea: "All this is a mandate for authoritarianism and brainwashing. Singaporeans get the government they deserve. I don't want to hear any more complaints." Singaporeans, in my experience, are anything but dumb, and talking down to those voters isn't smart. Last week, in their choice of who shall continue to serve as their "nanny", they chose well.

When I first visited, in 1996, I left impressed and wrote a Los Angeles Times column saying that. But American journalists, not one ever bothering to visit or interview Lee Kuan Yew (New York Times columnist William Safire actually called him "Little Hitler"), thought I had lost my mind. But I began to wonder whether the US media had lost its.

Two decades later, much of the Western media finally got the story right — that Singapore is a huge success, with a verifiable, empirical reason: it offers good governance. So where can we find more nannies like that?

I sincerely hope the leaders of China are taking all this in. The late Lee Kuan Yew could be grumpily frank about his tepidity for one-person, one-vote elections. He would tell you that such a system risked producing erratic results (and inferior leaders). But he also accepted that it gave people a sense of purpose in the polity, and more reasons for the ruling party to stay close to its constituencies.

The Singapore system is obviously not for everybody. That's not the argument here. But there's no reason not to take it seriously, not to mention not to treat it with the respect it deserves.

By the way, have you been following what's going on in neighbouring Malaysia?

P.S. That last line referred to the mountain of corruption allegations then surfacing against the federal government in Kuala Lumpur, headed by Prime Minister Najib Razak. Modern Singapore has yet to face anything remotely so enormous. Good government is honest as well as efficient. It does much more than simply make the railways run on time. Good governance is difficult to achieve, but a marvel to observe; and an achievement worth noting, and honouring.

AND THEN THERE'S...

"What '*liberté, egalité, fraternité*' meant to the French Revolution and to the making of modernity in the West, 'wealth, strength, and honor' have meant to the forging of modern China."
— *Wealth and Power: China's Long March to the Twenty-First Century,*
  by Orville Schell and John Delury, The Random House Publishing
  Group, 2013

09

OF DINNERS AND DEALS: THE DIFFERENT DIPLOMATIC STYLES OF CHINA AND THE US MAKE NEGOTIATION ALL THE MORE NECESSARY

SOUTH CHINA MORNING POST, MONDAY, 28 SEPTEMBER 2015

Tom Plate says relentless engagement, rather than aggressive containment, offers China and the US the best chance of achieving their ends

RETROSPECTIVE:

The ideal diplomatic diet with China is the one rich in diversity of connections and depth of contacts. Yes, Beijing can be difficult but so can any other major power; and, after all, dealing with the US these days is no fun run through Disneyland.

All's well that ends well? Start with this: guess who's been coming to dinner? In the otherwise Diet Coke blue-jeans Barack Obama years, a hip span showcasing the fewest number of formal White House state dinners of any administration since Harry Truman, only China has been graced with two prandial extravaganzas – just one for Japan, just one for anyone else. It's been a double dollop of dinner-party diplomacy for China. Let us all – including the anti-US faction in Beijing – dwell on this.

Each of the two state White House mega events for China – the first in 2011 with Hu Jintao when he was president, then last week with President Xi Jinping – produced results, which, mixed or unmixed, were better than no results.

Right now, the US media is picking holes in the cyber warfare agreement – but, really, who understands this problem fully? Notably, the Xi government's commitment to climate control and global de-warming increases with every diplomatic event. Perhaps Chinese people don't like breathing filthy air any more than anyone else. Western media critics continually – if correctly – point out that China's anti-earth emissions are double those of the US; but with its economy under stress in many sectors, and its population almost four times that of the US, how could it be otherwise? (Maybe China should stick with tea farming and forget all about modernisation?)

If Xi returned home believing his diplomatic venture was a success – it was – in part that's because he is Chinese, the Western business suit notwithstanding. What counts for him and his government is not so much the trip's actuarial pluses and minuses but the very fact that it took place – twice. Chinese needs are different from the American's.

Americans go for quarterly reports and five-year plans that tend to get scrambled every 18 months. By contrast, the bottom line for the Chinese is harder to achieve but more enduring: they want to get re-established the relative colossus that their country was centuries ago, before (in their eyes) the rest of the world was walking all over them.

The American leans towards (to quote a book title) "the art of the deal". Specific commitments of time must yield specific payoffs; otherwise the effort is seen to have been a flop. Some patently obvious metric assesses the result; computations are binary. This can annoy a true Chinese. When James Baker was secretary of state under President George H. W. Bush, he had his admirers, but not Chinese foreign minister Qian Qichen, who would cringe whenever his US counterpart would approach him with "let's make a deal". His view was that Sino-US relations belonged, by their nature, in a higher realm of being than, say, organizing a stock swap or pricing a used car.

Relentless relating between China and the US is an end in itself, because what else might lead to bilateral bonding? Not pushing forward is to risk accepting, inadvertently or not, a new Cold War – or worse. Sure, not everyone in Beijing thinks America is as great as America thinks it is; and sure, US domestic political pressures will limit the options of any president.

And – let us note – China's leaders somehow need to ignore every bit of the inevitable anti-China campaign rhetoric for the idiocy that it will represent. Trying to contain China in its own backyard – as if to slap onto such a vast people and civilisation an ankle bracelet of geopolitical house arrest – is a fool's errand. What Chinese government (Communist or not) would allow it? Smart Americans know that.

A mutual commitment to aggressive engagement has a far better chance of success than one of ill-conceived aggressive containment. At a minimum, it shows reciprocal respect rather than enmity. But where is the wise American voice that can convince the quick-hit American mentality that such is the best way? How can anyone in China really believe the path will not be a lot harder if America goes totally sour?

Consider the issue of the South and East China seas. News reports said there was no progress, the Chinese were obdurate, etc; but the very fact that both sides are working on this mess without stalking away in a showy huff suggests adults, not children, are at the negotiating table. The goal for Sino-US diplomacy is not to trump the other with some headlining win-lose gambit, but to work together to create some enduring liveable space in which both can find oxygen for their core needs.

This goes for both sides: if Beijing moves arrogantly, the Americans will be back in the barracks of Subic Bay, a non-sandy patch as big as Singapore – and rather closer to China than, say, Hawaii. And if the US moves arrogantly, it may find more of its allies tacking towards the pragmatic British position, leaving Washington looking petulant and old-fashioned.

The Philippines and others are alarmed by Chinese naval expansionism and seek relief from an international tribunal based on the UN Law of the Seas. But Beijing points out that the convention is too vague to be definitive. With contrary legal positions hardening, a smarter approach is needed: perhaps a grand bargain for Asian resource sharing. The path to that historic, needed settlement won't be found in "the art of the deal". China doesn't work that way, and in its most careful diplomacy the US doesn't – or shouldn't – either. What all sides need is a persistent process of relentless engagement that offers everyone something valuable and no one party everything under the sky. That would be real deal-making.

Let's say it again: all's well that ends well.

P.S. It is hard to believe either side will wish for a trade war to poison the bilateral relationship. The gains for each would be too marginal to warrant the erosion of forward movement. How much is geopolitical stability worth in monetary terms? It's not something easily monetarised but common sense tells us it's invaluable. In the mid-nineties, when the Clinton administration's trade hawks were bumping into Japan and blaming it for the big trade gap, President Bill Clinton intervened at one point and called them off, remarking that US trade with Tokyo was not the only aspect of that relationship that was significant. With China, then, you would have to say: Let's have a comparable proportionality.

AND THEN THERE'S...

"In 2014 the president of China, Xi Jinping, and Li Kequiang, China's premier, visited numerous countries as they worked to build strong relations directly with the political leadership of other nations. In a speech by President Xi given to Mongolian lawmakers, Xi said: 'China has always regarded its neighbours as cooperative partners and sincere friends for common development, peace and stability.' He went to quote an old Chinese proverb: 'A good neighbour is not to be traded for gold.' Xi continued to speak of mutual benefits: 'We will never do things that could result in 'one wins and the other loses' or 'one wins more and the other gets less'.

"China will unswervingly follow the path of peaceful development and in the meantime, it will push for peaceful development among all countries."

– *Fearing China, Asking the Question: Should We Fear China?*,
  by Terry D. Wittenmyer, Zebra CAT Publishing, 2015

10

SLOW AND STEADY IS HOW CHINA IS LIBERALISING THE RENMINBI — AS IT SHOULD

SOUTH CHINA MORNING POST, MONDAY, 12 OCTOBER 2015

Tom Plate says China is right to delay opening up its capital account before reforms are fully carried out

RETROSPECTIVE:

What the US wants another country to do may or may not be best for that country. In fact, the urged change may not be best for the US in the longer run. We are not always right, though we act as if we are. But because we still aver and believe that we are the "exceptional nation" – our motives are always pure; our integrity always pristine – and that we are the only exceptional nation, we will continue telling others how to run their country, no matter what. But guess what? The world is listening less carefully than it used to, including China.

The long march of the American campaign that ends in the crowning of our new president is well under way, as you have noticed. But I am not sure the great Chinese people should be allowed to watch.

Former top US national security official Zbigniew Brzezinski, who, at a fairly bouncy 87, is moving into the professor-ish throne of foreign-policy zen master, the one long filled by 92-year-old

Henry Kissinger, said he worries about "an increasing uncertainty as to what exactly ought to be the definition of China's role in the world".

Tell me about it! The more the US can talk to China "seriously and responsibly", he said, "the greater the chance that perhaps we can do more together instead of increasingly becoming preoccupied with suspicions that each is deliberately turning against the other". Let us give that a standing ovation – but also note the limitations of a process that works best only when trust is maximised.

US advice to China hasn't always been that great, and its conduct hasn't always been that inspirational. The Chinese are increasingly as aware of our flaws as we of theirs. Neither one of us always does the walk after giving the talk.

In the bad advice category, let's start with the early 1990s when Washington began pounding Beijing on the need to swing open its capital-conversion door. Then comes the Asian financial crisis to reveal exactly what happens when you mix wide-open currencies with pathetically weak institutions. Surveying all the currency carnage around Asia back then, Beijing drew back.

That financial crisis may well have been the tipping point. "Chinese policymakers studied the 1997–1998 financial storms, and they drew the right lessons," admitted Barry Eichengreen, professor of economics and political science at the University of California, Berkeley, in an enlightening interview in the October issue of The Oriental Economist, the smart New York-based monthly newsletter.

He added: "More than a century of historical experience teaches that open capital accounts can be an engine of volatility, that capital flows can reverse on a dime, and that financial markets, economies, and political systems can find it hard to cope with the consequences."

Even so, there would be a big upside to easy convertibility of the renminbi. Banks and corporations have a constant need to accumulate reserves in real money or liquid securities. Over the past several decades, something like 60 per cent of all central bank reserves have been deposits of dollars, which account for no less than 85 per cent of worldwide foreign-exchange transactions. Close to half the world's exports get priced in dollars.

In Washington and New York, this amounts to a tremendous ego trip, and yields absolutely enormous global US financial leverage. But given the pressures of the expanding global economy, the smart money is betting that, before long, another currency will have to step up to the plate; by itself, the US dollar is spread too thinly. Would logic not suggest that the currency of the world's other largest economy should be an option? The euro has been a weak player, and the world long ago lost its yearning for the yen when the Japanese economy went sleepy-weepy in the 1990s. So who's left? The franc?

Beijing's reluctance about swinging wide open its currency to global interchange is certainly understandable. You run huge risks if you have an open capital account without strong markets and financial institutions. No one needs to lecture the Chinese that they're not there yet. "China is trying to build deeper and more liquid financial markets, but in the last few weeks, it's tightened a variety of capital controls because of the weakness of the currency and the instability of financial markets," Eichengreen explains.

Rocked by sinking equity price levels and a slowing economy, the Chinese have been knocked off balance.

They do want to rely less on foreign trade and grow more from domestic demand. So Beijing would be doing everyone a favour – not just itself – by staying the course that is best for it, even if it seems slow for us. Internationalising the renminbi has to follow reform. Go the other way and you might just blow up the stability of the world economy in trying to "firecracker" reform into existence overnight.

Beijing is the first to admit much is to be done. The dark side – the shadow banking system – needs to be lit up like the Lunar New Year; the corporate bond market has to move towards international standards; and the stock market brought into at least some measure of transparency before the Chinese currency can go major-league global. After all, a prematurely totally open currency could trigger floodgates of renminbi outflow – and would have the wholly ironic effect of reducing its value in international currency markets. (Tired congressional hectoring about the evils of an artificially weakened renminbi has no real currency today – and from the get-go was always overstated by US politicians fronting for Wall Street.)

A solid Chinese renminbi as an international option for currency holders could be a very desirable development. But on this issue – unlike, for instance, global warming – Beijing will be listening to its own best voices and not US advice.

They have heard it from us all before. As Brzezinski put it, in a larger context: "We have to face the fact that we're now living in a world that has the United States pre-eminent but not really dominant." Our money still talks but we're getting near bottom with the dollar as the only conceivable glue for the international currency system.

P.S. Under President Trump, the "currency manipulation" quarrel has been restarted. I may be wrong of course, but this topic will prove a dead-end. The complexity of the two economies, their currencies and their inter-relationship has moved far beyond this point – let's get serious.

AND THEN THERE'S...

"As we enter the 21st century, we enter a world in which insecurities in one corner of the globe can almost instantly amplify insecurities elsewhere. This is a world in which changing currency values in China, Hong Kong, and Taiwan can affect America's prospects for stable growth and employment and the average citizen's most fundamental sense of economic well-being."
– *Same Bed, Different Dreams: Managing US-China Relations 1989–2000,* by David M. Lampton, University of California Press, 2001

---

11 | DEALING WITH CHINA'S RISE: US SHOULD LEARN FROM THE BRITISH THE ART OF THE DEAL

SOUTH CHINA MORNING POST, MONDAY, 26 OCTOBER 2015

Tom Plate says the US would be wise to follow in pragmatic Britain's footsteps and learn the art of the deal

RETROSPECTIVE:

The line between being principled and being stubborn is sometimes so fine it can be impossible to secure as a guide to conduct. America's views on communist ideology are well known, and in some ways (mainly economic) arc shared within China Itself. But politically, whatever you call it, a strong and determined Communist Party runs China, and a measure of respect has to be accorded – ideology, principle and indigenous stubbornness notwithstanding. America is not required to import China's political system simply because it accepts more of its exported goods than any country. Nor should China be required to import our political system simply because it works for America – but not in that many other places. Most of our serious shared problems are global, and require vast united coalitions of the non-ideological to solve. This column applauded the clarity, not to mention alacrity, with which the British government refused to let political principle becloud its legendary pragmatism.

Let us recall that, almost two decades ago, a cocky William Jefferson Clinton, then president of a country but two-centuries-plus old, bluntly informed Jiang Zemin that his country of many millennia, with a memory constructed, like the Great Wall itself, mainly along east-west lines, was "on the wrong side of history". This was in 1997.

Whatever the then general secretary of the Chinese Communist Party might have thought, he decided not to return the volley by impolitely laughing in the American's face. The exchange, after all, took place in Washington. But since then, the former Chinese president, now 89, has presumably enjoyed a few chortles with colleagues. China, governed by one-party communist rule that's often depicted in the West as the root of all possible political evil, may be on history's wrong side; but if so, isn't it rather odd that governments will jump to the Sino side quickly enough these days – or at least seek to play both sides of the ideological street?

And so let us also recall that, almost two decades ago, on a sodden night filled with images of British dignitaries all but holding their noses as they reluctantly handed over the keys to Hong Kong and tearfully boarded their outbound yacht, China looked to be less on the losing side than the receiving side of history. This was also in 1997.

So what do we have today? What we have is Brits cheering, as if he were David Beckham, the visiting president Xi Jinping, as if for all the world one big jolly Chinese Santa Claus – with Great Britain greedily peering into his goody-bag. You just had to love the sight of Xi's triumphant victory parade to Buckingham Palace (he and his glamorous wife Peng Liyuan royal guest-ing overnight), riding in a royal carriage, not to mention the solemnly attentive joint session of Parliament.

So history is flipping over on its back and landing on its "wrong" side?

The Brits know what they are doing. Outside of the average

successful Hollywood mogul, hardly anyone is better at feigning deep sincerity than a British official. With their own long history of hard knocks, the British are not about to permit past loyalty to block future survivability. The business bonding that took place between the British prime minister and the Chinese president was hardly designed as a geopolitical terrorist act to blow up the US-British alliance. But without rewriting the Magna Carta or slapping a Karl Marx wing onto the British Museum, London looks to be cutting commercial deals with the People's Republic of China as if there was no space for "ideology" on its bottom line.

America, fumbling anew in the Middle East, and well mired in its quadrennial domestic presidential campaign, seems off-balance. It is as if the US – despite all its carrier fleets and policy pivots to Asia – remains psychologically unprepared for the rise of China. Too bad America failed to hear out Asia's wiser voices, such as Kishore Mahbubani, the Singaporean policy-school dean and widely admired UN diplomat who back in the '90s was to lay out for the West the coming new global reality.

But precisely because they were forced out of Hong Kong, the British got that message and have been mulling it over ever since. London, despite the vaunted "special relationship" with Washington, was the first to break ranks and join the Asian Infrastructure Investment Bank that's key to Beijing's neo-Marshall Plan for the 21st century; and so now the city of London looks to be China's chosen pad for the launch of offshore renminbi bonds.

Who exactly are these Parliamentary reds cozying up to the Commies and yanking down the trans-Atlantic relationship? It's the blue-blooded Tory party of Winston Churchill and Harold Macmillan, not the crazy party with its dusty socialist tendencies and – Tony Blair aside – uncanny ability to scare the life out of most voters. It's the party of Margaret Thatcher, the Iron Lady who turned into silly putty at the hands of Deng Xiaoping when he insisted on the return of Hong Kong.

It is just possible, I admit, that Hong Kong is not the centre of the geopolitical universe, as many of its dwellers sometimes imagine. But it is not hard to make the case that the handover in 1997 was the political starting line of the 21st Asian Century.

And so here we are today, the pragmatic English cutting special deals to create a new relationship with the rising power of Asia. This is plainly smart, and I can only congratulate them on their historical consistency. Let me worshipfully recall Lord Palmerston's famous mantra (as nearly everyone does these days): "Therefore I say that it is a narrow policy to suppose that this country or that is to be marked out as the eternal ally or the perpetual enemy of England. We have no eternal allies, and we have no perpetual enemies. Our interests are eternal and perpetual, and those interests it is our duty to follow."

It's probably easier to wind up on the wrong side of history if you haven't lived through that much of it. Perhaps the British, with their gloried past as a naval power, can sense a sea change coming better than anyone. The Americans have not really begun to chart their own coherent course in the wake of the surfacing new Asian Century. And so the future going seems destined to get rough. Maybe, if the Americans won't listen to the Mahbubanis, they'll listen to the Brits? Maybe.

P.S. British government after British government has fairly well sailed this steady pragmatic course. What is the alternative? If one-party Communism is to fail in China, it will not be because of external invasion but internal erosion and ultimate implosion.

AND THEN THERE'S...

"And in Hunan, a youthful Mao Tse-tung attacked Wilson's failure in his first recorded criticism of the United States. The foreign community in China was astonished by the effectiveness of the movement, by the widespread expressions of patriotism, by the aroused state of the public. Many Americans, including businessmen, naval officers, and the visiting philosopher, John Dewey, responded with great enthusiasm to the awakening of China. For the first time, Chinese intellectuals expressed the desire for a complete transformation of Chinese civilization. They had come to realize that the modernization of China required the destruction of the traditional society and they were demanding precisely the kinds of social and intellectual changes that Americans had long believed would result in the 'civilizing', Westernizing, modernizing of China."
– *America's Response to China: A History of Sino-American Relations,* by Warren I. Cohen, Columbia University Press, 2000

12

In deal-making and handshaking Xi Jinping, China finds a new face of smart diplomacy

South China Morning Post, Monday, 9 November 2015

*Tom Plate says Xi Jinping has injected
welcome vigour into Chinese diplomacy*

RETROSPECTIVE:

I have to admit that I am not the biggest fan in the Western world of China's president. The best I know of him is that his wife was a very talented entertainer and gracious in person. From a distance, Xi Jinping seems no more magnetic than any other Asian authoritarian – and less than some. Personal admission: I suppose I do bear a grudge. I had formally requested interview with him for a book that would have comprised the next volume in my series "Giants of Asia". The request was approved by the Chinese Foreign Ministry, drawing on the recommendation of the PRC Consulate here in Los Angeles; but the project never got beyond that. Not being a particularly good loser, I sulked for a few weeks. Still, the government apparatus made a mistake. If China wants to be better understood, as it deserves to be, it has to do more than publish People's Daily and expect that to be enough to satisfy. Spending quality time with sincere and informed journalists from other countries and political cultures is a win-win.

China's new focused diplomacy, as viewed in an off-balance US, is close to remarkable. After all the past foreign-policy fog, through which it was sometimes hard to see where Beijing stood, we now have the Xi Jinping road show taking all sorts of stands at all sorts of splashy stops. It is an amazement of activity.

Today in the US, there may be almost as many think tanks, from Washington to Santa Monica, trying to parse Xi's new chess moves as pollsters tracking our many presidential candidates.

In recent weeks, you saw China's president in the US, addressing its business best and richest, then heading to Washington D.C. for a formal state visit; in London, hobnobbing with the queen, then all but being knighted by seal-the-deal Brits; in Hanoi, quick-stepping and happy-speaking; and in Singapore, shaking hands with Taiwan's leader, all in seeming respect.

Activity is not the same thing as achievement, of course. You can trot around the globe until your eardrums feel permanently popped and yet wind up with little more to show for it than yet more frequent-flier miles and business cards. Personal diplomacy that's solely personal won't stick unless a nation's core interests are behind the smiles. China's president and his glamorous wife Peng Liyuan, as much as they may relish the high life of first-class travel, are on a serious, if sometimes entertaining, mission to hike China's diplomacy to the next level.

Geopolitically speaking, the Taiwan impasse is one of the toughest on the diplomatic discord list, as it is the declared core interest of the People's Republic of China to lure, or compel, Taiwan to accept the sovereignty of Beijing.

Maybe half the people on the substantial island of Taiwan oppose integration, and maybe the other half support it – as (no maybes here) do countless mainland inhabitants, hoping for a kind of "come home again" sequel to the unforgettable 1997 Hong Kong handover.

Since 2008, Taipei and Beijing have not been getting in one another's hair, all things considered. One plus has been the Obama administration's inclination to keep its nose mainly out of it – and our annoyingly preachy voice mainly down. That has helped a lot: US diplomacy is sometimes best when publicly it says least (we are not always good at this). A related plus was the programmatic pragmatism of the greatly underappreciated president Ma Ying-jeou. Taking office in 2008, and immediately seeking out trade, tourism and other easy connections, Ma managed to downplay the icy-dicey stuff, particularly the fraught matter of sovereignty.

But in Taiwan's politics, as so often in life, no good deed tends to go unpunished for long: Ma can expect to leave next year after two terms with pitiful public opinion ratings – and the probability of his presidency ignominiously falling into the hands of the opposition whose independence party platform places Taipei directly at odds with Beijing and could try to undo everything Ma has achieved.

Xi would love to see his Singapore handshake somehow scare up the necessary votes to help Ma's Kuomintang party. Ah, but Beijing's track record is not good: the mainland's last run at Taiwanese voters, by unsubtly shooting off rockets in the island's very general direction before the 1996 election, only insured a romp for the very candidate Beijing loathed. Xi's weekend play in Singapore was far more subtle and statesmanlike, and commendable.

Beyond the January election, which every expert says is lost to the anti-integration opposition (and Xi knows this too), the Chinese president has now laid down a minimum standard of cross-strait diplomatic conduct – and one of his own making. Hold back no applause: sure, it's a charm offensive, no question, but it could help.

Regarding speculation that Xi timed the pulling of the Singapore rabbit out of his hat in anticipation of the Taiwanese election: maybe.

But it's just as possible the Chinese are focused on the unfolding American election.

Taiwan has been a campaign issue in the US before, notably in 1960 when Quemoy (Kinmen) and Matsu came under fire. Taiwan could come up as an issue again, but Xi's extension of respect to the leader of Taiwan puts his government in a better position to claim its rise remains peaceful, even over this issue.

The "one-minute handshake", as dubbed by the media, produced photos that offered a lot better image of China than missile tantrums.

In 2002, the then Chinese vice-president Hu Jintao bluntly warned America: "If any trouble occurs on the Taiwan question, it would be difficult for China-US relations to move forward, and a retrogression may even occur."

Everyone knows that the US military's backing of Taiwan annoys Beijing no end, but Xi's decision to shake that off, for the time being anyhow, suggests that quality relations with the US remain the higher priority.

The Democratic Progressive Party may well triumph in January, but Beijing is placing the bet that if China-US relations do deteriorate over new Taiwan tensions, the fault will be seen to rest with neither Xi nor Ma's party, but with people inside Taiwan who refuse to accept the reality of the 21st century.

In fact, Tsai Ing-wen, the DPP opposition leader, actually condemned the Xi-Ma meeting. This is unconscionable. China's rise will proceed apace, whether you like it or not. Everyone has to adjust their positions accordingly – and most preferably peacefully. No one will get everything they want. Including China.

P.S. I would not want Xi's job, of course. I imagine with all that communist palace intrigue, the atmosphere must be totally suffocating – not to mention the heavy air pollution around and over the capital. But I do think this giant of a man would benefit greatly – politically and otherwise – by granting this humble columnist interviews for that book I mentioned. What's the risk?

AND THEN THERE'S…

"My understanding then was that being a good journalist required excellent interpersonal communication skills. You needed to make people feel comfortable, and just being friendly wasn't enough; you had to be sincere, and then people would open their hearts to you. Sincerity – this is the calling card of a good interviewer." (Lin Gu)
– *China Ink: The Changing Face of Chinese Journalism,*
   by Judy Polumbaum with Xiong Lei, Rowman & Littlefield
   Publishers, 2008

13

THE BEAUTY OF RESTRAINT IN THE SOUTH CHINA SEA

SOUTH CHINA MORNING POST, MONDAY, 23 NOVEMBER 2015

Tom Plate welcomes the toning down of rhetoric and says Beijing should now consider taking the diplomatic initiative, given the need for China and the US to break through fossilised thinking to improve relations

RETROSPECTIVE:

The American view of the South China Sea tension is that it is all China's fault. Not quite. While it is true that Beijing this decade has pushed its weight around like a future hegemon-in-waiting, various claims and counterclaims have been bobbing up and down with the ocean currents for decades before. Beijing feels its turn to become feisty has arrived. One escape would be to take the position that the South China Sea is Beijing's Caribbean, and now China has its own Monroe Doctrine: Call it Xi's Doctrine, if you will. The problem with that simple solution is that it denies the counter claims of America's valid ally Japan and others with whom the US has longstanding relationships. Surely the Chinese understand and admire the quality of loyalty, especially when the going gets intense. And, as with most issues in a complex geopolitical struggle, the equities are complicated, if not impenetrable.

When feisty Chinese admirals or American generals fire off verbal macho-missiles, I either consider sliding under my earthquake-reinforced university desk or slipping over into the comfy contentment of denial that all is actually under control. And sometimes the latter is actually the case, as I hoped last week about China's admiral, Wu Shengli. While informing his countrymen and women that the PLA Navy deserved their patriotic acclaim for its "enormous restraint" in the face of US provocations in the South China Sea, its commander brassily added that China's navy would "defend our national sovereignty". This is the large mass of ocean that Chinese cartographic experts are allegedly thinking of renaming (or so goes the rumour) "Xi's Sea".

The American side baulked, of course, but its rhetoric seemed more level-headed than boat-rocking. At one stop during his latest Asia "pivot", President Barack Obama simply said: "For the sake of regional stability, the claimants should halt reclamation, construction and militarisation of disputed areas." This pitch was to the Association of Southeast Asian Nations, which includes lesser powers that have been doing their own share of land reclamation in "Xi's Sea". But the main target of Obama's remarks was the world leader in land, atoll and shoal reclaiming: China.

Even added up, these verbal shots across the bow from Wu and Obama did not sound like opening salvoes to war. It's possible that Beijing is starting to understand that it has pushed itself into such strong bargaining positions (possession being nine-tenths of international law) that it can now artfully proceed, in the wake of its blitzkrieg build-up, with a new-found diplomatic amity.

The timing for magnanimity is good. The US public, enduring the presidential campaign, would take notice of a Chinese bid to smooth South China Sea waters; and Hillary Clinton, the presumed Democratic nominee and poll leader, would benefit from a silencing, however temporary, of the Republican non-lambs (Donald Trump et al).

But supreme naval commander Wu is right about one thing: every time a probing warship or warplane from the US Pacific Command pokes its nose into what the Chinese believe is their righteous space, it creates a fateful opportunity for some trigger-happy PLA Navy officer (or some equally ill-advised American counterpart) to unleash bedlam. The risk would have no reward. With his former secretary of state leading the pack, not even our cautious and deliberative US president could turn a blind eye, much less the other cheek. But neither could Beijing, facing public opinion pressures of its own, afford to appear a pitiless, helpless giant. Both sides know this.

Beijing's top people don't like surprises any more than America's; behind-the-scenes choreography can work to reduce risk. The next US peacock-in-the-Pacific show is scheduled later this month; a pair of US warships will pop over to Mischief Reef to test the waters. But ask yourself: is this the best our two "bigs" can do? Whatever happened to President Xi Jinping's clarion call for "a new type of great power relationship"? Such a nice idea. And why not?

Sure, blame Washington, which, whether it's under an Obama or a Bush, cannot seem to escape the Dante's Inferno of the Middle East, so as to focus more on Asia. But the Xi administration needs to take a long look in the mirror, too. China may be destined to become the 21st-century power, but that doesn't have to happen tomorrow. Wanting something quickly sometimes means it takes longer for it to come to pass.

In his deeply wise new book Restraint: *A New Foundation for US Grand Strategy*, MIT professor Barry Posen agrees that powers that have the might will always believe they have the right. That China is climbing closer to the US on the power ladder requires us to understand that it figures it's in the right no matter what anyone says. Yet the US will stay in Asia as long as China thinks it shouldn't. Even Posen, who wants the chore list of the US military substantially downsized (now in the network: some 800 extraterritorial bases, ports and airfields in more than 80 countries), puts it this way: "Asia is a more difficult case [than other issues for the US] ... China may reach a point where it has sufficient power to bid for hegemony." But, speaking directly to Beijing, the professor notes that China "does not yet possess much offensive capability; it can punish and harass, but not crush or conquer. Its options are limited."

Logically, Beijing and Washington need each other and ought to do better by themselves. But how? Thinking out of the box is not easy when you are cooped up inside it. The Chinese act as if the South China Sea is their personal sandbox, triggering the inevitable US reply of "No, it's mine, too". Beijing takes the view that it is simply reclaiming what it used to own; Washington views the reclamation projects as archipelago empire-building. Both sides box themselves in at the very moment they need to construct a new box. Let China make the first move; showing a measure of flexibility might actually work to firm up its position, particularly in the court of world opinion. Two "rights" can make a big wrong when it comes to the bilateral relationship.

P.S. At this writing there was a relative calm in the South China Sea storm. Or is it merely the frightening calm before the fearsome storm? Perhaps President Xi accepts that China has pushed as far as it needs to for the time being. Give out some spiffy medals to his PLA Navy guys and focus on other projects. Give everyone a breather, thank you! Steady as you go, is the way to get on with your journey.

AND THEN THERE'S...

"... While China has consistently denigrated the US alliance system as Cold War relics and has trumpeted a new area of Asian multilateralism, it too demonstrates a penchant for bilateralism. Over the past decade, China has been quietly building its own China-centered regional architecture .... In the South China Sea, Beijing would much prefer to cut individual deals with each country with which it has territorial disputes rather than negotiate with ASEAN (Association of Southeast Asian Nations) as a group, because ... nervous Chinese security analysts [worry about] opportunities for the Southeast Asian Lilliputians to tie down the Chinese Gulliver."
– POWERPLAY: The Origins of the American Alliance System in Asia, by Victor D. Cha, Princeton University Press, 2016

14

US PRESIDENTIAL CANDIDATES' MISSTEPS ON CHINA A WORRYING REMINDER OF AMERICA'S INTERNATIONAL IGNORANCE

SOUTH CHINA MORNING POST, MONDAY, 7 DECEMBER 2015

Tom Plate says Republican Ben Carson's spurious claim about Chinese involvement in Syria raises disturbing questions about some White House hopefuls' lack of knowledge on foreign policy issues, and proves it's past time for the US to refine its thinking

RETROSPECTIVE:

This column called out former surgeon and former US presidential candidate Dr Ben Carson on one count of rank ignorance. Now a member of the cabinet of President Trump, the good doctor presumably has little recollection of the geopolitical gaffe described below. But to Asians, perhaps more than anyone else, the presumption that someone who knows so little about the world should be entitled to run for perhaps the most powerful single position in the world reeks of arrogance beyond belief. But this is America. And now Carson reports to someone who doesn't know much more about the world either. But this is my country. I still love it, but it is not always easy to defend... with a straight face, anyway. So be it. In part, this book is my penance for being a cosseted American.

At times, China and its ways are viewed from America as if little has changed. One of those times is now. This is our quadrennial US presidential campaign season. Sometimes, it is our silliest season.

One spurious claim about China recently marinated into a campaign issue and produced its first candidacy casualty – without Beijing having to lift more than one pinky of denial. Here's the story and the background:

In the arduous process of installing a new US president in January 2017, the China question has been simmering on the back-burner of the debate but not front and centre, yet. Several reasons explain.

One is the current US focus on Islamic extremism.

Another is that a non-posturing, truly substantive debate on any foreign policy issue is difficult to achieve when scoring voter points rather than unravelling complexities is the task at hand; but complexities are at the heart of all significant foreign issues, especially relations with China.

Yet another is that none of the candidates, except Hillary Clinton, former US secretary of state, can honestly say they know much of anything about China.

Of the two Republicans who in fact have chalked up headlines knocking Beijing, it looks as if only one will remain standing much longer. That would be Donald Trump. His campaign line, avoiding subtleties as any pitchman would, has been reductionist: Little good can come to the US when substantial good goes China's way. It's a one-way street. The Sino-US relationship functions as a competitive struggle, not as a common cause. You either beat them, or they beat you. At the moment they are "beating us". So we have got to beat them back.

It is true that, in America, domestic rather than foreign issues usually dominate presidential campaigns. But with skill, Trump has set up China primarily as a nexus issue of economic rather than geopolitical disadvantage. The real-estate tycoon's analysis is bogus, to be sure, but it is rather politically clever, and demonstrates anew his towering capacity for teeing up entertaining oversimplifications that capture some voters' rapture.

Less skilfully, the otherwise soft-spoken and provincial Republican Ben Carson, until recently close to Trump in the ever-roiling opinion polling, may have hit his tripping point when he slipped badly on the China question. Almost out of nowhere, the former neurosurgeon rhetorically wandered off the campaign trail into the Syrian desert, claiming to detect a sighting in that maelstrom of vast tragedy that no one else had: the presence of China.

The odd assertion, made about a month ago during a Republican TV debate, has been sticking to Carson like a celebrity medical malpractice suit. His Syria misstep was: "You know, the Chinese are there, as well as the Russians…" With that inadvertent revelation of incompetency, Carson strongly reinforced the point that not every American, not even a board-certified neurosurgeon, should be permitted to operate in the White House.

Be that as it obviously is, the poor doctor is anything but unique in a historically conflating China and Russia. For, something like a computer virus on the US political hard drive invariably prompts an automatic psychic recall of the former Soviet Union whenever the subject of China arises. The recall protocol includes the absurd notion that any country run by a communist party poses an inherent threat, as the former Soviet Union once did. But times change; even former "pure" Communists can marinate into BMW roadster capitalists; today's communist Vietnam, former all-out evil enemy, is now practically whimpering at the White House back door in a lost dog's effort to find a new pal; and lately Russia (these days terribly non-communist indeed) seems more the thorn in Washington's side than China.

Carson's clumsy Syrian slip prompted the question: Do we – or do we not – have the right to require presidential candidates to present at least a responsible level of knowledge about the big issues if they want the big job? America, which is not a dishonest society, knows in its heart that it must own up to aspects of its own international ignorance.

Every sane American now recognises that absolutely zero weapons of mass destruction were found in Iraq after we invaded, and that was the stated reason for the operation. And so now we have had tendered by a presidential candidate a phony claim that Chinese forces or agents (or … Chinese restaurants…) are in Syria, when they are not there and almost certainly never will be.

This unprepared candidate, blithely unfamiliar with core international fact, looks to have seriously deflated his presidential balloon. It's not often we see a candidate implode on a foreign-policy issue, but with the world getting smaller with every new, gruesome terrorist explosion, foreign policy questions no longer seem so foreign and ignorance no longer such bliss.

The instinct to conflate China with Russia is what mainland Chinese term America's "Cold War mentality". I have always thought this criticism a fair point, notwithstanding our differences with Beijing. So, in a sense, we should thank Carson for his inadvertent illustration of a recurring intellectual error and agree that it's past time our national thinking were updated and refined if we want to understand China and the world properly. Sure, China needs to understand America better – this too is true. But, sometimes, what our White House-ambitious politicians say and do seems inexplicable, incomprehensible and incompetent, even to Americans who, after all, are more or less used to this sort of nonsense, especially during campaigns.

P.S. Your humble columnist will have no more to say on this subject of inadequately prepared US candidates for the presidency, at least for the next four years.

AND THEN THERE'S…

"The reasonable man adapts himself to the world: the unreasonable one persists in trying to adapt the world to himself. Therefore all progress depends on the unreasonable man."
(George Bernard Shaw, Maxims for Revolutionists)
— *Superpower: Three Choices for America's Role in the World,*
   by Ian Bremmer, Penguin Publishing Group, 2015

15

For good Sino-US relations, the Americans must learn to listen, while the Chinese must learn to talk

SOUTH CHINA MORNING POST, MONDAY, 21 DECEMBER 2015

Tom Plate says China's government officials need to begin to speak up, and speak their minds, to foster understanding

RETROSPECTIVE:

Talk is not only cheap, it has the additional quality of being peaceful. I recommend that the Chinese do more of it and the US does less In front of the TV cameras and large public audiences. But talk is ineffectively one-sided if no one is listening. In this category the recommendation is for the US to do more of it, listening to the Chinese step up with the talking. One of my favourite world leaders, Ban Ki-moon, takes the view that there is little to lose and much to gain by avoiding the silent treatment in diplomacy. My trope is that while talk-diplomacy is no cure all, it is a *sine qua non* to peace and security.

As the influential sociologist and philosopher Jürgen Habermas was right to lecture us: conversations continuously conducted with rationality and thoughtfulness can ferment into a kind of symphonic repertoire for the civilised polity. You learn so little by talking: only the wickedly witty Oscar Wilde could get away with claiming to prefer talking to himself on the grounds that it saves time and prevents arguments!

That's perhaps an option for the poet or the playwright but not for the journalist; or for nations in their interrelations. We need to talk the talk before we walk the walk. To quote Habermas: "Society is dependent upon a criticism of its own traditions." This is now as true for our global society as for any nation state; and it is definitely true of the Sino-US relationship.

Listening to others – nations as well as people – requires respect. Without it, exchanges sour into shouting matches as if between the deliberately and defiantly deaf. Respect requires humility about one's own views and modesty about the universal applicability of one's own experiences. I know I've said this before – but there are always reasons for saying it again: America will never understand China if it talks and listens only to itself.

Sure, we have "track two" institutions (smart non-profits, heady think tanks) trying their best to engineer a two-way, 24-hour fast train to Beijing. But, overall, the project is not working well enough. Just one example: a former prime minister from Asia came to Los Angeles for a chat after an appointment-filled Washington visit. Basically depressed, he told me the American establishment will never understand the dynamics behind China's rise as long as it's viewing things through its usual military and adversarial periscopes. But did you not explain all this to them? "They hear but …[he paused]… they do not listen."

Arrogance can be a substantial bar to a healthy grip on reality. Listening to others is a time-honoured method of maintaining a measure of balance between the ears – a way of getting out of one's own head, which, as we all know, is sometimes a very strange and isolated place. All this by way of reiterating the obvious about China: if you want to understand it, you have to listen to it. But – and here's the "but", and it is a very big "but" – in all fairness to us in the US, it is hard to listen and learn when the other side all too often prefers not to talk.

And, yes, I'm getting a bit steamy now on this point: when Chinese officials do decide to say something, it is usually said so long after the fact that you feel you have heard it before. China needs to open up, at the highest levels, or – I believe – it may lose out in the global civic-conversation race.

Let me explain why we should worry. Looking back on my own occasional in-depth conversations with iconic Chinese officials makes the case – to me at least – that this Chinese government ought to be doing a lot more with its VIPs. I recall one session with then Vice-premier Qian Qichen, China's well-respected foreign minister in the 1990s. In a Diaoyutai guest cabin in Beijing, he laid out the core elements of Chinese internationalist thinking that served as invaluable markers for me for years. Then, in a Shanghai foreign ministry office, China's top official on cross-strait relations, Wang Daohan, offered up a riveting 90 minutes of emotional as well as intellectual context that had to be felt as well as heard. He took the listener from the depths of the Cultural Revolution to the heights of – well – the skyscrapers of Shanghai.

Canned press conferences do not measure up to real deals like these. But landing such sessions is rare; worse yet, this situation doesn't seem to be improving under the Xi Jinping government. So when China's top officials complain about being misunderstood, and while their complaint may well be valid, an available remedy seems not to occur to them: they should take their chances and open up. Heck, this is the globalised information age, not the Silk Road epoch of a thousand ox-carts.

Here's another illustration: Not long ago, the much-admired East West Centre of Honolulu, in alliance with the mainland's venerable All-China Journalists Association, brought to my university a VIP delegation of more than a dozen Chinese journalists and media executives. Represented institutions included China Central Television, China Radio International, People's Daily, Sichuan Daily Group, United Media Group of Shanghai, Worker's Daily, Xinhua News Agency and other mainland media megastars.

The topic of our seminar was "How China's rise is impacting its relation with regional neighbours; and China's future as a world power". It was a fascinating session that ended with the usual exchange of gifts. Mine were copies of the Chinese edition of my *Conversations with Lee Kuan Yew*. One journalist, noting that the book was part of the "Giants of Asia" series, asked why no mainland officials have yet been included: Is China not important – and is Singapore not so very tiny?

I answered as politely as possible: whereas Singapore and other governments reply to media requests for VIP interviews, yours ignores them. The journos shook their heads in dismay, for they knew I was right. I understand the longstanding official mentality on media relations, but I will stick to my guns: this is no good for China.

P.S. Again, I call on President Xi Jinping to meet the American press; or at least to meet with me (that should do it...). After all, what does he have to lose? And might not China have a lot to gain? Try it, Beijing, you may like it.

AND THEN THERE'S...

"China's diplomacy cannot be labeled simply as 'soft' or 'hard' line.... We Chinese believe in combining firmness and flexibility.... This means we must know when to fight, when to cooperate, and when to avoid direct confrontation."
(Assistant Foreign Minister Le Yucheng, 2011)
– *China Goes Global: The Partial Power,* by David Shambaugh, Oxford University Press, 2013

16

Why Xi Jinping remains an international man of mystery to most in the US

South China Morning Post, Monday, 4 January 2016

Tom Plate says even in informed circles there is little consensus about the Chinese president, who will be the most intriguing leader to watch, for most of 2016 at least

RETROSPECTIVE:

For an American journalist to profile a Chinese leader positively, a scent of treason might not be too far down the trail of accusation. At least you might risk losing your putative media membership card if you stray too far from the American party-line. Imagine proposing Xi Jinping for a Nobel Peace Prize! This cannot be, of course. But if one were to (very cleverly) propose a joint award for Xi along with the former president of Taiwan for keeping the political waters across the strait relatively calm, then you might be able to keep the FBI, the CIA and the NSA at bay! Read on, please....

Watch this man carefully. For at least until November 8, when who follows US President Barack Obama is to be revealed, 2016's most fascinating leader-figure will be Xi Jinping.

Although ensconced as president three years ago (with all the grandiose title trimmings attached), and immediately outward bound as China's globetrotting salesman in chief – opening doors, closing deals, scaring the West witless – this Beijing-born son of a Chinese icon remains a totally enigmatic figure. In the US particularly, the avuncular face of China has seemed frustratingly hard to read.

Even in America's best-informed circles, there is little consensus as to who Xi is. To optimists, especially hopeful economists, he is the keeper of the common-sense flame of Deng Xiaoping, the genius leader who undoubtedly saved Communism politically by all but abandoning it economically.

As Harvard professor Ezra F. Vogel put it in his masterpiece *Deng Xiaoping*: "Deng guided the transformation of China into a country scarcely recognisable from the one he had inherited in 1978."

On this reading, the 62-year-old Xi remains the committed Beijing-based gang Deng-er. But, to pessimists, Xi seems more the post-modern Mao man, grumpily chafing over the sins of materialism (now such the topic in the halls of the Central Party School) and the breakdown of party discipline. In some US circles, he is seen as using the current anti-corruption campaign to gin up some kind of loyal Chinese Tea Party. The fear is not only that this true-red Communist will concoct a cultural devolution and trigger a back-to-basics Chinese dynasty, but also that he will push East Asia into a tributary-traditional, Beijing-reliant geopolitical system.

Respected Columbia University professor Andrew Nathan offers pessimism: "I fear that Xi is creating great danger for China. By undercutting the institutionalised system that Deng built, he hangs the survival of the regime on his ability to bear an enormous workload, make the right decisions, and not make big mistakes. He is trying to bottle up a growing diversity of social and intellectual forces that are bound to grow stronger. He may be breaking down, rather than building up, the consensus within the political leadership and among

economic and intellectual elites over China's path of development …
As he departs from Deng Xiaoping's path, he risks undermining the
regime's adaptability and resilience."

Such polar-opposite portraits lack key nuances, especially in
dealing with one of the most complex systems in political history. As
an eminent source sees it: "It is true that Xi has concentrated power
to an extent not seen in a long time. But at the core is a life-and-death
struggle to re-establish the moral authority of the Communist Party.
The reasons for his doing it are not as your Columbia professor thinks
but much deeper."

Xi will always try to take the long view about his China, as if the
main monk of a new, emerging Chinese Confucianism. A few months
ago he wrote, remarkably: "Future China will be under a group of
people with the right view, right mindfulness and positive energy. The
real crisis is not of economic or financial, but it is the crisis of morality
and spirituality. The more blessed one is, the more energy one has. Be
friends with the wise ones, move with those who are kind. Always have
the people in mind with boundless great love."

Such warm words might well strike the Western eye as okay for
a spiritual pope but not a secular one – not to mention an avowed
Communist atheist whose government demonstrably does not love the
irreverent blogger or treacherous tweeter, much less the upstart Uygur.
Yet Xi's massive anti-corruption campaign, headed by the very capable
Wang Qishan, at times does have the feeling of a spiritual cleansing (or
is it just a commonplace political purge?).

Xi became China's maximum leader not so much through party
connection as policy competence. Highly regarded, he was put in
charge of the 2008 Olympics preparations and, back in the mid-
1990s, was Beijing's man hovering over the reacquisition of Hong
Kong to ensure it would not be bungled. To his party partisans, he

seemed the always-reliable deliveryman. One man very impressed by Xi was the late Singapore master Lee Kuan Yew, who said: "I would put him in the Nelson Mandela class. A person with enormous emotional stability who does not allow his personal misfortunes or sufferings to affect his judgment."

At the same time, Xi's climb to the top has made enemies of immense intensity (a nervous story all but hidden from mainland and world media), with attendant threats that have ballooned the size of his security contingent. In addition to the anti-corruption drive, Xi has pushed for a restructuring of the vast PLA military to nail down party control over a sector that sometimes careered toward the semi-sovereign. This revamp is a heavy lift.

Xi certainly deserves no Nobel Peace Prize simply for sweet thoughts in Confucian-like prose. But there is one area of achievement that does merit a look from the committee: he and Taiwan's leader Ma Ying-jeou as joint candidates for the 2016 Nobel Peace Prize for easing cross-strait tensions. In Singapore recently, this political odd couple put on a most welcome public display of diplomacy in the first such cross-strait meeting at that high a level since 1947. Absurd to propose Xi and Ma for the Nobel Prize, you say? I might agree if someone can explain why it's any more absurd than the 2009 Nobel Peace award to Obama … just nine months after he took office. That was ridiculous. The Xi-Ma idea is not, and has some charm.

P.S. The joint Nobel never happened, of course. I think it went to songwriter Bob Dylan or someone. Never mind, I'll be quiet. Some of his songs are pretty good, of course. So are some of Xi's … oh never mind.… Not to mention Ma's … oh never mind!

AND THEN THERE'S...

"A prosperous and stable China will not be a threat to any country. It will only be a positive force for world peace."
(Vice-president Xi Jinping, 2012)
— *China Goes Global: The Partial Power,* by David Shambaugh, Oxford University Press, 2013

17

WHY THE CASE OF THE HONG KONG BOOKSELLERS IS MORE OF A WORRY THAN CHINA'S MARKET WOES

SOUTH CHINA MORNING POST, MONDAY, 18 JANUARY 2016

*Tom Plate says while the economy will surely recover,
the same cannot be said of "one country, two systems"
unless Beijing moves to clear up the mystery*

RETROSPECTIVE:

Forget about anything like a strong American-like First Amendment governing the media in China. The Communist system is different, and unapologetically so. The media – whether newspapers, magazines, books or TV – exists to reflect the wise views of the Party, which exists only to mirror the wishes, will and hopes of the people. The American media exists to hold power accountable, while making profits. In the column below, a bookstore in Hong Kong (of – it must be said – tremendously marginal literary quality) somehow ran afoul of the mainland; even today the full story is not clear. The kerfuffle went global. But there was a reason: If Hong Kong were no more than a regular province of China – one of almost two dozen – then the story would not have had such legs. But because Hong Kong is quite special – and has been officially granted status as a "special administrative region of the People's Republic of China" – different standards of conduct for the PRC apply. In the column below, the sense is those standards were violated.

Overall, the unfolding drama of China – as viewed on this side of the Pacific, in sunny Los Angeles – has, in the past week or so, seen the vigour of its vim dimmed somewhat.

My worry is not so much the mayhem of the markets and the attendant gangling neuroticism of the gigantic mainland economy. While reports in the world media have been fulsome with negative detail, the fact is that an expanding, multifaceted economy such as China's was never going to unfold as daintily as a blooming rose or as harmoniously as a Mozart symphony. It was always going to jerk this way and that – imagine an especially neurotic octopus suddenly with even with more legs than normal and a central brain system constantly struggling just to keep count of them all.

Worry not excessively. China now fields smarty-pants economists as cunning and well schooled as any, anywhere. They will figure a way out, over time, especially if their political masters permit them enough time to do so and display the political guts to back them up. At the end of the day, politics does tend to trump the economists. Consider the highly political – and bizarre – story of the Causeway Bay bookstore and its missing team, including the owner. This macabre mystery rattles many nerves even more than the roiling markets.

Balance and perspective must be maintained until enough verifiable facts are out, and right now there are not many. Over the weekend one of the five, in Thailand, outed himself as a fugitive from mainland criminal justice and turned himself in. But what about the other four in the bookstore gang of five? That's the Hong Kong worry.

From China's hypersensitive viewpoint, "one country, two systems" goes out the window if and when Hong Kong morphs into a base of subversion on its southern flank. If President Xi Jinping's internal enemies (presumably growing in number and intensity with every new corruption crackdown) are using Hong Kong to spread tawdry and demeaning rumours in order to lower the angelic glow around the boss, mainland security people will want to know every who and all the how. Until his rocked economy regains its footing, Xi might want to dial down the intensity of the ethical evangelicalism. It is not for show that Xi travels with a noticeably large security detail wherever he goes.

Beijing does not wholly trust Hong Kong. Note that Article 23 of the mutually agreed Basic Law says: "The Hong Kong Special Administrative Region shall enact laws on its own to prohibit any act of treason, secession, sedition, subversion against the Central People's Government, or theft of state secrets, to prohibit foreign political organisations or bodies from conducting political activities in the Region, and to prohibit political organisations or bodies of the Region from establishing ties with foreign political organisations or bodies."

Beijing, for its part, takes notice of the fact that, almost two decades after the historic handover, Hong Kong has not done this.

On the other hand, if the allegedly subversive bookstore gang, in whole or part, was spirited or somehow lured over the border by nefarious methods, as many in characteristically suspicious Hong Kong suspect, then this is of course a serious violation of the spirit of "one country, two systems". Although perhaps not on the same elevated philosophical shelf as the Magna Carta, "one country, two systems" has a lot going for it; for sheer practical ingenuity, it is often underestimated. It's also a trademark political legacy of Deng Xiaoping, who, though he did not invent the idea, was surely its driving, principal proponent.

Until now, it has seemed unthinkable that the Xi government would regard "one country, two systems" as anything other than canonical. So, was the bookstore bust an instance of the "Mao" Xi at clandestine work behind the scenes; or, instead, of just some "Mission Ridiculous", Watergate-style bozo operation designed to ingratiate provincial security agents with higher-ups? The bookstore's shelves stocked tabloidian tomes of Clintonesque-type flings by Chinese VIPs.

At this writing, technically, based on the scant facts that exist, no law has been broken. Still, Beijing should clean up this mystery, make an example of the "Mission Ridiculous" boys (if such is the true story), and work better with Hong Kong on the vital job of making "one country, two systems" an exemplar of very smart 21st-century international politics. But Hongkongers have to accept reality: Beijing is sovereign. A famous Chinese saying applies here: "However ugly your parents are, they are still your parents."

But Beijing cannot behave as the beastly bull in the greater China shop, especially if it wants smooth sailing in Hong Kong and prays, some day, for the historic mainland docking by Taiwan. One notes that the island's pro-independence political party just nailed a smashing victory to regain power with the island's first female president. This is not the best news for any unification timetable. Unless the PRC plans an invasion, then endless patience for Taiwan as well as Hong Kong (as prickly as the wonderful territory can be) remains the smart policy approach. Exercising the force option would set back China more than any number of market corrections – and launch a thousand unfriendly new books, on sale almost everywhere.

P.S. The kerfuffle calmed down, but similar intrusions into Hong Kong's sense of new autonomy pop up from time to time. The question, in the paranoiac mind, is whether these apparent violations of the territory's semi-sovereign space are part of a whittling-down campaign, or simply the erratic product of a government up north that willy-nilly does this or that. Your humble columnist inclines tentatively toward the latter view. In America, we tend to believe that it is easy to over-estimate the coordination capabilities of government.

AND THEN THERE'S...

"We are still preoccupied with domestic problems. US leaders have a global perspective, but our leaders are thoroughly preoccupied with domestic issues." (Vice-foreign minister Cui Tiankai)
– *China Goes Global: The Partial Power,* by David Shambaugh,
  Oxford University Press, 2013

18

The rich history of mistrust behind China's warning to George Soros

South China Morning Post, Monday, 1 February 2016

Tom Plate says Beijing's suspicion of Western financial advice has its roots in the Asian financial crisis

RETROSPECTIVE:

There are many aspects of my culture – economic as well as political – that I like immensely; but short-selling against struggling companies and speculation against sovereign currencies are common Western money-making strategies not near the top of my honor roll. Whenever Beijing financial authorities seek to ban these practices, the Adam Smith part of my soul recoils in horror, but something in my heart tells me that, whatever the motives, the Chinese are right. Making money is an absolute good only if it is the only absolute good in your value system.

There are more than a few financial figures in China circles who no longer trust Western financial advice (or most advisers) any more than they have to. There is a rich, as it were, history behind the mistrust. And in this, George Soros, no less, has a role. Here is the story.

We start our narrative with the Asian financial crisis of the late 1990s. For years, China had been relentlessly advised by US Treasury experts in the Bill Clinton administration, and by other prominent experts in the West, to stop babying its coddled currency and let it go outdoors onto the international markets to play fair and square with other big-time currencies.

For decades, this has been the constant whining pitch of the geek chorus in the West.

In fact, the argument has merit if China is to secure its place in the competitive world marketplace, of which central cosmopolitan idea Zhu Rongji, the great former premier, was China's world champion.

In fact, years later, Beijing itself moved in exactly that direction, in part to satisfy the International Monetary Fund that its currency would be cleanly convertible and so globally market-worthy.

But two decades ago, China was not ready for the big bad sandbox, felt both crowded and rushed by the West, and so held back.

Surprise: Suddenly a vile regional currency crisis swept across Asia, from Bangkok to Seoul to Hong Kong. Western speculators, allegedly including Soros (in 1992, he hit his billionaire jackpot with a nervy mega plunge against the sodden British pound), dumped bundles of cash on the bet that weak Asian currencies would lose value, and pocketed fortunes via massive "shorting" campaigns that in effect ground down Asian currencies even more.

China, whose renminbi-exposure caution was then working in high gear, escaped all that pain – and to that I say thank goodness.

So did our more globally sensitive Western souls who were unnerved by the global turbulence, by the frailty of the fraying "international economic architecture" – and by the heartless display of sheer amoral speculative greed at the expense of the Asian people.

After all, everyone knew that massive currency speculation can rock even relatively well-managed small and medium-sized economies – just as easily as a tsunami can overwhelm the most competently installed roofing over a house. Soros, the mega investor turned philanthropist, knew well of what he spoke when he depicted predatory financial speculators as the destructive "al-Qaeda" (his words) of the financial world.

Now for a quick side note: If you claim that "al-Qaeda" short attacking, derivatives spinning and hedge funding more or less belong in the same foul and corrupt financial fruit salad, you might be accused of committing a category mistake. But surely such a broad definition is forgiveable given the delicate, easily fractured interconnectedness of the global financial architecture. Caution and respect are in short supply where greed is abundant. And so sure enough, in 2008 – only a decade after the near-death experience of the Asian financial crisis – the US economy itself almost collapsed into depression.

The reason: a new financial "al-Qaeda" investment house of cards known as the "subprime" credit default crisis. Need a quick primer on "subprime" but were afraid to ask? See the Hollywood film *The Big Short*, inspired by the book of the same name. I am serious. Do yourself a favour – don't miss pop star Selena Gomez popping up at a 21-table in Vegas to explain with almost didactic charm collateralised debt obligations. Priceless.

With the ground shaking from the US financial quake, Beijing then put into rush status long-planned, Pharaoh-like public-sector works infrastructure investments to push the domestic economy forward and provide as many jobs as possible.

While this bold 2009 move ran the risk of inserting bubbles into the Chinese economy that, down the road, might inevitably lose their pop, some Western financial figures applauded the "flash-flood stimulus". One was repentant Soros himself, who accepted that the 2008 "Bush bubble" was nothing less than an economic existential threat, and told the Chinese their stimulus response was spot-on.

A Beijing shaken by the US housing collapse greatly appreciated that support. But that was then, and this is now – so guess what?

The other day, Beijing unloaded on speculators who might have thoughts of wanting to "bet on the 'ultimate failure'" of the suddenly rocky Chinese economy, in the words of Xinhua, the giant Chinese news agency, which added: "Reckless speculations and vicious shorting will face higher trading costs and possibly severe legal consequences."

Where did that offended outburst come from? It turns out that, at the recent annual retreat in Davos, one famed Western figure airing the view that China is "doomed to a crash" was Soros himself.

While the old "shorting" master is no longer active as he used to be (and surely Xinhua must know this), in some eyes he remains the international icon (for all his commendable philanthropy) of sadistic currency and equity profiteering.

The People's Daily chimed in: "Soros' war on the renminbi and the Hong Kong dollar cannot possibly succeed – about this there can be do doubt."

These warnings are really directed generically rather than individually – at the global class of fast-buck investment jackals that care for no one's welfare other than their own. It's not hard to believe in the potential sting of the Xinhua threat. It's also not hard to believe that Chinese officials won't move to shelter the currency again.

Even some Western authorities won't blame them for that. They know how predatory their speculators can be. Sometimes, it is only common sense to get the heck out of the sandbox when the bullies in them are trying to pull off their shorts.

P.S. During the Trump presidency, with its emphasis on deregulation, another "2008 plunge" from the West is close to inevitable. If Asia and China seek any consolation, it should come from the realization that the poison originated in the West, not in Asia, where one regional financial crisis helped most economies clean up their financial act.

AND THEN THERE'S...

"The Chinese approached the moment with a mixture of triumphalism and concern. They began lecturing Americans instead of the other way around. In January 2008, Wu Yi, one of China's vice-premiers, criticized the US policy of letting the dollar fall. For years, America had blasted China for keeping its currency low, and here was a Chinese leader with the temerity to denounce America for doing the same thing. 'The Chinese people,' she told the group of American officials, 'are being hurt because they have invested in your dollars.'

"But it wasn't just American currency policy that got stuck in China's craw; it was the American way of life. At the fourth meeting of the Strategic Economic dialogue in June 2008 in Annapolis, Maryland, (Chinese official) Wang Qishan condemned America's waste. 'It's a hot summer day, but it's cold in your offices because you've got the air conditioning on,' Wang said. 'In the winter you've got the heat blasting out. For exercise you work out in air-conditioned gyms, then take hot showers, then get in air-conditioned cars. This is America! In China, we don't live that way. We can't afford to.' Wang Qishan's boss, Premier Wen Jiabao, picked the World Economic Forum at Davos in January 2009 to reprimand the United States for its 'lack of self-discipline' and 'blind pursuit of profit'. America had been weakened, he said, thanks to 'an unsustainable model of development characterized by prolonged low savings and the high consumption'. Clean up your act was China's message to the United States."

— *The Beautiful Country and the Middle Kingdom: America and China, 1776 to the Present,* by John Pomfret, Henry Holt and Company, 2016

19 WHEN IT COMES TO CHINA, AND US FOREIGN POLICY IN GENERAL, BERNIE SANDERS NEEDS ALL THE HELP HE CAN GET, INCLUDING FROM HENRY KISSINGER!

SOUTH CHINA MORNING POST, MONDAY, 15 FEBRUARY 2016

Tom Plate says the Democratic candidate's dismissive comments about the former secretary of state during a debate with Hillary Clinton reveal his lack of understanding of international relations

RETROSPECTIVE:

While Henry Kissinger is reviled by many Americans for work as America's top foreign policy official that was either illicit or even illegal, on the one issue of China he has over the decades been mostly right. Since this is no minor issue on which to have the right view, to dismiss this former Harvard government professor seemed to me infantile. But Senator Bernie Sanders, who has been right on many issues, did exactly that during his campaign for the Democratic nomination for the presidency. On this issue, he was wrong.

Henry Kissinger is a source of pride for some Americans and rage for others. Over the decades, our most famous former secretary of state (aside from Hillary Clinton) has turned into something of a lightening-and-ethics-measuring rod for the longitudinal validity of US foreign policy. Now, at 92, he looks to have a new role to play:

as a punching bag on the China question during the ongoing US presidential campaign.

Here's the back story: America has been both saint and sinner; it has conspired to concoct coups against democratically elected leaders, despite all our public blather about human rights, but has also interceded to save legitimate leaders from assassination. Our clandestine services have buttressed American corporations abroad that had no more interest in human rights than Pol Pot, and yet our armed forces, when not booked into foolish and illegal occupations, have jumped in heroically to rescue peoples and nations time and again from the most horrendous natural calamities. Often, this is forgotten.

Simply put, America does not offer simplicity of categorisation, and neither does Kissinger, the former Harvard professor suddenly caught in the centre of contention between Clinton and US Senator Bernie Sanders. During a televised debate, the two candidates for the Democratic Party nomination to succeed President Barack Obama next year differed on the national value and true character of this famous man.

Clinton pushed Sanders to name even one expert on whom he relies for input on foreign policy, a topic that's not the Vermont senator's strong suit. But, surprising everyone, he took advantage of the joust, turning it on the former secretary of state with more than a bit of burn: "Well, it ain't Henry Kissinger – that's for sure."

His sally relayed the liberal critique of Clinton as so deeply embedded in the American establishment as to be unable to see its serious shortcomings. In the minds of many liberal Americans, Kissinger, though a Nobel Peace Prize honoree, is nothing less than an unindicted war criminal for actions that included the Richard Nixon presidency's infamous Cambodia bombing, support of Pakistan's genocide in Bangladesh (then East Pakistan) and covert cheerleading of political executions in Latin America. All things considered, his is indeed a very mixed CV.

Against this, admirers of America's best-known living statesman bring up his seminal work with Nixon in breaking the historical ice with China during the Cold War – and for keeping the relationship warm decade after decade. But for Sanders, playing the China card does not do the trick. As he said: "Where the secretary and I have a very profound difference ... she talked about getting the approval or the support or the mentoring of Henry Kissinger. Now, I find it rather amazing, because I happen to believe that Henry Kissinger was one of the most destructive secretaries of state in the modern history of this country. I am proud to say that Henry Kissinger is not my friend. I will not take advice from Henry Kissinger ... So count me in as somebody who will not be listening to Henry Kissinger."

Clinton pushed back: "You know, I listen to a wide variety of voices that have expertise in various areas. I think it is fair to say, whatever the complaints that you want to make about him are, that with respect to China, one of the most challenging relationships we have – his opening up China and his ongoing relationships with the leaders of China is an incredibly useful relationship for the United States of America."

On the surface of the tense exchange (quality content for an American primary debate, usually little more than a podium for posturing by poseurs), is the implication that the Sanders position looks to the future whereas the Clinton position is stuck in the past. Paradoxically, the opposite is the case. Here's why.

Kissinger's sins, however grievous, are national sins more than those of an individual acting beyond his remit. The fact is that all major foreign policy decisions are presidential decisions, whether a given secretary of state is cunning and influential or, alternatively, slow-footed and marginalised, American foreign policy is set by the president. During his years of power, Kissinger worked for Nixon and Gerald Ford, not – as over the past four decades – for himself.

To be sure, this fact of governance provides no exculpation – no more than the capo of an organised crime family is blameless for the ordered sins of the godfather. But if the only relevant issue is about the future of US foreign policy, then Clinton was spot on: Without at least a satisfactory working relationship based on a measure of mutual strategic understanding with China (representing 20 per cent of the global population, no less), without such a fundamental ship-of-state bottom, the US will drift and sway dangerously – though perhaps not keel over – as it sails forward through the 21st century.

Kissinger's Beijing perceptions and experiences (for me, his 2011 *On China* is canonical) cannot be anything but welcome. Advice need not come from a saint to be useful to a secular president; one is wise to consult even Lucifer if real insight is the pay-off. Let us invoke the wisdom of Max Weber, the legendary sociologist and philosopher of a century ago: "It is not true that good can follow only from good and evil only from evil, but that often the opposite is true. Anyone who fails to see this is, indeed, a moral infant." If you see what I'm getting at.

Whether Asia finds itself content with Obama's successor or dismayed, it will have no choice but to live with him or her – just as we in the US accept President Xi Jinping, like it or not. In the US case, though, one would wish that the new White House occupant would not need a crash course in "Intro to International Relations Reality" from day one.

P.S. As it turned out, the new occupant and successor to Barack Obama did need exactly that. But his name was not to be Bernie Sanders.

AND THEN THERE'S...

"In general, since 2012, more Americans see China unfavorably than favorably. Despite increasingly negative perceptions, US-China relations will be vitally important in future. These two titans are tangled together in innumerable ways – strategically, diplomatically, economically, socially, culturally, environmentally, regionally, internationally, educationally, and in many other domains. The two nations are the principal powers in the Asia-Pacific region and globally. The two possess the world's two largest economies on aggregate, two largest military budgets and navies, are the two largest consumers of energy and importers of oil in the world, are the two largest national emitters of greenhouse gasses and contributors to climate change, contribute the two largest numbers of PhD's and patent applications in the world, and are the two true global actors on the world stage today."

– *China's Future,* by David Shambaugh, Polity Press, 2016

20 | In the end, Pope Francis' 'kowtow diplomacy' towards China will show itself to be smart diplomacy

South China Morning Post, Monday, 29 February 2016

Tom Plate says America has much to learn from the pontiff's open and humble attitude towards China

RETROSPECTIVE:

It takes just a bit of imagination to perceive the Vatican and Beijing as parallel in form. Highly centralised. Highly ritualised. Struggling to reform. Worried about the core ideology losing relevance. Accordingly, the thought here is that if Beijing and Rome can come to some kind of concordat, a circle will be squared, and the world will be advised that it is rare that harm comes from talking out a problem, no matter how long it takes.

You don't have to be a saint to be a great and effective leader, but you do have to be audacious. So when an audacious leader comes along that a good many admirers suspect to be a saint, you have probably got something special in front of you. May we presume this, for the moment at least, of Pope Francis?

The restless pope: after a papal visit to Mexico, about which US presidential candidate Donald Trump (audacious, but no saint) had something negative to say, Vatican sources floated the thought that perhaps Francis might soon visit China.

In his observations about a country with more than 21 per cent of the globe's population (but only 12 million in mainland China are Catholic), the pope will emphasise the positive: "For me, China has always been a reference point of greatness. A great country. But more than a country, a great culture, with an inexhaustible wisdom."

Yet, for noodle-brain elements here in the United States, Francis's diplomatic charm offensive may come across as classic kowtowing – an unseemly, un-audacious genuflection to the rising power of communist China. But effective diplomacy, especially when in public light, usually requires a premeditated emphasis on the positive (the negative comes later, behind closed doors). What's more, a posture of kowtowing can be potent when the target is known to be susceptible to it – as shown throughout the history of China.

So the Pope's kowtow diplomacy towards China is smart stuff. What he wants is to be able to improve the condition of his Catholics in their spiritual development; so he not only dreams of a semi-normal relationship between the Vatican and Beijing, he also envisions his church and the Chinese state working in polite, respectful parallel on the appointment of mainland bishops. Such accords would hardly undermine Beijing's national security and would certainly boost China's global image.

Diplomacy takes patience; you could come up short this year but come out long the year after. "Dialogue does not mean that we end up with a compromise, half the cake for you and the other half for me," the pope has adroitly explained. "Dialogue means: Look, we have got to this point, I may or may not agree, but let us walk together; this is what it means to build. And the cake stays whole, walking together." If President Xi Jinping and the pontiff are able to crack the Catholic mainland problem, they will take the cake – and maybe a joint Nobel Peace Prize as well.

Far from all international issues are cakewalks, of course. The South China Sea continues to boil and bubble like a perfect storm, where almost all boats are taking on trouble. China has moved too quickly to reclaim old littoral territory and manufacture new ones, scaring the daylights out of lesser area powers. Even communist Vietnam is now playing both sides of the diplomatic street – "kowtowing" to Washington! The South China Sea policy of the US is little better. Its knee-jerk pushback against China's reclamation campaign might make sense were we still in the last century when America ruled the world and China was still asleep.

But that was then, and this is now. Long-time Asia-watcher and economist Kenneth Courtis, chairman of Starfort Investment Holdings and managing partner of Courtis Global & Associates, is coruscating: "We note from history that a rising power, to be integrated into the system, changes perforce the balance of power ex ante. However, the status quo powers seldom, if ever, accept such change willingly … virtually always to their regret later. This is precisely what is occurring today."

America will fall on its face over its "pivot" to Asia, if it is based on the premise that China must rise no more and must be made to lose face. With the clarity of great scholarship, Professor Graham Allison and Harvard's Belfer Centre research team have laid down the markers of catastrophe for status quo powers that blindly oppose rather than cleverly adjust to rising powers.

And why pick on China? Americans might recall from its Asian experience last century that it was not China that launched a surprise attack on America; but it was China that worked as our ally in the second global war. The US has had a serious – and disastrous – military problem with communist China only during the Korean War, when UN/US forces brainlessly pushed towards the Chinese border. That triggered a massive ground counter-attack from insecure Beijing, easily spooked when barbarian foreign forces are at its gate.

The overly advertised US pushback in the South China Sea is less than shipshape and might even reactivate China's insecurities. Flaunting our naval capabilities in East Asian waters (and inviting the likes of CNN along to show all the world) is to shove the ghost of General Douglas MacArthur into China's face. One hopes our well-educated Pacific commanders will reflect on history and curb their confrontational enthusiasm.

Not all the world's geopolitical fish worth frying bob within the dark depths of the South China Sea. Last week at the United Nations, China stood with the US and others on the Security Council to pile yet more sanctions on erstwhile ally North Korea for its unwelcome nuclear weapon testing. Sino-US cooperation of this kind could prove the wave of the future if both sides avoid assuming they can continue to live in the past.

China knows it does not want to return to a condition of poverty. And the US, which sometimes doesn't seem to know what it wants, might wish to formulate policy around this pithy, pointed remark from the pope: China is "a great culture, with an inexhaustible wisdom". With an attitude like that, Francis will get some good things done with Beijing, while the US, with all its military might, splashes around pointlessly in the South China Sea.

P.S. At this writing, a Roman Church, China State concordat seemed closer than ever. But the issues on both sides are real, if seemingly mostly symbolic. And so the talking continued, but seemingly less futile with each passing month.

AND THEN THERE'S...

"Missionaries, frustrated by their inability to find converts to reach beyond the hunger of 'rice Christians' to the upper reaches of Chinese society, found a new lure: the Christian colleges, which offered China's future leaders access to Western science and technology."
– *America's Response to China: A History of Sino-American Relations,* by Warren I. Cohen, Columbia University Press, 2000

21 If it cares about its global standing, China should allay concerns about Hong Kong's missing booksellers

SOUTH CHINA MORNING POST, MONDAY, 14 MARCH 2016

Tom Plate says Beijing should be guided by common sense, rather than principles, in its response to international criticism of its handling of the case

RETROSPECTIVE:

Two cities in Asia that are as special as any on the face of the earth – at least to my mind – are Singapore and Hong Kong. Easily and happily, I could live in the tiny city-state (but not that tiny: Singapore has a larger population than Norway, New Zealand and so on) or in the "special administrative region of the People's Republic of China" (catchy, eh?). Because both are clearly special places, and because world-travellers visit both and become fond of both, they both enjoy a cosmopolitan cache that puts them into a special existential category. Macau or Moldova, not to mention Vanuatu, they are not! But given the difficult neighbourhoods they are in, they require special care and handling. Feisty, savvy, self-contained Singapore aims to take care of itself, but Hong Kong now enjoys the not-always tender embrace of Mother China after a long time under the colonial government of the United Kingdom. And so we tend to worry about the one more than the other, especially when the occasional optics of the treatment by Beijing seem better suited for the wrestling ring than the diplomatic arena.

There is a way one can be wrong even when technically one is right.

This happens upon approaching (what I call) the famous "twilight zone" of common sense. When you find yourself entering this zone of cosmic uncertainty, the recommendation here is to, as quickly as possible, "rise above principle" (see John F. Kennedy's Profiles in Courage) and notch down to a less elevated posture.

This is the best way to avoid severe political turbulence.

Consider the "twilight zone" experience of a senior diplomat from China at a UN Human Rights Council meeting in Geneva who flipped out when Security Council members, ginned by the US, tried to make political hay out of the unresolved case of the "Five Missing Booksellers".

Taking the view that this matter is under the authority of the People's Republic of China – and, thus, no one else's darn business – Fu Cong, the Chinese deputy permanent representative in Geneva, pulled few punches in countering the American diplomat who raised the issue. That was US ambassador Keith Harper, for whom the "unexplained recent disappearances and apparent coerced returns of Chinese and foreign citizens from outside mainland China" raised doubts about the commitment to its "one country, two systems" principle for Hong Kong.

Fu went ballistic: "The US is notorious for prison abuse at Guantanamo prison, its gun violence is rampant, racism is its deep-rooted malaise," he declaimed. "The US conducts large-scale extraterritorial eavesdropping, uses drones to attack other countries' innocent civilians, its troops on foreign soil commit rape and murder of local people. It conducts kidnapping overseas and uses black prisons."

Fu's bombast has some basis in fact, of course. Truth be told, many Americans also wish we'd invest more energy and enthusiasm cleaning up our own backyard instead of complaining about others' maintenance of theirs. But little ever seems to cause us a moment's lecturing pause.

Fu's fulmination was also completely consistent with his government's proclaimed policy of official non-interference in the internal affairs of other countries.

However, the reality of Hong Kong is that it hovers in a global "twilight zone" – not in a normal political realm. Since the 1997 handover, its astonishing high profile has not gone away; even two decades later, it remains a premier global city. Normal sovereignty standards do not apply; but the reality of "one country, two systems" does. Hong Kong is not, after all, Wuhan, much less Macau. Fu, it seems, was splashing around in the bumpy international political twilight zone and didn't realise it.

A grounded position on the Missing Booksellers Case came recently from the Press Freedom Committee of the Foreign Correspondents' Club of Hong Kong. It urged the Chinese government "to engage in good-faith dialogue when legitimate concerns are raised over possible breaches of international legal norms and human rights, such as in the case of the five Hong Kong residents". Its statement called for the immediate release of the five detained to "prevent further weakening of damaged confidence among the local, international and business communities in the robustness of Hong Kong's rule of law and protection of free speech guaranteed by the Basic Law".

In principle, Hong Kong is now an integral part of China. There is no quarrel with that.

But the issue here isn't the sovereignty principle; it's common sense, especially when you're in the political twilight zone. Yes, we offer Fu the courtesy of acknowledging that he was speaking from principle, as he saw it. And I cannot say that his outburst seemed insincere or out of line; the US provoked him.

But what to think? Principle or common sense?

In this context, the rumination of hard-charging Chinese author Yang Jisheng, in acknowledging an award from the Neiman Foundation of Harvard University recently, acceded to the need for modesty when entering the twilight zone of issues impossible: "[Ours] is an unfathomable profession; while journalists are not scholars, they're required to study and gain a comprehensive grasp of society. Any journalist, no matter how erudite and insightful, will feel unequal to the task of decoding this complex and ever-changing society."

But Yang would also be the first to reject a journalism of hedging that reflects intimidation by hard issues of significance. The constant worry that history may reverse the view we have today for a deeper, more rounded one in the future cannot handcuff us from trying to decode the present.

So, to me, there remains a special brilliance and deep cosmopolitan validity to the policy of "one country, two systems" originally recommended by Deng Xiaoping that is vital to maintain — not just for Hong Kong but perhaps as much for Beijing. Thus, the Xi Jinping government might well consider offering a full and un-redacted report on how this bizarre bookseller case came about; why it is not good for Mother China; and what measures will be implemented to insure against its like happening again. Only due diligence of this high level can bring this unnerving affair to a proper end.

The political wisdom and maturation thus displayed would increase China's soft power around the world more than any number of Olympic-size edifices. As for diplomat Fu, he was not wrong; he was just caught in the twilight zone. It's a tricky place for anyone.

P.S. I am not happy with the Republic's governors in Beijing. They need to treat this jewel of a special place with more tender care. But I don't think they meant it — in the sense of premeditated transgression of the "one country, two systems" understanding. The eruptions seemed to me to represent surface manifestations of a deeper power struggle within the Chinese Communist Party. They were undertaken foolishly oblivious to the optics of the actions. But the eyes of the world are on Hong Kong, as with few other places, and optics can count for a great deal in the general global perception of your country's "brand".

AND THEN THERE'S...

"As China becomes an increasingly international actor and power, its global relationships are becoming more complicated and strained. This is natural, and it can be expected to continue indefinitely into the future. While China's government rhetorically pursues 'win-win' relationships and a 'principled foreign policy' build on 'Peaceful Development' and the 'Five Principles of Peaceful Coexistence', it inevitably encounters unanticipated situations and nations that do not view China in such a benign light."
— *China's Future*, by David Shambaugh, Polity Press, 2016

22

Why the Chinese are so territorial about the South China Sea

South China Morning Post, Monday, 28 March 2016

Tom Plate says the bitter disputes are not so much a cold-war-style face-off between communist China and the West, as they are a clash of perspectives between the Chinese and the rest of the world

RETROSPECTIVE:

Transnational communication is not a subject commonly taught at universities. Most courses on international relations are conducted in the classroom of only one country, with one professor of a given nationality, and a set of instructional material that reflects mainly that national culture, not more than one – and surely no cosmopolitan diversity. In an increasingly tight and interconnected world, there is no reason for such a provincial pedagogy other than national censorship or academic lethargy. The consequences for future generations could be ruinous. Here is what I mean:

They say some things have to be seen to be believed, which is probably why the sight of a jaunty Mark Zuckerberg jogging through Tiananmen Square was almost unbelievable – unless you were there. Am I saying that the chairman, chief executive, and co-founder of Facebook rather made a fool of himself? Well, yes, I am. But in one way or the other, at one time or another – whether peddling a bicycle or bloviating on a mainland lecture tour (me) – we all have made fools of ourselves about China. In this sense, the multi-billionaire Harvard dropout loses no more face than any of us, myself surely included.

China is hard to get right. Once the anti-social network of violence associated with Islamist extremism is contained – and it will be (in part because of the emerging dynamics of the larger peaceful Muslim world) – China will stand alone as the West's prime number.

One reason for this can be illuminated by philosophy's hypothesis of the Twin Earth. Use your imagination, the late Harvard professor Hilary Putnam would urge his students, and envision two planets existing at the same time which appear virtually identical – person by person, tree by tree, barking dog by dog, annoying child by annoying child – except for one thing: their water.

Now this is key: On Planet Earth, water is exactly as we earthlings know it: H_2O. But on Planet Twin, while its water would look to Planet Earth-ers just like H_2O, its chemistry is different – let's dub it "Shui Too Oh". So if a Planet Earth person were to visit Planet Twin, people on both sides might understand each other well enough indeed, until they came to the subject of water: then they would be talking about two different things.

Such confusion now roils the politics of the South China Sea. This simple metaphor helps fathom the intensity of the current political storm over the slender islands, rocky islets, and semi-manufactured sand-landing strips from Planet Twin, which sees the world one way; whereas Brunei, Malaysia, the Philippines and Vietnam, on Planet Earth, see the water in another. The reality divide has become fearsome. Chinese fishing vessels swarm the waters as if they own it; smaller nations push back in anger. Boats are bumping, crew are jumping, politicians' fists are pumping, and US warships are intruding and over-

flying … so who's losing or has lost their mind?

To the West, it's the People's Republic of China that's lost its bearings. It would seem that in the span of a handful of years, the China policy "brand" has gone from "peaceful rising" (acclaimed as sensible) to "in your face" (viewed as confrontational). But the Chinese view is that the waters of the South China Sea are not just H$_2$O, as the West would have it, but Shui Too Oh: "The South China Sea islands and their surrounding waters were first discovered, named, and used by the early Chinese, as well as administered by successive governments, and have been considered inherent national territory and waters since ancient times, as is attested in numerous historical records, local gazetteers, and maps." There's more: "The Nansha (Spratly) Islands, Shisha (Paracel) Islands, Chungsha (Macclesfield Bank) Islands, and Tungsha (Pratas) Islands (together known as the South China Sea Islands) were first discovered, named, and used by the ancient Chinese, and incorporated into national territory and administered by imperial Chinese governments…. Any claim to sovereignty over, or occupation of, these areas by other countries is illegal."

That seems rather in-your-face coming from the communist People's Republic of China, don't you think?

But hold on a minute: This alternative definition comes not from Beijing but from Taipei. In fact, it is the official position of the government of Taiwan, known as the Republic of China; and it is virtually the same as the mainland's. Thus the fierce South China Sea bifurcation turns out not as Communist China versus The West, but more as the Chinese Civilization versus The Rest. What we have then is not a new Cold War (Beijing replacing Moscow), but a history-based resurrection of claims and counterclaims pressing onto the present.

Planet Shui Too Oh views its chemistry as critically different from that of the West because it bubbles up from a different place. For the hundred years prior to the ending of the war against Japan, the Chinese felt oppressed, their huge wartime contribution against fascism under-appreciated, and their post-war status as a major country patronised. Here is the consensus Chinese view: "From 1842, when the Treaty of Nanjing was forced on China by the British imperialists, to the War of Resistance against Japanese Aggression, Western Powers imposed upon China up to 1,000 unequal treaties by means of force and fraud ... China had become a semi-colonial country." This comes from a volume – *China in the World Anti-Fascist War* – that is little known in the West, but skilfully put together by Peng Xunhou, a professor at the Academy of Military Science of the People's Liberation Army.

The gap won't be smoothed over by billionaire jog sessions or by legalistic decisions of a UN court. Again (to lean on our metaphor), where the West sees seawater, the Chinese see ever-present currents of their tortured past. This is the lesson of the Twin Earth metaphor: However you look at it, the South China Sea ain't just bubbling up H_2O.

P.S. I give my little university on the US West Coast a little credit. My betters have always supported the efforts of our Asia Media International to pioneer courses on international relations taught from a true multi-national perspective. To date we have had live virtual classes (via Skype-type technology) with Fudan University in Shanghai, Yonsei University in Seoul, and United Arab Emirates University in Al Ain (outside of Abu Dhabi). I especially wish to commend Yonsei's Prof Hans Schattle for sharing the vision that courses on international relations greatly benefit from having more than one perspective, especially when students from one country (say, South Korea) vigorously interact in real time with students from another (say, the US). America needs to more aggressively pioneer this pedagogy.

AND THEN THERE'S…

"But the legacy of that imperial past is a system of international law that, when it comes to territorial disputes, prioritizes discovery over proximity. [...] The result in the South China Sea dispute is the apparently ridiculous situation whereby Britain or France might have as strong a legal claim to the islands as any of the states that border the Sea."

The South China Sea: The Struggle for Power in Asia, by Bill Hayton, Yale University Press, 2014

23

Don't be too quick to write off China's future based on a partial view of Xi Jinping's leadership

SOUTH CHINA MORNING POST, MONDAY, 11 APRIL 2016

Tom Plate says seeing a vast country like China through the personality and politics of one man will result only in assessments that, as many examples have shown, are often proved wrong

RETROSPECTIVE:

Donald J. Trump does not reflect all of America and does not constitute even half the story. So to look at all of China through the statue of Xi Jinping is misleading as well. But we the media have to latch onto this simplistic methodology for many reasons, not least being the press of deadlines that requires judgments right now. In the world of the journalist, there is never enough time for the longitudinal studies so common in the academic world.

Begin with the unpretentious wisdom of the late Yogi Berra, a notably inarticulate Hall of Fame baseball player celebrated for memorable "Yogi-isms": "It's tough to make predictions," one went, "especially about the future."

But the wish for the better can give birth to premature thoughts; the caring media always wants to believe that a negative status quo cannot endure. Consider North Korea. It's still there – how can this be? On the surface, the stocky figure of Kim Jong-un, all of 33 years of age, is said to rule. But you rarely see an official shot of him without ribbon-bedecked military brass hovering nearby, almost as if babysitting. They must burn at reporting to someone so lightly grown up. Is a military coup not conceivable?

Further, consider this: we hear from an authoritative source that China is agitated with its erstwhile historical ally. Sure, there are good reasons for leaving matters with North Korea exactly as they are – geopolitical need for a buffer state, ideological/historical fraternity, and so on.

But we are also hearing that the Beijing boys are blue beyond belief with their bumptious border baby. In his 3½ years as general secretary of the Communist Party of China, in fact, Xi Jinping has not bothered once to met Kim (in fact, Kim has not met a head of state from anywhere). China rarely shows enthusiasm for sanctions, but last month Beijing might have surprised even itself when it signed off on a tough round of UN pain for Pyongyang.

Given China's evident falling out of love, how can North Korea possibly go on?

Recall, however, that all past predictions of political climate change have been wrong, and wrong again. In 2005, the media cheered when the six-party talks in Beijing appeared to commit Pyongyang to halt nuclear weapons development. But that, for a number of reasons, never happened. So here we are, 10 years later, with the northern Korean peninsula more nuclear-equipped than ever.

I have certainly learned my lesson and, after joining "Predictions Anonymous" (like the original AA, the aim is for sober level-headedness in all things), I promise I have made my last flat-out political prediction. Furthermore, in the crusading spirit of all new sobriety converts, I'll alert you if I catch sight of media vehicles edging towards the prediction cliff.

Right now I have two such premature predictions for you – an otherwise totally respectable pair. They involve Xi, who is being regularly "shorted", as it were, by the Western media. We are told he is something of an emerging disaster. If he is not quite a modern Mao Zedong, neither is he a forward-looking Zhu Rongji, or a careful step-by-step Deng Xiaoping. He is cracking down on enemies, perceived or real; blocking the Internet; causing giant waves on the South China Sea; and smiling over a personal power cult that reminds one of the bad old days.

In the elite *New York Review of Books*, long-time China analyst Orville Schell paints a sad picture of China's diminishing freedoms. In his *Worse and Worse – The New Terror in China*, the former American journalism school dean concludes: "His authoritarian style at home and belligerent posture abroad are ominous because they make China's chances of being successful in reforming the economy – on which the entire world now depends – increasingly unlikely … Because such policies also grow out of a deeply paranoid view of the democratic world, they make it extremely difficult for China to effectively cooperate with countries like the US".

It gets worse. From *The Economist*, surely the world's most referenced English-language political weekly, you get a blunt, depressing, predictive, splashy cover story: "Beware the Cult of Xi. It asserts: "Not since the dark days after the Tiananmen Square protests in 1989 has there been such a sweeping crackdown on critics of the party … In the past 66 years of Communist rule in China, the most troubled times have usually come about when tensions break out within the elite. Mr Xi's style of rule is only serving to stoke them."

Do we sense the suggestion of a coup brewing here?

As both of these long-respected observers are too sophisticated to be simplistic, neither is prepared to brand Xi the Mao of today. Nonetheless, both view China though the personality and politics of one man, just as many of us imagine North Korea as if summed up by the young Kim.

This is history through the lens of personality. And it is absolutely the necessary crutch of the journalist, sweating out deadlines – barely finishing with one thing and immediately having to go onto the next. This is not the more pastoral remit of the historian, endowed with the leisure of as much time as is needed, whereas the journalist works with relatively little time, precisely in order to be comparatively timely.

But without more time, we won't know for sure who Xi is and what he will mean for his China. Maybe a kind thought might surface in our rush to judgment: that a man who has made so many enemies because of his anti-corruption campaign might be trying hard and sincerely to clean up China. This involves great personal risk (Xi travels with a larger security force than the US president), but countless millions of honest, non-wealthy Chinese are cheering him on. For them, Xi is the hope – maybe their only hope.

So, along with them, I am hoping for the best. But I am predicting nothing. Nothing at all – no more. About the future, you see, predictions are tough.

Hope is easier.

P.S. I said it once and will say it again: President Xi Jinping should sit with me for a few 90-minute sessions for the next "Giants of Asia" volume. But enough said.

AND THEN THERE'S...

"Xi's brand of modernism, analysts said, could mix bolder economic policies with anti-corruption campaigns, a vigorous military build-up and a muscular foreign policy. The combination is reminiscent of the Self-Strengthening Movement in the late 19th century, when some reformist political leaders and intellectuals sought reforms to revive a weakening Qing dynasty (1644–1911) harassed by Western powers and Japan."

— *The China Renaissance: The Rise of Xi Jinping and the 18th Communist Party Congress,* by the writers, artists and editors of the South China Morning Post and edited by Jonathan Sharp, World Scientific Publishing, 2013

24

How a little-known chapter in Sino-US cooperation may have helped save the planet

South China Morning Post, Monday, 25 April 2016

Tom Plate says talks between Li Zhaoxing and Condoleezza Rice 10 years ago, over who should be the next UN secretary general, paved the way for the Paris climate change agreement

RETROSPECTIVE:

If China's president Xi Jinping and America's Barack Obama had had more time together – more of an overlap – perhaps more might have been accomplished. Why can't the two superpowers get their top-leadership rotation in perfect symmetry? Here is a sample of the one time they did.

On occasions when China and the United States do manage to get together – landing and working on the same side of an issue (if not lovingly, arm in arm) – the result can seem a touch transformative. Conversely, when they cannot get together (quarrelling couple syndrome), the fallout can be alarming.

But for this week, at least, we shelve apocalypse instincts and mull over a couple-reconciliation scenario. Our story will go back 10 years – and then intimately connect with the present – thanks

to China-US get-togetherness. And to push the believability of the loving metaphor even further, the linkage involves the two most powerful members of the UN Security Council working with the UN secretary general in New York.

The denouement came last week with the sweeping and promising Paris climate control protocol – a necessary first step in meeting the fearsome global-overheating challenge. Not only did 175-plus nations put pen to the protocol's papyrus, but also – and more to the point – the Beijing-Washington odd couple led the political parade for the UN Framework Convention on Climate Change, put together in Paris in December.

These titanic economies dump down on us 40 per cent of all global greenhouse gas emissions, for which both presidents Xi Jinping and Barack Obama should be ashamed. In a sense, thankfully, they are, and last month signalled their intent to sign the Paris Accord, thus raising the UN-driven effort from the dead after the deeply unsettling climate-control negotiation collapse in Copenhagen in 2009.

It is true the new deal is but preliminary in the sense that the teenager is preliminary to the adult: further time will be needed for commitments to be actually honoured, to determine whether Paris will grow into a true unique historic achievement, or revert to some horrid teenage sequel (Copenhagen II?).

This week, I vote for the former and ask you to offer a rare standing ovation for Xi and Obama.

The irrefutable fact of current geopolitics is that Chinese-US concordance offers the greatest potential transnational force for good (or evil) on this planet. When Beijing and Washington can get together, and then can get it together, the effect can be stunning. To add to the background of this much-headlined Paris accord, we recount a quiet event 10 years ago in New York about which much less is known. It was a meeting between Condoleezza Rice and Li Zhaoxing in the US ambassador's suite at the Waldorf Astoria Hotel, there to exchange views on the tricky selection of a successor to Kofi Annan.

The outgoing UN secretary general had been media-genic, even charismatic, but he also had been immensely capable of irritating the permanent members of the Security Council, especially Washington and Beijing. The two foreign ministers quickly agreed they did not want to have to go though any more diva-drama, and when Rice brought up the candidacy of the low-key but well-regarded foreign minister of South Korea, who by then had straightforwardly declared for the job, Li's face brightened – even though Ban Ki-moon's South Korea was a key US strategic ally, a place where tens of thousands of US military were stationed, all allegedly because of North Korea. But the often in-an-airplane foreign minister Ban had made enough trips to the foreign ministry's gigantic headquarters in Beijing's Chaoyang District to make friends and influence very important people that he had become a regular, welcome and convivial face.

At the UN headquarters in New York, when China and the US agree on something of this nature – sensitive, difficult – the news tends to whip through the corridors faster than morning coffee carts. And the immediate reaction is usually relief: so when Beijing and Washington shook hands over Ban's ambitious candidacy, that was pretty much the end of the search process.

It is fair to generalise and say that classic Asian diplomatic style does not prioritise flamboyance. And while hammered relentlessly by the charisma-obsessed Western media during the first year or two on the job, in time Ban has shown himself to be a cunning choice. Careful by nature, discreet to a fault, but goal-oriented to the specific and achievable, the South Korean career diplomat committed his entire tenure to climate harm-reduction as his first priority.

He had other worthy goals – women at the UN, in particular– but the climate issue remained pre-eminent and he could never get it out of his head. After the collapse of the 2009 Copenhagen climate summit, he was dispirited almost to the point of severe depression. Yet his face hid the pain and anguish, and he pushed on, retreating to no safe harbour in the storm. Critics of the low-key Asian style can say what they want, but there is no quit in this honourable Korean's DNA.

When New York and Paris were conjoined last week, the convergence came about in part because of Ban – and thus because Rice and Li had worked together in that quiet 2006 meeting to make such a solid choice. Said the exultant UN secretary general last week: "Paris will shape the lives of all future generations in a profound way – it is their future that is at stake." Referring to the planet's record of ever-hotter temperatures, he added: "We are in a race against time." If so, no one can say of Ban that, on this issue at least, he has been wasting his. Still, without that Chinese-US cooperation, there would be no secretary general Ban, and no Paris climate agreement. This is a lesser-known chapter in the roller-coaster history of China-US bilateral relations.

P.S. Ban Ki-moon, the quiet-spoken South Korean foreign minister who was to become the eighth secretary general in the history of the United Nations, underwhelmed the media but may impress historical judgment as the steadiest of the UNSGs. Smart, experienced, but anti-charismatic, he worked his tail off for 10 years, tailing off at the end when the miserable disfunctionality of the sprawling organization got to him. I liked the man and his quiet ways. Let my grandchild and his children make the proportional judgment for history. My guess is Ban will come out of it well.

AND THEN THERE'S...

"Global governance is met with much skepticism in China. Another common view is that China has so many domestic problems that it does not have the luxury of contributing much to global governance."
– *China Goes Global: The Partial Power,* by David Shambaugh,
  Oxford University Press, 2013

25 | Anyone but Hillary? Why that's not China's best bet in the US presidential election

South China Morning Post, Monday, 9 May 2016

Tom Plate says Beijing should resist the temptation to root for Donald Trump instead of the more hawkish (in its eyes at least) Hillary Clinton. In fact, it should stay as far away as possible

RETROSPECTIVE:

Your humble columnist at least had this one right. The Chinese are not the only ones in the world who prefer the steady to the unsteady – so do sane Americans. At this writing, it seems as if Moscow tried to tilt the election toward Trump for reasons of national interest. And at this writing, it seems as if Beijing stayed out of the mess. Guess who in retrospect is looking smarter and wiser?

From Russia with love? Things are definitely getting weird.

Sure, with China's rise, nations in the vast neighbourhood of Asia are recalibrating their foreign policy and military-security portfolios with a view towards alliance diversification.

But … I give you Japan: not sure what China will be throwing at it next, Prime Minister Shinzo Abe has been flashing hungry eyes at Moscow.

That's quite a play-date proposition even for Japan's happy warrior: Putin as partner? Good luck with that! Looking for love in all the wrong places? Perhaps, but maybe it is worth a shot. What are his options? India? Or – yet again – good old Uncle Sam, the usual default? And perhaps now more fault than default: These are times that try one's pro-American soul as America's volatile political atmosphere continues to boil.

To succeed Barack Obama as president, the fight looks to have come down to a duel between a know-nothing and a know-it-all – between a candidate who has never held any political office, and one who has held only high office and, further, is destined to be nominated in July for the highest.

Beijing, as well as Tokyo, must be asking themselves whether they look for a horse in this race. They don't get to vote in the US election, but they get to suffer (or flourish) from the outcome.

For Tokyo, the know-it-all candidate would seem preferable to the know-nothing candidate. Foreign policy choices are often cruelly complex, their downstream effects murderously difficult to predict – except (of course) in the smuggest of hindsights.

So far, the presumptive Republican nominee Donald Trump would apparently let America's embrace with Japan slacken, even to the point where the world's third-largest economy and closest Asian ally might drift off ... right into the world nuclear club – Hiroshima be damned!

Is this real estate mogul mad? To quote well-known University of California macroeconomist Peter Navarro in his provocative (but depressingly China-negative) new book, *Crouching Tiger*, "Once the reliability of the American nuclear umbrella comes into question, all bets – and the brakes on nuclear proliferation in Asia – are off."

As for China, the Xi Jinping government might well imagine

anyone-but-Hillary as their best bet. After all, the former US secretary of state has been the proud proponent of the so-named "pivot to Asia", not exactly conceived in the Pentagon as a kindly kowtow to China; and by crooning sympathetically towards the anti-China claimants in the South China Sea – including the Philippines, Vietnam and Malaysia – this world diplomat, former US senator and once-upon-a-time first lady has not hesitated to throw sand in Beijing's face.

Regarding the swirling South China Sea-sickness: "Clinton's intervention in this dispute may have been one of the most consequential actions in her time as secretary of state," concluded the New York Times' Mark Landler, in *Alter Egos*, his crackling new book on Clinton and Obama that's superbly revealing about both of these iconic Americans: "If there is a military clash between the United States and China in the next decade, it is likely to break out in the South China Sea or the equally troubled waters to the north, in the East China Sea."

A patriotic Chinese reader digesting the psychodrama of *Alter Egos* – say, some whip-smart career climber at the Central Party School – could spin it to make a case for the know-nothing choice. More or less militarily cutting off Japan (and even South Korea), as Trump has suggested, could simplify China's job in East Asia, after all.

But wait: Beijing should also consider that the presumptive Republican nominee's stated belief that China is "beating us" by running up those trade deficits might fuel a kind of American consumer boycott of Chinese goods under relentless White House Stars-and-Stripes flag-waving. In fact, China-phobic Navarro recommends something of this ilk: "We … consumers are helping to finance a Chinese military build-up that may well mean to do us and our countries harm." He believes that China might be inflicted with as much harm with punitive economic measures as military.

Stephens.

Better, then, for China to be quietly rooting for the devil it knows rather than the devil that knows basically nothing?

Clinton, it seems to me, will present China will fewer surprises as president. It's true that her Republican upbringing beclouds her emotional ability to feel the flow of modern history finally giving China its right to fully rise; but decades of adult experience have taught her the need for pragmatic calculation in all things dangerous. (As Margaret Thatcher once said to me, it was one thing to take on Argentina over the Falklands, but it would have been quite another to sail the British navy towards China over Hong Kong.) As the ancient Chinese saying goes, it's a losing proposition to try to "hit a stone with an egg".

What's more, the know-nothing approach assumes that one can enter the White House with a blank slate and do whatever, more or less, one wants. "To catch a fish on a tree," I believe, is the relevant Chinese wisdom (that is, it is never going to happen). The wise move for Beijing, then, is to stay as far away from this election as possible, make peace with neighbours (enough grabbing and land-filling in the South China Sea for now), and certainly don't expect to catch a fish on a tree with a Trump.

Oh, and Abe should know better than to look for love in all the wrong places; to quote that non-ancient American saying, "Don't bite off more than you can chew".

P.S. This one came out about right in the prediction column. PM Abe made a splash visit to the Trump White House about six weeks after the American's inauguration that played well back in Japan. But the yo-yo tendency of Trump "policy" makes any successes or gains inherently transitory. As for the Chinese, what can they do? Watch, wait and hope for the best — like the rest of us.

AND THEN THERE'S...

"There are no walls which completely block the wind."
(From a Chinese guide on espionage)
— *Tiger Trap: America's Secret Spy War with China*, by David Wise, Houghton Mifflin Harcourt Publishing Company, 2011

26

Can China lead the world on reducing the threat of nuclear war?

South China Morning Post, Monday, 23 May 2016

Tom Plate says while Obama's visit to Hiroshima is welcome, Xi Jinping has a real opportunity to steer the world away from the use of nuclear arms as a defence option

RETROSPECTIVE:

It would make for a stunning reversal of expectation if the Chinese government somehow wound up as a nuclear disarmer. It would also make for colossal world leadership. We have to reduce our expectations that the United States can any longer fill such a role; with the end of the Cold War and the deconstruction of the Soviet Empire, the West had its chance. Even with a sophisticated American president in the White House – George W. H. Bush – the US did not seize the moment and commence unilateral disarmament. This was a tragic lost opportunity.

Way back when, rather long ago, a youngish, greenish post-graduate student, obsessing about nuclear war, devoted his first book to it. "Doomsday," I declaimed in *Understanding Doomsday: A Guide to the Arms Race for Hawks, Doves and People*, "the moment when all the energies of all the nuclear bombs are released over the heads of the inhabitants of the earth. Not a pleasant thought, and, to be sure, there's nothing to be gained by dwelling on it; but a lot might be lost by ignoring it."

No one in power should.

In 2010, the far-sighted Ban Ki-moon, barely into his first term, pointedly chose to become the first UN secretary general to attend the annual peace memorial ceremony in Hiroshima. The fact that he was from Korea, with all its issues with Japan, didn't stop him. It was a simple matter of conscience, he said.

Now, in 2016, "leading" yet again from behind, President Barack Obama this week is to become the first active US president to visit the Hiroshima memorial. Better late than never…

For their demonstrations of remembrance and concern, we applaud both, while devoutly wishing that President Xi Jinping would choose to do the same some day soon. It would be so impactful for the world to see China's president free himself from the familiar chain of enmity with Japan by visiting Hiroshima. In all-out nuclear war, after all, China could lose more people than anyone.

Japan, once Asia's No 1, will always have hanging in its closet the brutal ghost of having served as the first target of an atomic bombing: Will history record Hiroshima and Nagasaki as the last ones? The war-ending consequences of the A-bomb decisions by US president Harry S. Truman still reverberate. Among other things, politically, they include helping breed a populace that rates among the world's most consistently pacifist; and, paradoxically, supporting a political and military elite that at times seems to suggest Japan was somehow innocent for what preceded its nuclear nightmare. But please do note sympathetically the patient endurance of the largely pacifist Japanese people with a political system (engineered by conquering America) that has produced too many moral dwarfs and politically deaf figures.

In his 2014 novel, *Colorless Tsukuru Tazaki and His Years of*

Pilgrimage, Haruki Murakami might have been speaking for many Japanese with these words spoken by one of the characters:

"You can hide memories, but you can't erase the history that produced them … If nothing else, you need to remember that. You can't erase history, or change it. It would be like destroying yourself."

This would seem an implicit rebuke of his countrymen for actual or feigned memory loss.

To the rest of us, the passage might also serve to recall the disturbing fact that not only were atomic bombs actually dropped on the heads of human beings, but that the delivery of the atomic attack was by America, the reputed ultra-good nation always and forever on the side of God.

The very fact that America still sincerely believes it did the right thing (by ending the war without further major cost) suggests it is not inconceivable for another nuclear power to seek some day to similarly justify the nuclear option. What's more, the Obama administration itself, notwithstanding its laudable Hiroshima symbolism, has allocated colossal lumps of additional funds to "improving" and "modernising" its nuclear arsenal.

Talk about "leading from behind" by stockpiling!

What an opportunity for China, which should not fear to lead from ahead. Russia and the US are the nuclear-armament leaders with roughly the same high piles of nuclear stock. By contrast, China holds far fewer – in the same comparatively modest league as Britain's bomb pile; and, to its credit, has trumpeted an official policy of forgoing the option of ever being the first to use one, claiming deterrence of evil enemies as the sole motive for possession.

But the deterrence argument is bogus and should be buried deep underground, along with all the world's defused bombs: if the reason for deterrence is that others have them, logically it follows that a far less costly and far less risky way of "deterring" nuclear warfare would be if no nation has them at all. Whatever is the world thinking?

Master Murakami again, this time on the topic of human brain lock: "Like a man who has lost his sense of direction, Tsukuru's thoughts endlessly circled the same place. By the time he became aware of what his mind was doing, he found himself back where he started. Finally, his thinking process got stuck, as if the folds of his brain were a broken screw."

Can we cease circling the same deadly dangerous place, as if targeting ourselves for future nuclear war?

This is the issue for someone of Xi's high position in the global pecking order to consider. In Paris, Beijing worked out a noteworthy climate deal with Washington. Why not a noteworthy nuclear deal? China is currently the target of international fire for its pushy policies and aggressive actions in and around its South and East China seas neighbourhoods. Nothing would show its "peaceful rising" DNA better than helping lead a nuclear downsizing, trending towards eventual nuclear disarmament.

But is Xi up to it? Time will tell, of course – but maybe time is not on the world's side. Just consider the consequences of non-state terrorists getting their paws on these evil instruments of doomsday.

P.S. It might be argued that the opposition to nuclear weapons of any kind is more an ideological – or moral – position than a purely empirical, pragmatic one. Is not the world a safer place with the "good guys" in possession of them than only the "bad guys"? Perhaps on this one issue, I am an ideologue. To me it is axiomatic that we live in a safer world if we can move forward without the threat of nuclear doomsday over our heads.

AND THEN THERE'S...

"Chinese nuclear strategy presupposes that America's interests in Asia are not as compelling as its interests in Europe were during the Cold War. [...] In fact, as the United States and China compete for power in Asia, the possibility of conflict is very real, and the more intensely they compete, the more likely conflict becomes."
– *The China Choice: Why We Should Share Power*, by Hugh White, Oxford University Press, 2013

27

WHY THE WORLD NEEDS BORING BUT EFFECTIVE LEADERS LIKE HU JINTAO, RATHER THAN TRUMPETING SWANS AND POLITICAL PEACOCKS

SOUTH CHINA MORNING POST, MONDAY, 6 JUNE 2016

Tom Plate says on a global stage full of loud-mouthed politicians, there is definitely a role for Hu's style of supposedly staid, colourless leadership

RETROSPECTIVE:

Stumped by Trump? Horrified by Hillary? Apprehensive about America? As a therapeutic aid, dear distinguished reader, this column proposes to examine – and even appreciate – a totally different style of public leadership: the low-key. Yes, that kind.

Remember the old days? Remember Hu Jintao, the predecessor to China's current leader Xi Jinping? The uber-quiet Hu was widely assessed as so low-key as to not even require a key chain. But maybe second thoughts are in order about this whole business of political peacocks that strut their stuff even if they don't have any.

Let's start with a little insight from the late, great US writer E. B. White, in his tale *The Trumpet of the Swan*: "'All [trumpet] swans are vain,' explained the cob. 'It is right for swans to feel proud, graceful – that's what swans are for.'"

Now apply this to the less graceful world of politics – as in: "All politicians are vain, but it is right for them to feel proud – that's what politicians are for." Like swans, perhaps we might say, politicians when they are in full crowing, obnoxious mode are simply being true to themselves. Expecting a political figure to be humble, as for a swan not to be vain, is to fight the nature of things.

And so this year, as almost everyone in the world knows, a bevy of American trumpeter swans have been winging their way towards the White House. Last week, one of the last still wedging forward – Hillary Clinton – did a sort of politician's swan dive from the heights of serious public policy to honk back at Donald Trump's many prior public insults. Originally billed as a foreign policy address, the speech was anything but. Many pro-Hillary commentators and her outright allies applauded, as in: This lady can honk with the worst of them!

Maybe, but as we see it: really, there's nobody that quite trumpets like The Don. Perhaps all Clinton's swan dive proved is that birds of a political feather do flock together: in public politics, it sometimes seems as if nothing is too vulgar. The Don has already denounced the former US secretary of state and first lady as "crooked". What could be a worse charge than that?

Ah – there is at least one other calumny of consequence far worse than "crooked".

It is, in today's value system, the sin of being "colourless". Colourless – we recall – is exactly what our hard-hearted, colourful Western media dubbed Hu Jintao, who, between 2002 and 2012, served as paramount leader of China. This meant that, for 10 years, he was one of the two most powerful leaders on earth. But the man got scant respect, at least in the West. A US news magazine once dubbed him "the kind of guy you wouldn't ordinarily think twice about – cautious, colourless and corporate".

It's time for a reappraisal of Hu's true hue – and of "colourless" politicians in general – in a recalibration of leaders whose colourlessness might simply hide a healthy measure of calm reflection. Maybe the Hu style, reflecting collective leadership, was less colourless than properly cautious. "Colourful" flares can trigger explosive flare-ups; a low-key style can prevent relations from hotting up.

Here is one telling example: the little-known story of Hu's state visit to the US in January 2011. To almost everyone's surprise and relief – on both sides – it went quite well. For his part, China's president returned home impressed by the possibilities of reducing bilateral tensions and instructed the central government's propaganda department to tone down the anti-American stuff. That moment of good feeling did not last forever, of course. But the story illustrates the point that colourlessness is not necessarily the enemy of effectiveness. It might even be a symptom of a statesmanship that values quiet results over prideful flamboyance.

By contrast, the current, successor administration in China is anything but colourless. But all the pushing and shoving – rhetorical as well as naval, especially by Beijing, but Washington, too – can make one nostalgic for the balm of calculated colourlessness. The escalating language over who owns what in the South China Sea is producing new tension, triggering an Asian arms race and colouring the very way America and China view each other.

As the experienced and extremely knowledgeable Susan Shirk, now a University of California professor, and former State Department star in the Bill Clinton administration, once pointed out in a discussion on the US-China relationship: "Over the past several years, Americans have noticed with apprehension a steady drumbeat of [mainland] media messages about America's supposed 'containment' of China that have undoubtedly been officially encouraged. The precedents of Germany and Japan show how this kind of commercialised semi-controlled media, by creating myths and mobilising anger against perceived foreign enemies, can drag a country into war."

China is, of course, a nuclear power. The entire world would be better off, to be sure, if the US relinquished a substantial portion of its nuclear vanity and compacted it down to China's more modest arsenal. But, for that day of epiphany to ever come, considerably more mutual trust, reasoned discourse and deft diplomacy will be needed. That's one good reason to leave open the possibility of appreciation of political leaders who offer the calm of colourlessness rather than the trumpet of The Don. The non-grandstanding Hu style has so much more to say for it than perhaps heretofore acknowledged.

But you can always honk if you don't agree.

P.S. I like this column even better today – a year later. When it first appeared, I think I was the Only Man on the Planet who had such nice words to say about the "colourless, but also odorless" Hu Jintao. A year later… I may still be!

AND THEN THERE'S…

"Zhu said that for Hu, the status quo meant first and foremost the party's monopoly on power and he tended to see grievances and growing disobedience resulting from an avalanche of social woes, such as a yawning wealth gap, rising food and housing prices, corruption and pollution, and calls for Western-style democracy, as threats to his leadership."

— *The China Renaissance: The Rise of Xi Jinping and the 18th Communist Party Congress*, by the writers, artists and editors of the South China Morning Post and edited by Jonathan Sharp, World Scientific Publishing, 2013

28

Let's hope the Hong Kong bookseller saga does not mean the end of 'one country, two systems'

South China Morning Post, Monday, 20 June 2016

Tom Plate says one must believe that the treatment of the Causeway Bay booksellers is an idiotic misstep on Beijing's part, rather than a change of heart on a cherished principle

RETROSPECTIVE:

Perhaps I was overly optimistic in 1995 with a series of columns about the handover of Hong Kong that were supportive of the notion that the Communist Party and the Chinese mainland government were not stupid. Perhaps my penchant for going against the conventional wisdom led me too close to the cliff. But for the immediate years after the 1st July 1997 handover, the judgment looked pretty good. Nothing lasts forever, of course. And lately "one country, two systems" seemed destined for some Third Way that no one could quite imagine in detail.

Might it be permissible, under the rare circumstance, of course, for an American journalist to speak positively about a Communist leader and a particular policy?

If yes, then permit into evidence one Deng Xiaoping, the diminutive chain-smoking maximum leader who, though with almost as many major faults as California, probably carried around a political brain the size of Texas. His achievements include two that remain particularly relevant to the issue at hand: the future of Hong Kong and its principle of "one country, two systems".

Deng's recasting of China's economy to unleash the entrepreneurial work ethic of countless Chinese meant curbing his government's grinding enthusiasm for intervention in the economy. That one big forward burst of self-recognition and policy flexibility (too bad India's Nehru never developed such vision) helped tee up a second Deng brilliancy: setting down as policy upon the future acquisition of Hong Kong a sensible formula to protect and enhance its success while keeping sovereignty firmly in Beijing.

And this meant curbing the enthusiasm of know-it-all comrades in Beijing inclined to intervene like mad in the affairs of the former British colony. Bluntly put, Deng was smart enough to know that his comrades, however otherwise capable, could not possibly be smart enough to micromanage from up north, and certainly not without greatly unnerving capable Hongkongers: and so came "one country, two systems", the label for maximising autonomy.

So smart; but now that legacy is being put to the test by the latest twists in the Bizarre Case of the Disappearing and Reappearing Booksellers.

In recent days, the plot has been thickened by allegations of secret-police-style snatching and interrogating – and enlivened of course by a proper street protest against alleged Beijing thuggery.

Allow me a personal note first, OK?

By the maniac metrics of American time keeping, I go back a ways with Hong Kong. In 1995, I vowed in the Los Angeles Times to seek "to overcome my patriotic American inheritance" – that is, bias – "and arrive at a balanced, non-ideological assessment of China's takeover from the British of the jewel known as Hong Kong". This sentiment appeared in my first column on Asia – around the time that Fortune Magazine infamously predicted on its cover "The Death of Hong Kong".

My optimism came from the people I talked to and the best thinking of the time.

The underrated Tung Chee-hwa, the first Hong Kong leader appointed by Beijing, seemed so sincere in his patriotism for Mother China that it had to seal Beijing's trust (which was the only way "one country, two systems" could ever possibly work). The outgoing, ultra-articulate governor Chris Patten was so slick in his manoeuvres that I had to distrust the British pitch. And the near-pathological negativism of the Western news media, exemplified by the funereal Fortune Magazine cover, made me sad and angry – and eager to uncover a less fatalistic narrative.

Sure enough, post handover, Hong Kong flourished economically, and while the boys in Beijing had talented officials detailed to the Hong Kong remit, they otherwise sought to maintain a proper Dengian distance. Though Deng died just months before the handover in July 1997, the wise and restrained premier Zhu Rongji hovered uncle-like over Hong Kong until retirement in 2003; and the presidency of the quiet but very solid Hu Jintao that ran until 2012 must be credited for its policy of laudable minimalism.

But, now, things are starting to make a pivot for the worse.

In late 2014 – with a rather different administration settled in Beijing – Hong Kong erupted into semi-charming if annoying demonstrations designed to embarrass Mother China into redefining Hong Kong's election policy into an almost perfect textbook model. That was not going to happen, of course. (Hey Umbrella People – we don't have perfection in the US, either; recall that, in 2000, George W.

Bush became president over Al Gore, even though the latter got more votes; and now there's Trump; and so on.)

Beijing did give a little ground – but not nearly enough for the Umbrellas, as for utopia they cannot wait. Protests ensued.

But utopia always plays a waiting game, and by its infinite inaccessibility will outwait us all. For Beijing, the ultimate issue of the management of Hong Kong was not a matter of conscience but of sovereignty – of power, not principle. Who is the boss – us, not them!

To reinforce this point, I revert to the timeless insight of Albert Camus. "By definition," concluded the French literary giant and journalist, "a government has no conscience. Sometimes it has a policy, but nothing more." It is always foolish to believe otherwise, whether the government is communist, capitalist, religious – or allegedly utopian.

So, logically, if Beijing (and not some band of one-off, overreaching idiot security people in the south) is in fact responsible for the abduction of the irreverent, but ultimately pathetic booksellers, hoping to harvest mainland renminbi by peddling dumb, gossipy books about President Xi Jinping, then we know that such action must reflect new policy. This means Hongkongers may have to learn to live with the current sovereign government that is their present lot – and that is not as wise as ones of recent past.

But because of my optimism about Hong Kong – and about the enduring power of Deng's insight – I cannot believe this to be so. I prefer the hypothesis that what happened was not policy but idiocy. China's top leaders simply must be too smart for such nonsense, though they are not, as surely Deng would have told them, smart enough to micromanage Hong Kong.

The best move for Beijing's leaders is to conclude, at least among themselves, that the handling of the case of the Causeway Bay booksellers is not one of the high points of their reign to date, and that when in doubt, it is always best to revert to "one country, two systems" as if it were chiselled in stone.

It is, after all, one of the wiser legacies of modern China's most forward-thinking maximum leader.

P.S. It's very complicated: Hong Kong is different from China and yet now legally and formally part of it. But it is more like Manhattan to Des Moines than cut from the same cloth. There will always be problems — as with Taiwan.

AND THEN THERE'S...

"My thesis said that, even if you're unwilling to talk about it, the concept of freedom of the press is very useful, a technique to make society safe, including the government itself. If you don't permit reporting and then everybody listens to Voice of America and the BBC, is that any benefit to you? We are facing an open world and people have diverse channels for obtaining news, so you can't cover things up. If you try, you will reap just the opposite of what you wish." (Wang Jun)

— *China Ink: The Changing Face of Chinese Journalism,*
  by Judy Polumbaum with Xiong Lei, Rowman & Littlefield
  Publishers, 2008

29

Xi Jinping, the champion of Marxism, may find unlikely comrades in critics of Western capitalism

South China Morning Post, Monday, 4 July 2016

Tom Plate says while Xi's reassertion of ideology may be a bid to legitimise the Communist Party, his rejection of the Western status quo chimes with a growing number of voices pointing to capitalism's failures

RETROSPECTIVE:

It's hard to make the argument that Communism works better than capitalism, that's for sure. But it's almost as hard to make the argument that capitalism works well enough to purge from our mind any thought that there might be a better alternative, even if it is not Communism. But when the leader of the world's largest titular communist state makes a pitch for the moral relevance of socialism, it would have carried less weight if our global capitalist system had not been the culprit in many calamities, including the colossal global scare of 2008–2009.

True transparency is hardly the calling card of many governments, and, certainly, the People's Republic of China wins no awards for openness. But about the central ideology behind the Communist Party, President Xi Jinping could not be more transparent. The party is all about Marxism, he averred recently – and not some Scandinavian milquetoast graduate-school Marxism – but a serious Marxism, in Xi's view the only known government system for addressing structural inequality.

Xi, who is also party general secretary, laid down the party line anew on the occasion of its 95th anniversary celebration, in the Great Hall of the People on Tiananmen Square.

Only Marxism, he insisted, could have provided a scientific guide for the development of China, the party and the people – melding his complex nation into one of reasonable unity. The president admitted that this Marxism had to be suffused with Chinese ways to work, but that the party would be nowhere had Marxism not been its primary operating system.

To be sure, Xi's reassertion of ideology was calculated to counter any flirtation in the party with pure neoliberal market economics, not to mention Western-style democratic governance. Just check out this revivalist line: "The whole party should remember – what we are building is socialism with Chinese characteristics, not some other – ism." Xi's address, televised nationally, was no discourse in economic theory, but an emphatic effort at legitimising the party's continuance in power on the march towards the nation's "great rejuvenation".

"Marxism must be the basic fundamental, guiding principle, or the party would lose its soul and direction," Xi said.

Xi failed to mention it, however, but outside China, arguably, no Marxism in continuous practice has ever proven exemplary as a method of managing a nation's economy. For China to have added those many touches of "Chinese characteristics" is not proof of the validity of pure Marxist orthodoxy but rather of the innate genius of Han improvisation.

What's more, sceptics and critics will be quick to note that, without the inherent Marxist need for control, the party might have lost power entirely. They will view Xi's declaration as no more than an effort to rally ideological belief. For, as China's growth rates slow (though still among the world's highest), the view is that, without some secular religion for justification, Han society might come to seem no more than one big Chinese casino in which some gamblers lose, some gamblers win – but the party's house management never loses.

Even so, while Xi's primary target for the revivalist speech was the party elite (speaking of inequality!), the message might well offer a touch of appeal to a broader, non-Communist audience. Even in the most intelligent and best-performing Asian economies (say, Singapore and Hong Kong), the gap between rich and poor is widening, seemingly beyond immediate amelioration. Xi's pitch echoes growing global doubts about the equity utility of neoliberal capitalist economics, which, though a proven wealth-producer, seems incapable of yielding broad-based fairness.

And so in the West, where capitalism has dominated, a neo Marxist or postmodern Marxism now gets a second long look. If the richest 1 per cent hold more wealth than ever before, and the other 99 per cent are struggling as never before, and the physical globe overall looks to need a massive urgent injection of ecological protectionism, consideration of alternative approaches to running economies and setting priorities will be necessary.

In American academic and foundation circles, for example, one detects the slow surfacing of a "postmodern Marxism" that does not foolishly propose to stamp out wealth-creating market forces (clearly a cure worse than the disease) but insists on a humanitarian neo-socialism that requires a governance system which stifles corruption and obscene profit-taking, and curbs the power of wealthy elites to shape social and economic policy so as to line their offshore pockets while pocketing preferred politicians.

Professor Philip Clayton, a California colleague, has put it this way: "Most people find it counter-intuitive that a system motivated exclusively by greed and cut-throat competition would bring the greatest benefits to the greatest number of people. We now see that there is a good reason people find this claim counter-intuitive: it is false. Abuses are only overcome when governments, multinational agencies, labour groups, consumer advocates and a well-organised system of checks and balances all serve as watchdogs over market competition." And let us get this out of the way: Clayton boasts a PhD from Yale University and a background that includes teaching at Williams College, Harvard and Cambridge.

In Europe, many agree with such views as that of Jacques Derrida, the late French philosopher – that the "triumph" of capitalism in the West has only served to "highlight its own failures, as human suffering continues and environmental catastrophe appears inevitable". At the least, the relentless ecological crisis and frightening rich-poor divide require us to open our minds to alternatives ways – or at least profound modifications – of current canons of governance and economic management.

This does not mean, as the saying goes, that one throws the baby out with the bathwater: capitalism, after all, does create wealth. But at what corollary costs? And for whom? The well-known Methodist theologian and Marxist theorist Joerg Rieger is fond of praising US billionaire Warren Buffett for saying that "there is such a thing as class warfare and that his class is winning it".

You don't have to be a Marxist – with or without Chinese characteristics – to seriously question the continued validity of status quo liberal-democratic governance. Xi is hardly the only one in the world who appears to find this transparently obvious.

P.S. I am frankly not sure where the trail goes from here, but I plan to follow it closely if I can. And it might not even prove a trail – but a transformation. International lawyer and emeritus Princeton Professor Richard Falk provides an overarching vision of such a last-gasp transformation in his latest book Power Shift, an important attempt to make a realistic case for a global procedural utopia. Think as a species, he writes, not as a tribe; and praises China its own "transformation".

AND THEN THERE'S...

"Finally, and perhaps most important, Xi is determined to reform and revitalize China's economy. He has championed his vision of a 'Chinese dream', defined as the rejuvenation of the Chinese nation and the opportunity for all Chinese to attain a middle-class lifestyle. [...] With a road map for financial liberalization, service-sector development, and a new stage of environmentally friendly urbanization, Xi has set a bold agenda for economic change that aims to be as consequential as Deng Xiaoping's landmark decision to pursue economic reform and opening in 1978."
– *Chinese Politics in the Xi Jinping Era: Reassessing Collective Leadership,* by Cheng Li, Brookings Institution Press, 2016

30 | Beijing may have lost the court case, but it still rules the South China Sea

South China Morning Post, Monday, 11 July 2016

Tom Plate says Beijing made a blunder in not settling its maritime dispute with the Philippines out of court, but after years of quietly reclaiming land and building facilities in the South China Sea, its actual position is one of great strength

RETROSPECTIVE:

All politics abhors a vacuum. Beijing saw one in the South China and grabbed the opportunity to fill it before a militarily revitalised Japan could. Yes, sometimes international politics is that simple.

The Obama administration was shocked and rocked by these words: "We recommend that the United States bring its [raised tariffs against China] into conformity with its obligations."

That, just two years ago, was the sharply worded ruling from an international body whose judgment Beijing roundly cheered. It came out of Geneva, from the World Trade Organisation, of which both the US and China are members. The WTO had found the Obama administration in violation of international rules with its set of aggressive US tariffs against China importers. How embarrassing!

So, what did Washington then do? What could it do? You either abide by an unfavourable ruling or get out of the organisation. Since you cannot expect to win all disputes all the time in any court, you stay in the system because you know you will win at least some of the time. The alternative is a completely lawless world trade system in which clouds of chaos might precede the more dangerous fogs of war.

Beijing's official reaction to the 2014 WTO judgment? "China urges the United States to respect the WTO rulings and correct its wrongdoings of abusively using trade remedy measures, and to ensure an environment of fair competition for Chinese enterprises."

That was the public statement issued by Chinese diplomats – and it was hard to blame them for its "we told you so" tone. After all, it was their diligent legal and deft diplomatic work that so paid off for the world to see.

But that was then and this is now: China's skilled diplomats have little to celebrate this week.

On Tuesday, a different international body ruled against Beijing in a different high-level dispute. This one concerned sovereignty and land usage, as well as maritime rights and jurisdiction issues, in the sprawling South China Sea, the heavily used and vast ocean water of East Asia.

The international organisation issuing the ruling was the Permanent Court of Arbitration in The Hague. In a case brought to it by the government of the Philippines, the court, with explicit reference to the UN Convention on the Law of the Sea of 1982, dismissed China's expansive territorial and sovereignty claims in the South China Sea as lacking legal foundation; scoffed at its island-enhancing-and-creating campaign as unsupportable under international law; and described all its oceanic filling-and-building and upgrading to be in serious breach of the convention's environmental aims.

From the standpoint of its world image, this therefore is not Beijing's best week ever. Although it had long ago claimed that Manila's case was frivolous and even provocative, it was, as a factual matter, a signed and sealed member of the Law of the Sea treaty and thus under some obligation to respect the process.

But it made a tactical blunder: Instead of "settling" the maritime dispute with the Philippines "out of court", before this embarrassing (and, frankly, anything but unpredictable) decision was to be handed down so loudly, China chose to hold defiantly to its position that the Hague court was not competent to address these issues, while continuing to landfill and build and expand facilities.

So, what next for Beijing?

Stay cool: As we say in America, "possession is nine tenths of the law", and no court order out of Switzerland – however proper, technically correct and well meaning – will fully dislodge the Chinese from their claims and facilities. Nor will the US, especially in a presidential election year, risk serious conflict with the People's Republic of China, especially at a time when American public opinion can barely bring itself to support the current policy of keeping 8,500 US troops in Iraq.

And, by the way, China should ignore any unctuous comments that may come out of Washington: notwithstanding, the US Senate never ratified the Law of the Sea treaty and so, unlike China and more than 150 good international-law-abiding nations, technically America is not even a member of this convention that it insists China must honour. Just tune out any lectures from Washington in response to the ruling.

The Chinese government's first wave of reactions to the Hague ruling will be probably prove negative, dismissive and even spiteful.

But, given enough time, cooler heads in the capital of the world's most populous country will locate an actual silver lining in this cloud.

Which is this: Having accomplished so much in its expansion of groundbreaking claims and indeed building a physical military presence in the South China Sea, it can now afford to take the high road on these high seas and begin to negotiate with Hanoi and Manila and other claimants and concerned countries.

Through sheer audacity and grand scheming, Beijing has attained a position of great strength. It will only strengthen its hand even further – morally (soft power) as well as geopolitically (regional leverage) – by giving back to its neighbours some of what it has claimed and gained.

If it does, it will still remain ahead in the great historic game of the South China Sea competition. Perhaps even further ahead than anyone thought possible.

Win some, lose some.

*P.S. The question of the relevance of international law, and international court rulings, is explored in a systematic way in the 2012 book **Legality and Legitimacy in Global Affairs**, edited by Richard Falk, Mark Juergensmeyer, and Vesselin Popovski. It is highly recommended for not flinching from the need to achieve an understanding of both the need for credible and applicable international law – and its very significant limitations, especially in a fast-moving and precedent-creating world order.*

AND THEN THERE'S...

"Today, the centerpiece of China's salami slicing is the clever use of large fleets of white-hulled boats like fishing vessels and maritime surveillance ships to advance China's territorial claims in very small increments, ergo the "salami slicing" metaphor. Of course, always waiting over the coercive horizon are China's gray-hulled warships should they be needed. To see how China's salami slicing now works – and how it could well drag the United States into a conflict – we need to look no farther than China's successful taking of Scarborough Shoal in 2012 from the Philippines."

– *Crouching Tiger: What China's Militarism Means for the World,*
   by Peter Navarro, Prometheus Books, 2015

CHINA AGAINST THE WORLD: A TALE OF PRIDE AND PREJUDICE

SOUTH CHINA MORNING POST, MONDAY, 1 AUGUST 2016

Tom Plate says seeing a vast country like China through the personality and politics of one man will result only in assessments that, as many examples have shown, are often proved wrong

RETROSPECTIVE:

There are many Chinas. The urban China, the rural China, the new China, the old China, the unknown China. The argument for trying to write the Big Picture column about China while living inside China itself has merit, of course. But so does the argument that to get perspective on the whole of it, the observer is better off a distance away. Here is what I mean: on the whole the best China "experts" I have met lived in Singapore.

The cafe in Los Angeles was well shaded from the glaring sun outside and not even half full and no one was within overhearing distance. My appointment was with a diplomat – a smart Ministry of Foreign Affairs veteran from China. I needed to talk to him – no; I needed him to talk.

This is what I do when I am not teaching or working on my next book; I try to listen carefully to people who know more than I do (a notably vast pool).

The diplomat arrived, and stirred the hot latte put before him without enthusiasm. His spirit was low. The Permanent Court of Arbitration in the Netherlands had ruled against his government on the Philippines brief in the South China Sea case. And his job was public diplomacy. For him and other Chinese "public" diplomats, it was not exactly the night before Christmas.

China is a riddled entity of profound vastness – one big Jupiter surrounded by many twirling Asian moons. Despite all the post-Mao openness, all the enforced globalised intimacy and all those Western think tanks, it has proven about as easy to unravel as string theory. I read academic journal articles and trudge through long books by China "experts", but sometimes wonder if the notion of a "China expert" is often more hope than realisation.

"There is an occupational hazard for anyone who chooses to write about Chinese politics in the second decade of the 21st century," admits Professor Kerry Brown of King's College, London, in his dazzlingly detailed new book, *CEO, China: The Rise of Xi Jinping*. "We may live in an age of openness and information, but the inner workings of the Chinese political system … remain one of the few bastions of opacity." More presumptive "experts" should follow Brown's lead and humbly offer their "expertise" with modesty. Few do.

With Beijing, Western arrogance grates. Representing a government atop a continuous civilisation that dates back thousands of years, my friend the diplomat parried my questions by seeking to elicit, sincerely, my thoughts on The Hague tribunal's anti-China decision on the South China Sea. This struck me as a trap, though not plotted: Anything this American might say short of saying that the tribunal was a CIA front might be viewed by him as anti-China.

In all fairness, Manila's decision to file its arbitration case, egged on by Washington, was never going to do much but add to the tension. President Xi Jinping's neighbourhood is no happier a place thanks to The Hague.

"Our public diplomacy must be improved," said the Chinese diplomat when he started to open up. In his view, Beijing's problem is that it is misunderstood by the world. Perhaps – but sometimes it is either understood all too well or deliberately misunderstood.

In the South China Sea, China has consistently put forth core sovereignty as the basis of its claims. What part of that stand did Manila, in pressing its legalistic case in The Hague, not get? Modern China draws the red line on sovereignty – including sovereignties, in China's mind, regained with its rise. No court in Europe could ever shake that sense of rectitude.

Even this polished professional diplomat cannot hide the deep well of emotion that comes from the sense that now is China's time – the era of catching up on old losses and evening-up causes once thought lost. "We're not afraid of Europe," is the diplomat's way of dismissing some full-of-itself tribunal in a far-off Dutch coastal city.

The sincerity (if not the wisdom) of that emotion is impossible to doubt but the time had come for a bit of bluntness. Trying to appear as casual as the young waiter seemingly avoiding our table, I asked why his government hadn't anticipated the inevitable "public diplomacy" problem from The Hague decision by working harder to defuse Manila's volatility. Why not throw a real concession or two its way?

The diplomat hesitated; I had hit a nerve, and took a stab at an answer myself: "Nationalism, right?"

He looked at me directly but responded with the slightest nod that I took to be yes.

I couldn't help myself: "But nationalism's also a force in the Philippines. They're people too, right? And Vietnam doesn't have nationalism?"

He said nothing but his eyes said a lot. China's problem is less with neighbouring nations than its own people. Its foreign relations are fuelled more by domestic pressures than by logical interactions with neighbours.

A long time ago, a wise American offered this enduring perspective:

"Today China stands isolated, mistrustful and hostile toward the outside world; her whole history has contributed to the view of herself as a superior civilization set upon by hostile barbarians … China's ancient pride may be an obstacle to communication, but it also provides the opportunity to breach the barrier of mistrust and hostility by treating China with the respect that is her due as a great and ancient civilisation."

This foreign-relations homily came from US Senator J. William Fulbright, the famous chairman of the Senate Foreign Relations Committee, in his classic book with the enduring title, *The Arrogance of Power*. This was written in the mid-1960s.

Now, it's half a century later: Can the West honestly say that it finally gets it?

But at the same time: When will China be able to tell us that it's finally over it?

P.S. My view of China is and has been as the late Fulbright's: a great and ancient civilization. No one has put it better.

AND THEN THERE'S...

"It is not impossible that the Chinese state is on its way to becoming a good regime of its own kind. Many outside observers have come to accept that it is. Inside believers are not naive. They know of the regime's blemishes but will argue that it deals with the problems and that people are better off. They may compare it with India, the other big Asian nation, which is democratic but where governance has not delivered, and people have suffered for it."
— *The Perfect Dictatorship: China in the 21st century,*
   by Stein Ringen, Hong Kong University Press, 2016

<table>
<tr><td>32</td><td>'BLAME IT ALL ON CHINA'—
US AND BRITAIN PLAYING A
DANGEROUS GAME WITH
TURN TO SCAPEGOATING</td></tr>
</table>

SOUTH CHINA MORNING POST, MONDAY, 15 AUGUST 2016

Tom Plate decries the increasing tendency of political and media sectors to see Beijing as the cause of all their woes, as it goes against the openness that has made America great

RETROSPECTIVE:

Very large targets are much easier to identify and hit than small ones. But their pushback is far more dangerous. America can invade a button of a nation like Grenada (1983) as easily as turning on the TV and not worry about retaliation. China is a different story. Logically, blaming China for this, that and almost everything else makes no strategic sense, and morally it is bankrupt. China is not 100% bad, just as the US is not 100% good. We live in a mixed swirling world of deficient players with limited talents and spotty capabilities. Self-examination instead of scapegoating is the productive way forward.

"China, China, China". Blame it all on China. Why not?

The scoop from the US mainland is that economic dislocation and unemployment problems are starting to be branded by the political and media sector with that provincial if semi-official moniker: It's China's fault.

Well, yes – China is a problem and it does create problems with its trade wins (but it also creates a lot of opportunities, right?); but China is not *the* problem.

It's our overrated political and overheated media system that defaults to scapegoating – as does China towards the West – that's becoming the problem. Even the Brits have jumped into this dumb, self-defeating game – toddling along as if a clueless puppy on the heels of the new government of Conservative Prime Minister Theresa May.

She pulled an 11th-hour plug on a forward-thinking nuclear power installation deal with Beijing that had been negotiated by the previous government of David Cameron and formally agreed to in good faith by both. At that betrayal, the Xi Jinping government is howling and I, for one, cannot blame them.

High-level agreements between governments should be mutually drilled and cemented into core national interests. After all, if every pact is to be subject to the revisionist whims of the next government, what's the value of arduous international negotiations? In the British case, one might have thought the political-ideological distance between Cameron and May, previously a member of his cabinet, could not possibly have been so great as to recall a signature agreement with Beijing.

May's betrayal of her former boss reminds one of Hillary Clinton's parallel perfidy with her own former boss. The Democratic presidential candidate (egged on by traditionally Democratic union leaders) now opposes the vital Trans-Pacific Partnership trade pact as written. Perhaps she has forgotten that it was her own former boss, US President Barack Obama, who put the deal together while she was his appointed secretary of state and was peddling the deal throughout the Pacific.

On balance, the deal is a good one: were the TPP to come together as Obama and his team imagine, the effect would not only boost US exports but could start to stitch together the Asia-Pacific region in a manner that Beijing might have found difficult to fight. In fact,

China might even have been wise – or flattered – enough to join, a development that could render the Pacific region more enduringly economically stable and presumably more politically peaceful.

Ok, so I'm dreaming. Even so, let us reiterate: populist, jingoistic paroxysms of politics are not the monopoly of the Chinese. It is true that the government and Communist Party of China have been indulging in the crowd-control technique of unadulterated nationalism. But this sin is hardly new – indeed, since the death of Deng Xiaoping in 1997 and the retirement of the sensible and grounded Zhu Rongji in 2003, China's once-appealing international interface has lost a measure of sheen.

Let us not sugar-coat reality by kowtowing to the proposition that everything China does with the West is now justified because of everything terrible the West has done to China over the centuries. That's a formula for geopolitical regression.

Beijing stroking its nationalism and counting on it to undergird its legitimacy is hardly news. What is news is a reviving Western primitivism. One senses it to be potentially as corrosive as China's. In a way, this too is not new. We recall the early 1990s when the economy of California, the best in the nation, began stumbling badly. The culprit then was not what we Americans were doing wrong but what the Japanese were doing to us. Now the alleged culprit is low-cost Chinese exports and low-cost Chinese labour, which have put some Americans out of work. The result is that, at least for the duration of our miserable election season, the very idea of globalisation is under siege.

Just blame it on China! What a fraud: international globalisation (which, one way or the other, is unavoidable) is not the problem; the problem is incompetent American governance and greedy, narrow-minded corporatism. It is said of the mainland these days that foreigners are viewed with increasing negativity – the crude souring effect of Chinese nationalism.

That may be true; but what is also true is that American politicians have been working hard to get the American people to forget about those nicely priced toys under the yearly Christmas tree that helped stretch the family budget and stymie price inflation; not to mention the magnitude of Chinese government investment in US Treasury instruments, which have helped finance our pathetically misconceived military adventures and illegal invasions.

Those who live in glass houses should not lob rhetorical rocks. The US and its historic ally, Britain, would be running a terrible risk in going down the scapegoating route – especially with the Chinese and American navies playing macho games in the South China Sea.

To my mind, maybe the most admirable and exportable American trait is the beautiful mentality of openness to outsiders and to outside ideas. This is America at its greatest. But close that mind, roll up the drawbridge, build walls around our heart and blame others for our shortcomings – this is the route to decline and the start of American mindlessness.

But Beijing must cut down on the nonsense, too. Why should either of us play such a dangerous game?

P.S. At the writing of this note – about a year later – the simplistic Trumpian blame-game seems to be subsiding, giving way to a more mutual-needs-based attitude and approach. And something of this trajectory marked the outset of all recent incoming US presidential administrations since John F. Kennedy.

AND THEN THERE'S…

"Reason is a very light rider, and easily shook off." (Jonathan Swift)
– *Superpower: Three Choices for America's Role in the World,*
  by Ian Bremmer, Penguin Publishing Group, 2015

The Singapore political system may prove a difficult model for China, whatever the West thinks

South China Morning Post, Monday, 29 August 2016

Tom Plate says a changing Singapore, though increasingly seen now as an acceptable model for China, may be a hard act to follow after all

RETROSPECTIVE:

Your humble columnist bears the burden of being among the first US journalists to appreciate Singapore for what it has become: a huge success, achieved on its own terms. Surely my many memorable conversations with the late Lee Kuan Yew led to my religious conversion. They also helped me see all of Asia in a new light. In terms of geopolitics, he was my most memorable tutor.

Singapore has been an upwardly mobile Asian phenomenon for decades. But Americans were the last to realise the extent of the achievement. Until recently, the US establishment media smugly scoffed at this soft-authoritarian-style city state. But, over time, facts do matter: lately, its role in Asia – especially as a non-ideological signpost for those leaders of China who wish to implant further mile-markers down pragmatism road – is increasingly apparent.

Singapore has been an absolute stand-out, particularly for a small city state (think Norway, sort of, but warmer). It bobs at the top of the charts in the gold-medal statistical metrics: high per capita income, exceptional governance, internationally lauded health care, scary-smart kids in well-run schools and so on. Its ministers and civil servants generally outshine other countries', especially in ethically challenged Southeast Asia. It has sported notable prime ministers: the late, legendary whizz Lee Kuan Yew; the underappreciated, charming Goh Chok Tong, and, since 2004, the well-serving, intelligently determined Lee Hsein Loong.

All were nurtured in the ultra clean, tightly wound People's Action Party (PAP), which until relatively recently hovered over Singaporean politics, not wholly unlike the Chinese Communist Party in the way no one seriously challenged it. But the PAP is now under a measure of other-party competition (with some even hailing the birth of genuine two-party democracy).

Recent health downturns within the reigning elite serve to remind Singaporeans that nothing is forever. Last year, at 91, founding prime minister Lee Kuan Yew died; earlier this month, current prime minister Lee, one of Lee Kuan Yew's two sons, suffered a collapse during a speech and had to be revived; also this month, an ailing finance minister emerged from hospital, and a former president, S. R. Nathan, passed on, to a proper state funeral.

Right, nothing lasts forever – except surely China, which accounts for about a fifth of the global population. It's not ever going away, but unwise Americans sometimes almost seem to wish it would, as if viewing nations and governments like imperious TV producers pondering whether to renew a sitcom series ("Gaddafi's ratings are down – maybe we should cancel?"). One father of that "wishful" thought is Cornell-University-educated Gordon Chang, who in his book

The Coming Collapse of China declaimed: "The end of the modern Chinese state is near. The People's Republic has five years, perhaps 10, before it falls." This came out in 2001.

For myself, predicting China's collapse seems joyless speculation. The resultant suffering and sadness (not to mention world economic collapse) would be immeasurable. Nowadays, our more sophisticated China-critical crowd narrows the scope of its Sino-failure prediction and focuses on the Communist Party, which has a public relations image in the West today not unlike that of Singapore's PAP decades ago.

One exemplar of the pessimism-revisionism school is Professor David Shambaugh, the respected director of the China Policy Programme at The George Washington University who – unlike Chang – sees a way out for China. It should draw on the political model of Singapore's PAP. His important new book, *China's Future*, makes the case that the Chinese government must turn away from its constant defaulting to the repression option that "like chemotherapy for someone who has cancer, can work for a while, but not forever". Instead, it should maturely accept a more evolutionary approach: "This would entail a real opening of the political system to embrace many of the elements and attributes of the semi-democratic systems currently operating in Hong Kong and especially Singapore." If it doesn't, Shambaugh predicts, the Communist Party "will gradually lose its grip on power".

To the far-flung, worldwide secular clergy of political scientists, this thought about a redemptive Singapore road is anything but new; but in America it is almost novel! Singapore's political system as the better way now for China? "It is not democracy as it is known in the West (indeed it operates more efficiently)," writes Shambaugh the pragmatic. "[But] even Singapore has rid itself of the more draconian

aspects of its authoritarian past. For China to go down this path would still require a significant and far-reaching transformation of its current political system."

Singaporeans deserve to enjoy a chuckle over its new status as a positive model after decades of detention in the public-opinion purgatory of relentless Western human-rights condemnations. But this brilliant country is changing, too. In 2011, the PAP was rocked when it got "only" 60 per cent of the national vote. It rebounded in 2015, but the theoretical possibility was set: the ruling party could be voted out.

On the mainland, of course, that prospect is about as easy to imagine as finding deeply discounted Mao posters for sale on Taobao. Shambaugh agrees. "Would the [Communist Party] be willing to undertake … constraints on its complete monopoly of power? The chances are close to zero."

Singapore's foreign policy also seems under reorientation. In the past, it emphasised a balance towards Beijing and Washington. Now, the tilt feels more US-leaning than Sino-US balancing.

Thus, as a model to emulate, it becomes a somewhat problematic target when it itself is in flux. Yet, nudging China into more suave, cosmopolitan politics would add to stability in Asia and the world, and merit Singapore something like a Nobel Peace Prize.

In that sense, one might almost wish that the city state stuck to its old ways but, of course, I personally cannot suggest this: after all, I am from America, which itself is stuck in its old ways.

P.S. Size does matter. In the jungle of the world, the elephant stands his ground while the little cougar runs up the tree. Each survives in his own particular way. While they learn from each other, the elephant is not the cougar. Everyone is its own model. Broad, transformative models tend to ignore the fact that most political reality is local.

AND THEN THERE'S...

"A pessimist sees the difficulty in every opportunity; an optimist sees the opportunity in every difficulty." (Winston Churchill)
— *Superpower: Three Choices for America's Role in the World,*
  by Ian Bremmer, Penguin Publishing Group, 2015

<table>
<tr><td>**34**</td><td># Why 'macho' Putin has the lead over Xi when it comes to American minds</td></tr>
</table>

SOUTH CHINA MORNING POST, MONDAY, 12 SEPTEMBER 2016

Tom Plate says US media and the likes of Donald Trump have made Russia's president a hero while Xi and his China remain a somewhat unfathomable mystery

RETROSPECTIVE:

Journalists, reflecting human nature perhaps only too well, tend to view a country through an iconic visage of its leader. It's a methodology filled with risk, of course. If China is Xi Jinping, and Xi is China, what happens to China if something terrible (coup, death, whatever) befalls Xi? China, after all, does not disappear.

Perhaps you're not going to believe this. The fact is that if a poll were taken of American public opinion about Russia's Vladimir Putin and China's Xi Jinping, Putin would get the higher recognition rating, and easily.

Two cheers for Putin? In part, credit Republican presidential candidate Donald Trump. With odd consistency in a campaign otherwise peppy with inconsistency, the garrulous New York real estate mogul has been peddling the notion of Russia's autocratic president as a great leader, inspiring some Republican Americans to whine (utterly without irony) that President Barack Obama is no Putin.

And what a lovely thing that is!

"Few leaders have caused more suffering and conflict today than Vladimir Putin. It shows just how far down the rabbit hole some Trump fans will go to defend their guy," sighed one dispirited Republican national security expert. "It's a national case of Stockholm syndrome, one that makes decent Americans turn their backs on values and traditions that they've held dear for their entire lives."

Against Putin, Xi lies second, not because he is not as "strong" a leader (he is undoubtedly the more formidable, more steeped in the complexities of Chinese civilisation); but because he is not as readily categorisable or as identifiable. Once at a seminar with *China Daily* journalists in Beijing, I asked if most Chinese citizens could summon up the name of the US president; and they looked at me as if I were nuts – of course they could! I then asked if they could guess the percentage of Americans that could name the Chinese leader. A guess came in at "50 per cent?" I tried not to laugh: "Sorry, it would be less than 10 per cent." The journalists gasped in dismay, and, as an American, I was embarrassed.

Blame our national ignorance entirely on our news media – why not? Almost everyone, from academics to taxi drivers, makes it the go-to culprit for almost everything. But there are deeper reasons why hardly anyone in America knows Xi, and we might as well start with this: if China's obviously talented president does care a great deal about his international image, he might try harder to soften it.

He is certainly no baby-kisser like former premier Wen Jiabao, or self-effacing press conference jokester like, say, Wen's predecessor Zhu Rongji.

In all fairness, Xi is obviously no faceless bureaucrat putting in time to retirement; and in conversations with Chinese officials, I hear only praise for his bold strikes against corruption. But in America there is doubt – doubt as to whether his campaign aims to destroy, impartially, only the corrupt.

One expert's view: "Within China, President Xi Jinping's anti-corruption campaign has targeted previously untouchable members of the ruling Politburo Standing Committee, though it remains unclear whether the campaign is motivated by a desire to truly root out corruption or to weaken Xi's political opponents." That assessment comes from Kurt Campbell, a famous US diplomat, in his valuable book, *The Pivot: The Future of American Statecraft in Asia*.

The truth of the matter is that Xi is the most important world leader that Americans know least about, when as head of China he should be a world leader about whom they are at least knowledgeable.

Might China's public diplomacy do a better job of conveying what Xi is trying to do?

For all anyone knows, Xi may have the softest heart and sharpest brain of anyone in his fifth-generation class. Or he might make Putin look like a positive pussycat by comparison – who knows? Does Xi receive the best possible advice on America from the experts in his party and government on which he must draw? Sometimes leaders are told by their minions only that which it is known they prefer to hear.

In life, as we say, timing can be everything.

Xi took power as general secretary of the Communist Party of China and chairman of the CPC Central Committee in the aftermath of the convulsive worldwide economic downturn of 2008–2009, triggered mainly by serious evils in the ethics and operating systems of Wall Street America. Here is the problem: since this epiphany of evil, almost everyone from the mainland I talk to views the US as in historic decline. But, in fact, are America's best days only yesterdays? I wish some Chinese would not be so quick to count America out. After all, China's elite still sends a generational avalanche of its children to our colleges and universities, and there's good reason for this. It's that many in China's moneyed elite are smart, not dumb, in advancing their children's prospects. It would be a serious error if the government were making decisions on the simple-minded presumption that America were slowly crumbling like some exhausted cracking wall, when its elite is dramatically voting with its tuition chequebooks the other way.

It is painful to believe that China and Xi do not respect the US. The flap over Obama's disembarking from Air Force One when it landed at Hangzhou for the G20 summit last week cannot be anything but a regrettable one-off botch job. With characteristic forbearance, Obama reacted to the tempest on the tarmac with a well-considered shrug.

Too bad some Americans jumped on the incident as if looking for a serious punch-up opportunity with China. Foremost among the jumpers was Trump. Presumably he figured that his hero Putin would have reacted with more machismo. But the US president's cool conveyed self-confidence, not frailty. It's bullies who lose their cool. Smart Americans have figured Putin out; but, alas, Xi, from an entirely different system with different political values, is still a mystery, at least to Americans.

P.S. At this writing, Xi still remains a mystery to Americans.

AND THEN THERE'S...

"We should pursue mutually beneficial development featuring openness and cooperation, develop China by securing a peaceful international environment and, at the same time, uphold and promote world peace through our own development."
– *The Governance of China,* by Xi Jinping, Foreign Languages Press, 2014

35

US and China need more soft power, not military hardware, to resolve their differences

South China Morning Post, Monday, 26 September 2016

Tom Plate says history is moving in the direction of China and Asia, and America would do well to favour understanding over grandstanding

RETROSPECTIVE:

As this column clearly or even effusively admits, I have considerable admiration for our military leaders who do their social science and history homework – and for the political science departments of the US service academies that are so first-rate. But my stomach sinks when military leaders offer too many policy speeches, or assume too high or loud a profile in our national debates. I just find it worrisome – if you know what I mean.

Embedded in my otherwise dogmatic pacifist DNA is honest respect for the military officer steeped in history and political science. Perhaps in part because my late father, who was an honourable US marine, was not, alas, so steeped. Steeping, one has to believe, is a prerequisite to understanding our complex world.

In writing for newspapers about Asia and China since 1996,

informative exchanges would routinely arise with members of the US military, especially the razor-sharp heads of the Pacific Command at Pearl Harbour. Standouts in my mind included admirals Joseph Prueher, who was later to become ambassador to China (and help defuse the nasty 2001 Hainan Island incident); Dennis Blair, later President Barack Obama's first director of National Intelligence (and famous as the first skipper of a destroyer to water ski in his ship's wake); and Thomas Fargo, a charismatic submarine commander behind the character "Commander Bart Mancuso" (Scott Glenn) in the action film *The Hunt for Red October*.

The current Pacific Command head is Harry Harris – the first Asian American to make admiral (this has got to be generally good for Asia). Born in Yokosuka (and raised in the US South), Harris is the navy's highest-ranking Japanese American (this perhaps being less good for China). His fabulous education: the Naval Academy (of course), Harvard's Kennedy School of Government, Georgetown's School of Foreign Service, Oxford University and even MIT.

This articulate and personable navy aviator not only saw his career zoom, but also touched down in Washington at one point as a joint chiefs of staff speech writer. And it was his verbal dexterity that shone during a recent speech at a hotel in Los Angeles, courtesy of the Asia-alert LA World Affairs Council. The navy fly boy had previously caused a buzz (famous in Washington, infamous in Beijing) for this wise crack about the South China Sea: "[China is] creating a great wall of sand."

In LA, though the admiral did not throw any sand in China's face, his talk did plainly pivot on the assumption that the best response to China's push in its own neighbourhood was to push China back, even though it's China's own neighbourhood. Noting China's rejection of an arbitral tribunal's South China Sea ruling, and – as a key factor in

North Korea's nuclear buildup – fingering Beijing's tepidity in failing to stare Pyongyang down, Harris' pitch was rather brutally binary "good guy, bad guy". He was pushy on the need for more military hardware, sparing on the need for deft and aggressive diplomacy.

Washington has been posting more and more ships to the Asia-Pacific but Harris cannot hide his glee at the new ones coming his way: "The lead ship, USS Zumwalt, is scheduled to be commissioned next month … This region is getting a ship even the Klingons would fear. And the destroyer skipper's name is Captain James Kirk. You just can't make this stuff up. Jokes aside, this is serious business. If we have to fight tonight, I don't want it to be a fair fight. If it's a knife fight, I want to bring a gun. If it's a gunfight, I want to bring in the artillery…"

The few Chinese diplomats from the local consulate in the ballroom audience sat admirably quiet. They did not jump up to ask whether the prime cause of North Korea's buildup was Beijing's timidity – or, rather, Washington's diplomatic frigidity. And the admiral was little short of a travelling salesman for THAAD, the brutally expensive missile defence gadget proclaimed by Washington not to be offensive to Beijing but defensive only as regards North Korea.

Will it actually work? There are doubts about that – but in the North Korean mind they have no doubt that a working Terminal High Altitude Area Defence system arms the US with a first-strike nuclear capability. THAAD is thus effective in not only irritating Beijing but also motivating Pyongyang to keep nuking.

What China and America need is not more arms but more diplomats – not another carrier of soldiers but an armada of diplomacy. Military power will not force China to back off on its sea claims; it will only dig in its heels, if in yet more sand. Chinese public opinion has a different historical narrative than does Harris and would support nothing less. Just as the Caribbean and Atlantic oceans are American seas due in part to their proximity, the seas around mainland China are not widely viewed in Asia as primary American waters.

From an Asian perspective, the great wall of the Cold War fell more than a quarter of a century ago. So history moves on, but this time in the direction of China and Asia.

America's quarrel is thus not only with China but with history – and with many parts of Asia. Even some otherwise pro-US stalwarts in Australia are starting to have doubts. Former prime minister Paul Keating, in a riveting conversation on ABC radio recently, urged the Chinese and Americans to forgo the gun-fighting and try power-sharing: "The United States is still fundamentally pursuing the policy for the maintenance of primacy against the obvious rise of China and therefore resisting the whole idea of sharing strategic power in Asia, which I believe the United States should do with the Chinese," Keating said. "We [in Australia] both need and deserve a nuanced foreign policy which does take account of these big seismic shifts in the world." Keating, now 72, urged Aussies not to fight reality: "Strategic hegemony by the US in the Pacific is incapable of preservation."

My last quote from Admiral Harris: "Everything that's 'new in cool' in the US military arsenal is coming first to the Pacific." Oh my. Even America's best-educated military leaders need to keep steeping.

P.S. We all need to "keep steeping", including China's top military brass. They have their share of boisterous battle-ready brigands, too!

AND THEN THERE'S...

"Or we can stop fearing China as a superpower and accept them as a partner in the real challenges of our world. When we consider the cost of being the world's only superpower, we can see that they're quite high. When we look at the benefits of being the world's only superpower, we can see they're minimal. Looking at what China will do with its growing power, we may find that to fear China becoming a superpower would be the worst possible decision we could make."
— *Fearing China, Asking the Question: Should We Fear China?*,
   by Terry D. Wittenmyer, Zebra CAT Publishing, 2015

36

The constant gardener: why the US needs to stick to its time-tested role in Asia

SOUTH CHINA MORNING POST, MONDAY, 10 OCTOBER 2016

*Tom Plate says turning geopolitical maestro instead
could prove a tall task, given that the 48 Asian
nations may well play to their own tunes*

RETROSPECTIVE:

The notion of likening a foreign policy to puttering in your garden seems quaint and rather English. But it has the value of seeming unaggressive and indeed nicely pastoral. You can decide for yourself if the metaphor beloved by a former US secretary (courtesy of a British novelist) to describe the US role in Asia paints a correct picture – or offers the best vision. But the image of the "constant gardener" seems a great deal more sensible than the "constant intervener".

It is cleverly and famously said that electoral democracy is the worst political system we have to endure in our mixed-up world, with the notable exception – and this is the key point – of all the others.

But is this well-travelled bromide still salient? Are you still a happy fan? Have you listened to what is coming out of the mouth of the elected president of the Philippines? Have you followed the

US presidential debates, with all that campaign slurp and candidate mea culpa? And yet you still believe? If so, good for you; but candour compels me to tell you I have lost the faith.

I used to be as faithful as anyone. For a time the inspiring Sir Isaiah Berlin was my political Einstein, whom I read religiously. His mind was a library of great books that in his essays on liberal freedom talked to you with wisdom. The Oxford-based political philosopher and historian of ideas died in 1997 – the same year, we note, as did Deng Xiaoping, the sly Great Innovator who represented quite a different political faith.

It was another innovator that urged me to think less dogmatically than either: Lee Kuan Yew. Planting himself somewhere between Berlin and Deng, the fiery but wonderfully polished leader of the People's Action Party that founded modern Singapore was anything but a one-citizen, one-vote fan. It was a risky system, he would warn, that, left on its own, could yield "erratic results". And so it is in a way fortunate that Lee, who left us last year at 91, is no longer around to have to witness the juvenile misogyny and risible amateurism of one US candidate, and the hubristic duplicity of the other.

I'll never forget the anxious face of Lee Kuan Yew, in 2007 inquiring about Hillary Clinton, when he was told by a visiting American professor she'd probably prove "good enough". That caused him to pause: "Good enough?" he said. "Hmm … whomever you elect, we'll have to live with."

Trying to predict which one of the current duo would prove better for China is a complete waste of mental activity. This presidential campaign is roiling on emotions, not on ideas or policies. One poses as the candidate of urgently needed major change (of some kind), the other of continuing successful reform (of a mainly Obama kind). To avoid serious frustration, try not to delve beyond this.

Trump mentions China mainly when he is fishing for votes from the unemployed or job-rattled. Mrs Clinton says little about China (otherwise a blessing) but is said to be "tougher on Beijing" – whatever that means.

Unaddressed is the massive challenge of how to make the bilateral relationship better, or at least not worse. The fate of the 21st century will depend on this. Long after the Islamic State is bagged and placed into the dustbin of history, China and America will be bumping into one another. This power pair will never couple contentedly but the forced intimacy of the 21st century global order will not permit them to be all that separated.

China is further along in fashioning what it wants to be and how it wants to fashion its Asian future; we in the US, bogged down as usual in the Middle East and too often leaning on our warriors more than our diplomats for wisdom or resolution, have not thought it through. Only our wiser minds have done any deep thinking. The illustrious George Schultz, the former secretary of state and of the Treasury, and now a senior Stanford Solon, has likened the US role in Asia in the 20th century to that of the attentive and well-equipped gardener.

Americans tended to the honourable, if pedestrian, chore of pulling out destructive weeds, ministering to our allies' spatial and nutrient requirements, and sprinkled around garden-variety plant food (although also, tragically, napalm or Agent Orange sometimes instead).

With the withering of the Soviet empire, more than a vegetarian approach was thought needed – something grander, bolder, meatier. And so for the 21st century, Kurt Campbell, the well-travelled former US diplomat, conjures up for the entire world to see an image of Asia that cannot possibly proceed apace without the undergirding of American wisdom and power. America's 21st century role will be that of the orchestra conductor – the geopolitical maestro that "coordinates the increasingly independent efforts of Asian states and multinational institutions in common cause to shape Asia's future," as he writes in his new book The Pivot.

Good luck with that, well-intentioned Americans! In case you have not noticed, Asia is rather grown up now.

With half the world's population, it is the world's leading regional economic actor. At the same time, it is quite true that dramatic American shrinkage from Asia would not do anyone much good (the Chinese elite, especially, needs to face this reality).

But there are 48 countries comprising Asia and some will be organising their own concerts. China and America may wrestle each other to lead but neither will get to monopolise the baton; and many of the 48 orchestra musicians will try to play one superpower maestro off against the other, probably successfully.

Cacophony is as likely to fill the huge concert of hall of Asia as will harmony. The honourable George Schultz has never said this and never will, so I shall: America in Asia needs to stick to its gardening. It worked once and it is the only role that can ever work, whether the next US president is the second Clinton or what's-his-name. Being the constant gardener is an honourable and healthy role. We will flourish in no other.

P.S. Another nice aspect of the gardening metaphor is its civilised sense of gradual careful improvement. It offers a sense of reassurance that a degree of consistency in the persistent practice of tender care will produce healthy, positive results.

AND THEN THERE'S...

"The United States and China are necessary partners, but ones with real underlying issues. For all their cooperation and joint interests, the two countries represent different visions of the world. Underneath their harmonious language towards each other there is implicit disharmony and latent competition."
– *CEO, China: The Rise of Xi Jinping*, by Kerry Brown,
   I. B. Tauris Company, 2016

37

Duterte's 'pivot' to China offers a reminder that all Asian diplomacy should be guided by subtlety and care

South China Morning Post, Monday, 24 October 2016

Tom Plate considers the changing geopolitical order in the region – brought home by Manila and Beijing becoming fast friends – as China's ascendency continues

RETROSPECTIVE:

It may well be that a new Cold War in Asia has already begin. This is in the sense that the little powers have begun to play the big powers off against one another – milking them for whatever they can get. Vietnam plays the China card to get the US re-involved in helping defend a country with which it once waged a vicious war. The Philippines plays the American card to get in favour with China. It is all very regrettable, and anything but inventive or even unprecedented.

Any history of the US impact on the Philippines would greatly suffer from rendition in short form; but the relationship has had its ups and downs, and now we have a serious downer period in that bumpy history. Philippine President Rodrigo Duterte's anti-American tantrum may seem Trumpian in its primitivism but, even so, the clear winner in this round of Asia's geopolitical "dating game" is China.

We should not be surprised. The central global political fact of our times is the gravitational pull of growing China, all but destined to become the Asian superpower. It will not be easily resisted. Wake up, Americans. It's the 21st century, not the 20th.

And so now you have the Philippines. With the finesse of a dump truck, one day Duterte decides to drop Uncle Sam in order to embrace the inheritors of Mao's China – now profiting from a quasi-market system that more and more seems to resemble that of the political one-party Taiwan of the 1990s. Visiting China, Duterte declaims for all the world to hear: "America has lost now". "I've realigned myself in your ideological flow," he told his Chinese hosts.

The mainland's success with state-guided marketisation provides the goodies for the likes of Duterte's Philippines. From his perspective, China can offer his country more than the US. Let's face it: Uncle Sam no longer has the wherewithal to be Santa Claus to everyone, all the time – as in the grand old days of goodies for all.

Is there risk for Duterte? The obvious would be that were China to invade the Philippines tomorrow, Washington might look the other way – but China doesn't need to invade anyone. Its inherent size and growing presence will ineluctably pull its neighbours closer to it, one degree of reduced separation after another. Osmosis rather than offensiveness will suffice.

America is otherwise engaged. From the Obamas on down, the White House is in what we term "Outbox" mentality. They are focused in on the margin of Hillary Clinton's victory, not on the magnitude of Manila's perfidy. Duterte's timing might be thought sly: the White House at this moment is distracted and on the campaign trail – and even thinking about how soon it will be packing its bags.

To be sure, the permanent national security government entity that includes the defence and state departments, not to mention the

CIA and the overall national security apparatus, are watching, however. This is the permanent locus of America's geopolitical wariness and obsessions; and it is one US elephant that usually doesn't forget. As long as countries in Asia, such as Laos, Cambodia and now, perhaps, the Philippines play proactive binary geopolitics – that is, either Beijing or Washington, one or the other; the new Asian dating game – the now ongoing regional reorientation – will prove bumpy and sometimes brutal.

My only advice to the nations rotating around the land of the rising Chinese sun is to avoid lurching and aim for suavity in diplomacy. Under the Philippines' prior president, the well-intentioned but ineffective Benigno Aquino, Manila's foreign policy tilted dramatically towards the US; but then the successor government in Manila starts leaning like a drunken sailor in the other direction. Neither extreme can be said to be in the country's national interest.

The Asian planets revolving around the China sun are best advised to organise their diplomatic reorientation with more subtlety and care.

Beijing played off against Washington; Washington against Beijing. This new Asian diplomacy aims to "yin-yang" the two superpowers with insincere tenderness so as to milk each cow for whatever each one is worth. Something of this mentality may well have arrived in Vietnam and Malaysia and, perhaps before long, Indonesia. Asian nations will enjoy many opportunities to benefit from the dating game. Even now, Japan, the US surrogate in the region, is expected to proffer a new US$48 million loan package to the Philippines.

It may all end in sadness. The wooing of Duterte was no casual afterthought on Beijing's part. Months ago, a Chinese government diplomat tipped me off about what was going on. Behind the scenes, Beijing was working hard on a deal with Manila well before the issuance of the Permanent Court of Arbitration at The Hague's negative ruling on China's entitlement claims in the South China Sea.

Any way you figure it, the Philippines pivot is a tactical triumph for Chinese diplomacy. But I wonder about its sustainability: the Filipino people probably have more fundamental affection for the Americans than the Chinese, whose sudden bonhomie may feel suspiciously – er – fishy. The US State Department, assuming the January inauguration of Clinton, can be expected to make another serious run at East Asia. As the presumed 45th president of the United States put it to a Wall Street audience a few years ago: "We liberated it. We defended it."

As of now, however, the reconfiguration of the diplomatic orbits of the nations of Asia – with the Chinese sun rising ever higher – proceeds apace. Almost no one in America is psychologically prepared for this new reality. Maybe Aquino swung too far one way, Duterte the other. But now the Chinese pull feels more and more ineluctable.

The better approach to geopolitical order in Asia and peace in general would be for Beijing and Washington to work together, hand-in-glove, like adults. This is not happening.

This bodes ill: I doubt that Clinton will ignore what is happening, and Beijing won't back down. So a measure of some sort of future conflict surely looms.

P.S. So, from the standpoint of China-US relations, was it "better" that Hillary lost and The Donald won? It's a ridiculous, impossible to answer question, to be sure. The most important factor here is the one "law" I always follow studiously, one of the greatest "laws" of all – The Law of Unintended Consequences.

AND THEN THERE'S...

"Originally its role was minimum deterrence: to provide assurance that China itself would not again – as it had in the 1950s – face nuclear blackmail. To prevent this, China has built-up forces sufficient to pose a threat of unacceptable damage to an adversary's homeland in retaliation for any nuclear attack on China. More recently, as China's conventional maritime forces have expanded, the nuclear arsenal has started to take on a wider role. It now also functions to deter the United States from mounting large-scale conventional strikes against China of the sort envisaged by the Air-Sea Battle Concept, by raising the possibility of a Chinese nuclear attack on US bases, such as the one on Guam, from which such strikes would be mounted."
– *The China Choice: Why We Should Share Power*, by Hugh White, Oxford University Press, 2013

38

How China and the US are spooking each other with their politics

South China Morning Post, Monday, 7 November 2016

Tom Plate says far from being a force for good, Sino-US interdependence is raising fears of knock-on instability

RETROSPECTIVE:

Scientists have a phrase called "spooky action at a distance". We use it in the column below to suggest the possibility of a dimension of unconscious intimacy in the bilateral relationship that passes understanding – but it's nonetheless as "real" as a copper pipeline.

These days, startling philosophical perspectives originate as much with our "crazy" physicists as our "wise" philosophers. What's more, thinking in effete code so much, physicists will offer memorable ways of phrasing things when they come down to Planet Earth to communicate in, say, plain English.

Consider their fun term for spots in space where gravity somehow clamps down so hard that even light is trapped, as if in a deep coal mine. Physicists have a term for it that has wormed its way into common conversation: "black hole".

Now, along comes another term of comparable transferable utility

– and gawkiness. It's called "spooky action at a distance". And it bodes, for several reasons, to become my all-time favourite.

One is that social science, a dog looking up to its master, will sniff around the physical sciences in a desperate search for comparable certainty. So, as with other scientific terms, "spooky action at a distance" may come to offer insight for social science analysis – as suggested here regarding the US national election and China's political evolution.

The background: the "spooky action at a distance" term is not new. Albert Einstein is said to have coined it while knocking the controversial concept – that two physically separated particles can be correlated – as voodoo physics. But over time, this genius began to doubt his own doubt: maybe, somehow, particles not in close proximity (having "locality") could directly affect each other – in a kind of inexplicable long distance intimacy, via hyper speeds faster than light. Today, the notion of "remote causality" finds considerable favour among physicists for whom quantum theory comes up short in explaining our complex physical world.

And so this American presidential campaign might be thought to fit like a glove the notion of "spooky action at a distance". Consider that two American figures have battled to occupy a place in the political universe that will have an undeniable tug and pull on China. They do so from far away, and are perhaps at times oblivious to the influences being exerted, precisely because the source is so out of direct sight.

The implications of such a geopolitical tightly wound "string theory" are unclear but possibly positive. Both sides may sense or feel a potentially tendentious tug every time one or the other moves out of normal customary space; thinking optimistically, "spooky action at a distance" may eventually embed a kind of distance learning on both sides of the Pacific that serves to curb truly risky behaviour.

The pull and tug is undeniable. For example, when the political camp of President Xi Jinping seeks to gather up as much power to itself as possible so as to emerge as the "core" of China's power structure, reverberations are felt in Washington almost as if invisible strings were strung between the two capitals. Similarly, when the US begins to replace its commander-in-chief with someone else, stress is generated from such "spooky action at a distance".

The bilateral relationship is so intertwined that it is practically strung out – as if in a constant state of intimate tension … in a sense, truly intrinsically neurotic.

One further implication: if geopolitics, in our rapidly integrating and globalising world, comes to resemble anything like a contiguous, holistic physical world, then win-lose outcomes will not offer resolution – they will be unstable isotopes.

Imagine the Sino-US relationship – two countries separated by 10,000 km – as modulated by a sort of iron law of "spooky action at a distance". Neither is now – or ever will be – independent of the other.

So if one side's political system returns inextricably into a throwback one-man dictatorship, or the other willingly elects a disturbed retro would-be strongman, possible disaster beckons. Thus, both China and the US have a huge responsibility, to themselves and to the world, not to permit an unstable leader to surge to the top of their political systems.

What kind of a job is each side doing in this regard? For China, if we believe famed emeritus Oxford professor Stein Ringen, the answer is not so great: "Xi Jinping has moved governance away from apparent softness and towards more undisguised hardness."

In his punchy, provocative and highly critical new book, *The Perfect Dictatorship* – published, interestingly enough, by Hong Kong University Press – the professor imagines China in the 21st century as a modern Mao-type one-man "controlocracy": brutal, wasteful and destructive, and rising irresistibly as a "power state".

In the harsh Ringen scenario, the culprit is not the political system, which the professor admits seems somewhat bendable in various directions, but the tendencies of the current leader himself: "Xi Jinping has gathered unprecedented, since Mao, powers to his own hands and is presenting himself as an ambitious and activist leader who may not have in mind a legacy of simply leaving the ship of state on steady keel. It seems he might be a man with a mission, and ... may have concentrated enough power in his hands to pursue it and may be determined or trapped into imposing his own will to the bitter end."

Ringen's vision is far, far too grim for me, but as one conceivable option in China's evolution, it would be irresponsible to dismiss it out of hand. Now, as to the direction of the United States, you should have a much better idea in a day or so.

Let's hope that what we will face is not too – how do we say? – spooky.

P.S. Sometimes they call CIA agents "spooks". Should I make more of this?

AND THEN THERE'S…

"In this time of prosperity after centuries of external disruptions and recent internal missteps, great opportunities have come to China – China is seizing those opportunities. Xi Jinping, the president of China, has spoken of the 'Chinese Dream' saying: 'Dare to dream, work assiduously to fulfil the dreams and contribute to the revitalization of the nation.' On the surface, this theme may simply sound like guidance for the future path of China, but more than a guide for the future, it's a recognition of the historic place China stands now."
– *Fearing China, Asking the Question: Should We Fear China?*,
  by Terry D. Wittenmyer, Zebra CAT Publishing, 2015

39

WE STICK LABELS ON CHINA – OR THE US – AT OUR OWN PERIL

SOUTH CHINA MORNING POST, MONDAY, 21 NOVEMBER 2016

*Tom Plate says generalisations only mislead when we're trying
to understand complex giants like China and America*

RETROSPECTIVE:

Would mutual understanding be advanced if the world dropped the
use of the catch-all word "China"? It's not going to happen, of course,
but just imagine….

It was a little awkward. The Council on Foreign Relations had
organised a fine luncheon to present an august policy report (many
months in the making) from a high-level independent task force of
US experts very concerned about North Korea. And herein lies a story.

The Council on Foreign Relations is a pillar institution of the
American establishment, its members offering views so carefully
mediated as to comprise virtually a power-elite consensus on
international issues, intended as all but official briefing papers for the
White House, the Pentagon and the State Department.

The luncheon, held in Los Angeles, was well attended, and the
report ("A Sharper Choice on North Korea") beautifully presented;

even so, it was awkward. The hard work behind it was probably all for nothing – as it was clearly intended for the woman who eventually lost the country's presidential election, as a kind of inauguration gift from well-meaning policy wonks.

But it is a him, not a her, moving into the White House; and the prospect of Donald Trump bothering to ponder the report issued by the council – or any of the other similar work products from Washington or New York think tanks that were lining up like toy soldiers to salute a Clinton administration – are next to zero. All those reports timed for Hillary Clinton's coronation might now as well be heaved into the Potomac.

Consider this: until the first Tuesday of this month, the entrenched New York/Washington elite was not just the life of the party; it hired the bouncers. Now they become the bouncees – the new policy outliers, red-faced with loss: another America is on top – the one not of our two flashy coasts so much as of our core interior heartland.

You see, the very term "United States" (50 states, but not so united) was always a sort of summing up – a dash of certainty blanketing a lot the normal eye could not see. So what you are now viewing of the American polity – and what the media is sure to label (the "Trump Era"?) – has always existed, it is not new; it is simply visible now, surfacing with a whale of political force.

The term "America" itself is a very broad generalisation, as, it has always seemed to me, is the term "Europe". I like to quote this from novelist Vladimir Nabokov, already a reeking genius at 27: "When people pronounce the word 'Europe' with … metaphorical, generalising intonation, I see precisely nothing." There is, he said "a very seductive and very dangerous demon: the demon of generalities. He captivates man's thought by marking every phenomenon with a little label, punctiliously placing it together with another, similarly carefully wrapped and numbered phenomenon ... into a neat little office."

Pity us journalists. Because of the automatic alacrity with which we are forced to react to contemporary history, and the time pressure under which we are required to birth our frail judgments, we are the commonest carriers of demonic generalities. Yet this is the satanic fate with which we live in order to perform for public observance in the currency of the historical moment.

All this is by way of trying to prepare not only for the gush of asserted certainties/generalities that are sure to greet this astonishing US election, but also from the continuing rise of China's president that will be aggressively processed – as Nabokov put it – with "the temptation of completely comfortable generalities". Observe the widespread use of the proper noun "China" to tent over that amazing sprawling and grandiose culture, nation, civilisation, people. (But what else, after all, to term it?)

Similarly, you notice the cascading commonality of Western commentary on Xi Jinping, the openly active but yet so-difficult-to-read president, since 2013, of the People's Republic of China. Yes, it seems that the world has entered a new Chinese "era" or "period" or "system" – the usual jaunty but suspect type of term strung together and hung on a generalisation wall as if a Degas.

In fact, in today's demonic world of "generalisation" filling in for insight, as derided by Nabokov in his 1926 talk recently translated, "China", it seems to me, generally gets the worst of the demonisation of generalisation. A book I have just finished tells of how China is heading towards a "new hard authoritarianism". While the author did concede that China's size and complexity might well be unique, this was no reason (it seemed he was saying) to spare it the criminal sentence of relentless generalisations of blanket negativity.

But isn't there? Some 1.4 billion human beings in that sprawling nation rumble along with more history in the DNA of their fingertips than in the entire corpus of America's comparatively brief existence. Today's "China" is, on its slowest day, an insane complexity of provinces (23), autonomous regions (five) and special administrative regions (two).

If anyone believes that the word "China" is anything more meaningful than a broad generalisation screeching to a halt just short of vapidity, then I am the second coming of Vladimir Nabokov, Xi Jinping, the second coming of Stalin, and Donald Trump, the new Lincoln.

I know enough "Chinese" people to know that I like the Chinese people, as I do the Japanese and the Korean, and so on; and not one of them that I have ever met reminded me of Stalin.

We must be more careful with what we say and think about others, especially those with whom in one way or the other we disagree. Generalisations about "them" just will not suffice, as they will not about "us".

Let us leave the final words to Nabokov: "We should not slander our time."

P.S. Generalisations have their utility, generally speaking....

AND THEN THERE'S…

"Man is by nature a political animal."
– Aristotle

<table>
<tr>
<td>**40**</td>
<td>

ONE PHONE CALL WON'T CHANGE US POLICY ON TAIWAN – OR RELATIONS WITH CHINA

</td>
</tr>
</table>

SOUTH CHINA MORNING POST, MONDAY, 5 DECEMBER 2016

*Tom Plate says Beijing is right not to lose its cool over the
unexpected talks between US President-elect
Donald Trump and Taiwanese leader Tsai Ing-wen*

RETROSPECTIVE:

Almost a year later, this prediction looks pretty cool. The famous phone call from Taiwan that the then US president-elect elected to answer with astonishing insouciance sent the global media into pandemonium. War was around the corner. The Trump administration has no use for the idea of one China; and so on. It is hard for the push-to-publish-or-post press to keep its balance and proportionality. In this story it didn't.

Even within the sombre cloister of Zhongnanhai, not often depicted as a rollicking laugh factory, a wan smile must have crossed the faces of a few Chinese government officials with a healthy sense of humour. Let's face it, Zhongnanhaites (but keep it a secret, because officially we are so angry…): She pulled off a good one.

The "she" being Tsai Ing-wen, the president of what this Cornell

Law School graduate and many Taiwan islanders term the Republic of China (but not recognised by the UN or dealt with officially by many of our 194 nations). By inducing Donald Trump, still on schedule to become US president next month, to accept her congratulatory long-distance phone call (what could be more innocent, right?), the island's anti-unification leader brought the global spotlight down on her 24 million constituents living in the shadow of the mainland – and managed to set ajar decades of delicate hard work between Beijing and Washington.

With one phone call! Viewed purely as a spectator sport, mark it down as a home run for Taiwanese diplomacy. Notwithstanding her bumpy public opinion ratings at home, Tsai is a clever woman. Maybe Zhongnanhai could learn from her – how in today's Twitter-diplomacy, less can be more

But was Tsai using Trump, or vice versa? A widespread view in the US is that the American president-elect may know his real estate game better than a Rockefeller but, on the evidence presented, he doesn't know his geopolitics from his mooncakes. What's more, every new president faces a steep learning curve – though Trump's all too often looks to be more a vertical line than anything curvaceous.

Perhaps the slow motion (as of this writing) in picking a secretary of state should actually be applauded – and is evidence that there is more to Trump the international tactician than meets the eye. As the face of American diplomacy, after that of the president's, this highest-profile appointment is important, especially in a know-little administration. The late Theodore Sorensen, president John Kennedy's storied speech-writer, would often remark that all major US foreign policy decisions are perforce presidential ones, no matter how forceful the sitting secretary of state. But Trump seems so categorically unschooled in international issues that perhaps, at bottom, he does really know what he really doesn't know. And that would be the start of on-the-job wisdom.

The time period between the election and the inauguration of a new American president is both too short – to get those cabinet executive positions filled – and too long. Much can go wrong with so much time to blab – or tweet.

In the book Difficult Transitions: Foreign Policy Troubles at the Outset of Presidential Power, by two highly accomplished career foreign policy officials, Kurt Campbell and James Steinberg, a tableau of no fewer than 20 guidelines are offered for transition managers. Two of relevance are: "Defer decisions, when possible, until confident of the facts, while recognising that there will be often gaps in information"; and, "Think carefully before reversing predecessors' policy decisions".

For that second point, the Trump people have put it out that the Taiwan phone call was premeditated, no slip in judgment. If true, however, this might suggest a fundamental rethink of the Sino-US relationship. This would be unwise both domestically as well as internationally. Trump won the electoral college vote – our bizarre system – not the popular vote (Hillary Clinton won that by more than two million). He had a mandate only to perform competently, not upend decades of American diplomacy that has helped avert major war in East Asia. Toying with the mainland's emotions about Taiwan is, rather, the road to ruin.

The Trump transition may prove a trying period even for the best-humoured officials of Zhongnanhai. Even so, Campbell and Steinberg, in recounting all the anti-China malarkey from past campaigns (Dwight Eisenhower, John Kennedy, Ronald Reagan, Bill Clinton and George W. Bush), would suggest they not worry: "Yet in every case, once taking office, the new president found himself adopting policies that bore a remarkable resemblance to those of his predecessor – a dramatic illustration of governing realities intruding on intended policies."

So what should China do? Barring some stupendously stupid move – say, a Trump invitation to the Dalai Lama for a round of golf, or for a weekend at Mar-a-Lago – the Xi Jinping administration should stay as cool as the mountains around Lhasa in May.

In fact, China's leaders, after thinking it all over, might want to plunge themselves into the tranquillity of rereading their Analects while ordering their staff to cease monitoring America's Twitter – the otherwise useful social media that pops out those Trump verbal intercontinental ballistic missiles. Why upset yourself? Have no serious worries that one transpacific phone call alone can erode the core of

Sino-US relations. Powerful forces swing China and America into comparable orbits. Indeed, forces of undeniable geopolitical gravity are slowly even bringing China and Taiwan closer together.

A last thought on "The Phone Call That Zonked Zhongnanhai": Probably because I am in Los Angeles, where Hollywood studios trade executives almost as often as stars get divorced, the other day I had this silly idea: that Beijing would consider pitching Tsai Ing-wen an offer to slip across the Taiwan Strait – give her a top job, stock options, the whole deal. But, no, this lady is not for poaching, even if Zhongnanhai suddenly went Hollywood. Simply consider my idea a peace-loving attempt at lightening the mood.

Over the weekend, the mainland government did harrumph up an official "solemn" protest but, before that, Foreign Minister Wang Yi got it right by simply dismissing the phone trick as "a shenanigan". Now that is the spirit. Let us never lose a sense of humour, eh? Haw-haw is much, much better, after all, than war-war.

P.S. When China's leaders decide to take the long view on a crisis issue, they tend to get the decision exactly right – as in this instance.

AND THEN THERE'S...

"On March 12 [2000], President Clinton gave a speech at John Hopkins University. In it, he said: 'there must be a shift from threats to dialogue across the Taiwan Straits.' I think a couple of words should be changed to make President Clinton's statement more accurate, namely: 'there must be a shift from threats to dialogue across the Pacific Ocean.' Thank you."

– *Zhu Rongji Meets the Press,* by Zhu Rongji, Oxford University Press, 2011

41 | UNDERWATER DRONE SPAT SHOWS WHY CHINA-US RELATIONS ARE TENSE — AND CAN ONLY GET WORSE UNDER TRUMP

SOUTH CHINA MORNING POST, MONDAY, 19 DECEMBER 2016

Tom Plate says the latest Sino-US tensions show both sides need to make a lot more adjustments to get along. For China, it means accepting a US leader who will certainly offend its sensibilities

RETROSPECTIVE:

Donald Trump had not yet been inaugurated when this column appeared. But as with many other journalists, my work was hard on him nonetheless. Too hard? The fact was that I was deeply worried that the lack of foreign-policy preparation and obvious absence of perceptible finesse would make a hash of Sino-US relations. The sheer negativity was no doubt premature, if not unfair; but as you know by now, your columnist is neurotic-nervous about this issue, and worries that stylistic incompatibilities will eventually negate the effort by Trump to personalise international relations. May I be proven entirely wrong.

And so the question is sure to arise: Who will be blamed for "losing" the South China Sea to China? That utterly passive/non-aggressive Obama crew? Or, instead, will the sea change be viewed in a more sophisticated way – perhaps as a simple matter of a newly energetic

China in full neighbourhood swagger?

The question resurfaces when the crew of a Chinese warship scooped up a US oceanographic sea survey drone and absconded, apparently without a care in the world – and with a fishy finger in the US Navy's face. Washington lodged a protest, of course – blah, blah, blah; and then the Chinese responded by saying the act was "professional and responsible" – blah, blah, blah.

In fact, according to a Hague tribunal recently, by the tepid authority of international law, central seas are everyone's waters; but China has dropped enough hard infrastructure onto various islands and sandy shoals that we might as well face facts and accept the notion of *uti possidetis juris* (as you possess under law; or, in other words, possession is nine-tenths of the law). As an honest analyst at the Centre for Strategic and International Studies in Washington put it: "China has radically changed the balance in the South China Sea and no one can do anything about it."

The US Pacific Command, mustering pushback, has been rhetorically flapping its sails, more for the calming of allies than anything else: "You can count on America now and into the future," declaimed Admiral Harry B. Harris Jr. in Australia. "Reports of America's abandonment of the Indo-Asia Pacific have been greatly exaggerated," he added.

In reality, the rarely speechless US Pacific Command boss is caught between a rocky shoal and a sandy soft place. In his remarks at the Lowy Institute in Sydney, the ranking admiral depicted the People's Republic of China as being "increasingly assertive". He is surely right about that, but nations fighting to regain their balance after being knocked off stride for ages do tend to come off as pushy in rebound.

Rather than throw curses at historical probability – whether via bombast or bombs – a responsible and visionary US foreign policy would focus more on the reality of the 21st century and China's rising role in it.

One trick is to comprehend this giant on its own terms, rather than on ours, while still honouring worthy treaties with Japan and Korea (Beijing must try to swallow this). That won't be an easy balance to maintain, but it will be easier and more prudent than if the US Pacific Command tries to regard the South China Sea with the same proprietary air as the US Fourth Fleet over the Caribbean.

Similarly, Taiwan is no run-of-the-mill issue but core to China's sense of self, as President Barack Obama aptly acknowledged last week: "The idea of One China is at the heart of their conception of a nation." This, after all, is the "Mainland Consensus", and sometimes even the "Washington Consensus": In remarkable respects, US diplomacy has handled the Taiwan issue with more delicacy than the South China Sea. Nuanced policy has helped foster functional autonomy for Taiwan, substantial economic growth on both sides of the Taiwan Strait, and peace in East Asia. That kind of result surely rates more than a passing grade in any professor's class.

It would certainly help to keep the bilateral blood pressure on an even keel were President-elect Donald Trump to control his tweets and be more careful about accepting phone calls from relative strangers bearing ego-stroking gifts. Again, Mr Obama: "And so if you are going to upend this understanding [about Taiwan], you have to have thought through what the consequences are." The Chinese, he said, would not treat any departure in US policy on Taiwan the way they would treat other issues – not even the South China Sea, "where we've had a lot of tensions".

The brittle personality and questionable global views of Trump are well suited to further roil the waters of the China-US relationship. As far as anyone can tell, his beliefs are that the world needs to remain

America's oyster; a treaty has no higher reverence than, say, a rental-lease arrangement; and alliances are solely for convenience – always shifting, never foundational, spare any emotion or foolish loyalty. International diplomacy is, at bottom, the art of the deal.

Based on any sympathetic understanding of Chinese diplomacy since 1949, this won't do. Pick up a copy of T*en Episodes in China's Diplomacy* by Qian Qichen, who from 1988 to 1998 was China's foreign minister, and you will see the problem. The Chinese find "deal diplomacy" extremely tacky. In Qian's 2005 memoir, the figure of James A. Baker, the US secretary of state under President George H. W. Bush, emerges not as a skilled statesman but as a vulgar discount-car dealer: "Baker handled foreign affairs as if he were doing business. At the negotiating table, he liked to say, 'Let's make a deal'." The irritation of Qian, who was respected among world diplomats, notwithstanding his hawkishness on Taiwan, is palpable throughout the book. America's incoming "Dealer in Chief" will grate against Chinese sensibilities; Trump is Baker without the finesse.

China's leaders need to regroup and review. For, whatever his faults (indecisiveness, fumbled Asian pivot, whatever) with Beijing, Obama was always properly cautious. Let the record show that, on his watch, no war between China and America came close to surfacing.

Trump is no Obama; he tweeted: "We should tell China that we don't want the drone they stole back – let them keep it!"

Yes, this is the social-media voice of the incoming 45th US president. If the Chinese are going to twitch over every one of his tortured tweety thrusts, they may be setting themselves up for an enervating and stormy four years. After all, Trump is, to use his very own word, "unpresidented". Of course, one means unprecedented. But perhaps we could begin to use the word "unprecedented" to describe someone who doesn't act like a president.

P.S. The deal-making point is a very interesting one. The Chinese party and government prefer to believe they operate on principle, but of course the Chinese themselves, like most other people on the planet, are flexible when they need to be. How this will play out, we should see soon enough. Best guess would be: Little room for negotiation on Taiwan (core), a little room on issues of trade (less core).

AND THEN THERE'S...

"Whether it is the United States as the lead state in Asia or China as the rising power, each is obsessed with its future position. Indeed, leaders or soon-to-be leaders have a stronger psychological tendency to expect the future to be worse than the present and therefore have a strong inclination to shape the future to their advantage. This may mean trying to improve one's position, but more often than not it means trying to keep bad things from happening."

POWERPLAY: The Origins of the American Alliance System in Asia, by Victor D. Cha, Princeton University Press, 2016

42

CHINA CAN LEAD IN 2017, EVEN AS A SLOWING ECONOMY TESTS ITS GRIP ON DOMESTIC STABILITY

SOUTH CHINA MORNING POST ON MONDAY, 2 JANUARY 2017

Tom Plate says the coming year is likely to defy many pundits' predictions about China and the US. For one, China can expect some instability in society, while Trump's presidency won't be bad news for bilateral ties

RETROSPECTIVE:

The terrible events in Beijing in 1989 set back relations for years — and floats in and out of the American mind even today. No one of goodwill on either side wishes for anything like this to happen again. Even so, maintaining domestic stability in China has got to be a great deal more difficult than in Switzerland or Singapore. This column makes the point that it is better to anticipate the unexpected than expect the anticipated. Or is this simply your neurotic/obsessing columnist in one of his worry dives again?

"It's tough to make predictions," an American baseball star used to say, "especially about the future."

But, toughing it out, we make them anyway, don't we? Especially at the onset of the new (Gregorian calendar) year, we scarcely hesitate to proclaim, for all the world to admire, our fearless forecasts. No doubt in short time, they should prove no more enduring or worthy than the fast-evaporating New Year Resolution or the predictable hangover.

It is especially perilous to make predictions about the China-US relationship, one of the greatest Godzilla face-offs in recorded history. The world's two most powerful nations do not always interact in predictable ways.

And now the Taiwan issue, until recently in semi-sleep mode, is again in play. The mainland economy's growth is not as buoyant as it needs to be, given its billion-plus inhabitants.

And with China's maximum leader still consolidating his power, while America's new leader is about to take power (and figuring out "what the hell" the top job is all about), any wager one way or the other would seem a fool's flutter. But making predictions "about the future", despite the risk of embarrassment, is what we narcissistic humans do. So here I go – yet again.

For China, most "experts" predict that the central government will effectively maintain stability – economic and political – at least through this year. This is, of course, quite the predictable prediction, telling us little; predictions so utterly predictable offer scant utility. As far as I can see, the only value in predicting anything at all is to illuminate the possibility of the unlikely. Such a mental effort – or, as physicists might say, "thought experiment" – can help us anticipate (perhaps even prepare for) the truly unpredictable.

My own work has tended to obsess over the unpredictable. The early plunge in the Thai baht that was to trigger the Asian financial crisis (I wrote in July 1997) would not be contained and would probably become regionally viral. Contrarily, the Hong Kong handover the same year to Beijing would not be a disaster, as the Western press was wickedly predicting. The 2003 US invasion of Iraq was a bad idea. Given the build-up of the PLA Navy going back a decade and more, China's assertions in the South China Sea were not Communist manoeuvres but deeply motivated Chinese get-evens and that would proceed apace as core China policy.

For many years, my favourite against-the-grain prognosticator of China's ups and downs was probably the public intellectual, Charles Wolf Jr. He was an admirer of China's breathtaking economic progress – only the heartless would not be. But as senior economist at RAND, the US think tank widely associated with lucrative Pentagon contracts, Wolf, who died recently after a fabulous career, used to brief me on the mainland economy. His worry point was always China's unemployment rate, which by his calculations clocked in at an unreported multiple higher than the announced 4 per cent or so.

Wolf never believed that official figure and was certain that the structural stresses from "the persistent masses of unemployed and underemployed labour" would in time erode core stability, notwithstanding the central government's many control programmes.

Today, with China's growth rate at or under 7 per cent and probably at a lower point than at any time since 1990, it would thus be my best guess – my prediction – that 2017 will be a year notable for worrisome and observable instability on the mainland.

With China, as with the United States, I have no appetite to see either giant stumble. But history is not infrequently stormy, unpleasant and unpredictable.

I remember well Wolf saying to the effect that experts are good enough at interpreting and explaining the past – but are pathetic with forecasts. "Their testimony [about the future]," he'd drolly say, "is often wrong."

As for China's superpower dance partner, the experts haven't been much better in predicting major developments in the US, whether the near-global depression of 2008–2009 or the outcome of the recent US presidential election (Wolf, by the way, was the only public intellectual

I knew who predicted the unexpected Republican White House victory. This was back in May).

Now we see experts betting on rough sailing in the bilateral relationship when Donald Trump hits the White House. Once again I have to go the other way: consider in evidence that his only actual non-Twitterish move to date has been to propose Iowa Governor Terry Branstad as ambassador to China. This is a solid choice – a man said to have worked some comity into his meetings with President Xi Jinping– and is anything but an in-your-face slap designed to poke the panda.

The political prognosticator must not assume the inherent asininity of Trump's every move; even a dumb broken clock, as they say, is right twice a day. China is hugely important to the United States. Anyone who does not know this is slacking around on another planet; so, managing to improve relations would put solid bedrock under his presidency.

But Trump's amateurism will present opportunities for the more experienced and professional Xi. The American's evident wish to downsize global issues, especially environmental, will create unprecedented public space in which China's president can make his case to be the true world leader. (The launch of the new ambitious China Global TV Network could not be better timed.)

So China's international image will improve even as its domestic stability declines (I'd wager a flutter or two on this).

That will especially be the case if Trump continues to embarrass himself with Russian President Vladimir Putin. Anyone who calculates Russia over China as the better bet for America needs to have his head examined. Come on, man! China is the future, Russia the past. Sure, this might seem a slight oversimplification. But that's my prediction and I'm sticking with it.

P.S. Since China and Russia share the sixth largest international border on the face of the earth (more than 4,000 kilometres, or about 2,500 miles), their economic and diplomatic relations will always be near the top of the worry list. But for China, the US will remain the number-one concern/opportunity for the foreseeable future.

AND THEN THERE'S...

"The fact that Russia is rich in oil, gas and many other commodities – as well as being its major supplier of weapons – clearly makes it a very attractive partner for China. But Russia has proved a difficult collaborator, loath to meet its needs, certainly on the terms desired by China."

– *When China Rules the World: The End of the Western World and The Birth of a New Global Order,* by Martin Jacques, The Penguin Press, 2009

43

CHINA SHOULD BEWARE
THE TRAP SET BY 'DUMB TRUMP'

SOUTH CHINA MORNING POST, MONDAY, 16 JANUARY 2017

Tom Plate says the US president-elect isn't known for his intellectual prowess, but he is wily: Beijing should not be riled into doing something reckless by his purposely provocative views on "one China"

RETROSPECTIVE:

The 2017 World Economic Forum policy-wonk and VIP-networking extravaganza opened the day after this column first appeared. As it turned out for China's international public relations, President Xi Jinping's appearance was a smash hit – his main address an almost canonical exposition on the economic benefits of open-globe trading. For the audience of mainly go-go international business leaders, mere multi-millionaires and out-and-out billionaires, it was as if Karl Marx had rose from the dead to reappear in Davos in a Brooks Brothers business suit. Observers concluded that Xi had deliberately – and skilfully – moved into the perceived vacuum of Trump's shrugging-off of globalization and evident embrace of more nationalistic policies.

With the World Economic Forum plenary meeting up and running this week in Davos, as usual in January, you may find this story poignantly relevant, even though it occurred back in 2000.

And so US President Bill Clinton, ever restless, orders Air Force One to fuel up for Zurich, where a Swiss military helicopter then lifts him, his then teenage daughter Chelsea, and what seems like half his cabinet to the Swiss Alps village of Davos, where upwards of 1,500 world CEOs, government leaders, political and literary figures, and a handful of mere journalists assemble annually to mull over global issues and hobnob like excited kids at a preschool.

The first US president to appear at Davos while in office, Clinton makes thoughtful comments on not just the bright but also the dark side of globalisation.

But it is his other appearance that day I remember best: a closed briefing for journalists, mainly from Europe; and though late, as usual, Clinton, with Chelsea in charming daughterly tow, hits it around with the media for a 90-minute back and forth. Halfway thorough the performance, I whisper to ask the journalist from Agence France-Press next to me of her impression of the US president. In a tone tinged with a touch of surprise, she says: "He's very smart, isn't he?" But of course he was; after all, as president of the United States, world leader, he had better be smart, right?

Perhaps you can see where I am heading with this. Later this week in Washington, as the big shots and prima donnas helicopter out of Davos, the US will inaugurate its 45th president, Donald Trump. Let me ask: Can you imagine Trump, in Davos in some future year, facing a barrage of European journalists and triggering the same impressed reaction: that he is "very smart"?

The question arises poignantly in the context of US-China relations as President Xi Jinping arrives in Davos this week – the first Chinese top leader to attend the World Economic Forum. Will the international press judge the Chinese leader to be "very smart", whether or not he lowers himself to a surprise press chat?

For starters, Xi's views generally seem more Clintonian than Trumpian. Although hardly unaware of the dark downsides of globalisation (roiling employment dislocation, structural equity, endless trade disputes, and so on), Xi accepts the inescapability of global interaction in this epoch of nano-second Internet communication. This line contrasts with that of President-imminent Trump, who campaigned crudely against international trade regimes.

By contrast, the Chinese government offers a vision of trade harmony and ways to harmonise. Such public diplomacy enlarges China's global stature and makes Trump's America, the world's richest nation, seem petty and nationalistically selfish.

In addition, the Xi government also seems, on the whole, open-minded on the nuclear arms limitations; at least, it seems to regard the option of further nuclear innovation with a lot less relish than the US. And, as everyone knows, China has long trumpeted a no-first-use nuclear policy.

Another Xi-Trump comparison concerns the Iranian pact. Why propose to ditch this admittedly flawed agreement (and almost all complicated multinational deals markedly fail a perfection test) when you have zip in your pocket to replace it with? It's an insane diplomacy.

In addition to looking comparatively sane on the nuclear issue, Xi's Beijing bodes to look more cosmopolitan than a Trump Washington on growing climate concerns. The latter appears to hold that no compelling global challenge needs to be unduly fretted over; by contrast, the former stoutly supports the 2015 Paris climate agreement. Especially if Trump proposes to undermine it, the accord having been signed by no fewer than 194 nations, China could come to resemble the world's only climate-sensitive superpower. Similarly at the United Nations, which in Trumpian rhetoric has already fallen to the status of some kind of multilingual bridge club, a higher, proactive profile from China, especially at the Security Council, could add to its leadership aura.

Xi is not only younger than Trump, but also patently smarter. The incoming American government is a jumble of ethical uncertainty and policy pugnacity, whereas the Chinese government's positions on some of the globe's most important transnational issues are supported by many nations – not to mention by well-respected scholarly and policy communities.

Yet, at the same time, China may risk underestimating Trump, as did countless allegedly smart American journalists during the campaign. For Trump is only dumb in the manner of the fox that was Ronald Reagan, the 40th US president. What's more, the shameless brutality of his political incorrectness and his savvy sense of smell for the rot of liberal complacency seems always keenly targeted for political kill.

Thus for China, the current public quarrel with little Singapore over armoured vehicles en route from Taiwan and the rising to the bait of the Trump-teasing on the "one China" issue could play right into his hands. Great powers should not be easily flustered. The smart advice for Beijing would be to avoid doing something dumb in frustration or anger. This we shall term falling into the "Trump Trap".

P.S. Since then, Trump has skated an erratic pattern internationally, and China's Xi has not rolled out a totally coherent challenge. But there is an international public-opinion tilt toward Beijing as the possible world leader of economic globalism. This is not by any means a minor development in world politics.

AND THEN THERE'S...

"Man has three ways of acting wisely. First, on meditation; that is the noblest. Secondly, on imitation; that is the easiest. Thirdly, on experience; that is the bitterest." (Attributed to Confucius).

– *CEO, China: The Rise of Xi Jinping*, by Kerry Brown,
   I. B. Tauris Company, 2016

44

TRUMP COMES UP SHORT – FOR BETTER AND FOR WORSE!

SOUTH CHINA MORNING POST, MONDAY, 23 JANUARY 2017

RETROSPECTIVE:

Except for one, all of the columns in this collection were written over a span of 48 hours. On Friday nights, I work up the main idea, possibly laying out a rough (usually, very rough) first draft of about 1,000 words. On Saturday I work up the second and third drafts. On Sunday, home stretch: drafts four and five, the latter finally emailed to Hong Kong from my home office in Los Angeles to arrive at the newspaper no later than 10 am on Mondays. In this case, however, the SCMP editors asked me for a news analysis on the subject of the inauguration of Donald Trump on 20 January, for posting in its 21 January online edition and thereafter in its print edition. So instead of having 48 hours to write, this one time I had only four. It was a rush, believe me!

[*Author's note: The following appeared in the SCMP not as an op-ed column but on the newspaper's front page as a News Analysis article to accompany the main news stories on Trump's inauguration.*]

Only a relatively few sprinkles fell on US President Donald Trump's inauguration parade. By contrast absolute doubt and worry descended in greater force, starting with the cloudy and overcast American capital city of Washington, then across the vast expanse of the North American continent, to all the way to San Francisco. Protests were held. Mostly untouched by the foul political weather was America's mid-sector, often termed Middle America. People there were reportedly mainly happy with what they saw and heard. In fact, the new president gave a clear, focused and blessedly short inauguration address that worked for them, but had the notable deficiency of not adequately addressing the other half of the nation.

This will surely prove the crux of the governance problem for the incoming Trump. He may well produce a good 50 per cent presidency – perhaps even quite a good one. Such a halfway achievement seems well within his capacity, as his campaign demonstrated: to be able to appeal to his base, even by repeatedly recycling baseless appeals to outmoded economics and international relations notions.

His emphasis on nationalism will warm the hearts of many who feel left out, but leave cold those Americans who are convinced that in a globalised world a simplistic psychology of "America First" will wind up leaving America Second. Already the president of the People's Republic of China has announced, at the recent Davos Forum, the birth of an emerging new Chinese national mentality that is as proud of its history as America is of its; but will not foolishly seek to chart a path forward in the 21st century by proposing to return it to the 20th.

The average American may well have a thirst to see America first, but it is the vision of the preschooler who must be the only one to play with all the Legos. Honestly: Trump's anti-establishment pose is as old as the hills; the protectionist position reminds us mainly of another great Depression; and his rank nationalism sounds as if America can do no wrong – which feels like a formula that could push America every which way wrong.

Much of what Trump said in Washington, mirroring with good proportionality what he has been telling his base for months, makes less sense than the new president may sincerely believe. Half his Republican Party doesn't agree with him, and little of the opposing Democratic Party does.

So here's his problem: the American Republic is not structured to accommodate the worldview of one man or woman – say, a dictator. Its governing system is a freeway always at rush hour with more than enough traffic jams and construction slowdowns to try Miss Daisy's patience, not to mention a hell-bent Nascar driver. Trump, to the extent we understand him, is built for speed, head-on; never for the lowly second gear. What he will face may thus prove a torture for him.

Unless he somehow changes or allows the bumps and grinds, not to mention stops and starts, of feral Washington to alter his straight-ahead course, he will find himself continually on his own – and this may plunge him into a personal self-isolationism deeper and perhaps even more troubling than any new national isolationism. This will be dangerous for him and for the nation, as well as the world. So it is important for Americans who can bear the burden of a measure of personal insincerity to emphasise as much as possible a respect for views with which it (half the nation) otherwise might quickly dismiss. As even Barack Obama will readily attest, no president is perfect; every one makes mistakes.

But, as much as anyone, the American news media will find this a hard line to follow, much less honour. Trump is right when he claims 'the media' is biased against him, in the sense that it is by nature inclined to jump on the negative, the un-genuine or the transparently ridiculous, precisely because it has experienced so much of it in American politics and knows it when it sees it – and so loves to report it.

His inauguration speech was in this sense prehistoric – to employ the title of a famous American movie – *Back to the Future*. It looked back in anger, as if America was nothing more than one huge downside and the only way to go now was up – and only Trump knew how to access the elevators.

It is perhaps a mistake to seek to wax overly profound over a speech that was designedly simplistic, and blessedly short. If the worried and watching world wishes to come away from this inauguration drama in non-panic mode, and go back quietly to its own national-interest business, it can do so most easily by recognising that the new president's priority is to focus first on US domestic foremost in order to achieve his utopian vision of always "America First".

This is not to say that complicated international issues such as North Korea and Iran nukes (top of the list?), Russia, trade-relations, Nato's future, coordinated international climate control and – last but not least- One or Two Chinas … that these monster items will mysteriously vanish from the president's desk in the Oval Office. But President Trump will not be looking for new trouble abroad, though he is of the instinctive mentality to push back as hard as it comes in if others come in looking for trouble. Perhaps the rest of the world might go about its own business and raise tough issues or challenges at a later date.

Trump now starts year one of what could prove a run as lengthy as eight years. Before long he will figure out, probably, that internationally problem-one is forging a coherent policy between America and Asia. At Davos last week, the great thinker Kishore Mahbubani, Dean of the Lee Kuan Yew School of Public Policy, noted that "… all responsible leaders need to have today a deep understanding of the key global trends driving change…. (and) the first is a return of Asia and the end of Western domination of history…. It is not enough to watch personalities like Xi Jinping and Donald Trump. We also need to understand the deeper forces driving their behaviour. Any leader who fails to understand this unique complexity of our time is ill-equipped to provide leadership to their society."

Sorry to end on a profound note. But, for better or for worse, there are many more Trump speeches to come. Patience may be more prudent than snap judgment.

P.S. I like this column, particularly for one written in just a few hours. Writing on a severe deadline is thrilling, but scary. There is no room for error; never enough time. But then ... when is there enough time?

AND THEN THERE'S...

"... The United States needs to maintain its forward deployment, superior military forces.... its alliances, and its enhanced relationship with other emerging powers. Chinese analysts are likely to consider all these traits to be hostile to China, just as every Chinese political and military advance, such as development of an aircraft carrier, will be depicted as a threat to America. Future presidents will need to find the right balance in China policy, so as to maintain America's strength and watchfulness but not fall into the classic security dilemma, wherein each side believes that growing capabilities reflect hostile intent and responds by producing that reality. I believe that President Obama struck that balance. I felt honored to be part of administration in trying to achieve it."

— *EO, China: The Rise of Xi Jinping,* by Kerry Brown,
  I. B. Tauris Company, 2016

45

WITH HAWKISH NAVARRO AS US TRADE TSAR, IT'S UP TO CHINA TO SHOW DIPLOMATIC RESTRAINT

SOUTH CHINA MORNING POST, MONDAY, 30 JANUARY 2017

Tom Plate calls on China to focus on a peaceful rise and avoid overreacting to provocations from the Trump White House, especially its National Trade Council head

RETROSPECTIVE:

Honestly, I had not an ounce of jealousy when the new American president tapped a fellow professor just a handful of miles away from another university where it worked to serve in the White House as his chief trade adviser. I would not have served if summoned, not because of Trump but because of propriety. Journalists who are serious about their role should not serve in government. And journalists should not denigrate academic colleagues. But in this instance, I could not help myself.

Not far down the freeway from my own university is the University of California – Irvine, for years the faculty home of one of the West Coast's better-known China-watchers/worriers. He is the controversy-prone professor Peter Navarro, of the Paul Merage School of Business. For the foreseeable future, though, you won't find him in classrooms lecturing or clinking cappuccinos at the faculty club, joking about yield curves. Instead, you'll find him in Washington – as head of the White House National Trade Council. And this is a concern.

Although technically his title is a nerdy "assistant to the president of the United States for trade and industrial policy", currently he has been given to shoulder the monster moniker "US trade tsar".

Pity this solitary man! American trade policy is the messy product of multiple economic and political forces, not to mention craven self-interests. But even if, in the end, Navarro proves far from a tsar, right now he is the hottest professor in the Donald Trump administration.

His academic work is neither solidly mainstream nor especially celebrated, but often bruited about by critics as that of an ideologue rather than empiricist. By his own descriptions, in fact, he would appear to almost welcome the buzz of negativity.

According to Navarro: "The role of government is to help a nation's businesses compete by providing technological assistance, subsidies and protectionist measures such as tariffs and quotas." For many Americans – not just academics – protectionism has an unpleasant historical association with the Great Depression of 1929–1939.

So stay alert: "trade tsar" Navarro might well become for Trump what Donald Rumsfeld was to George W. Bush, as the former president's warmongering defence secretary.

Navarro is a "panda hugger" in the exact opposite worst-case sense of the trope, sometimes wrongly applied to those trying with near-pacifist passion to steer clear of war with China. Rather, it's as if he'd like to hug the utter life out of Beijing.

His 2011 book (with Greg Autry), Death by China: *Confronting the Dragon – a Call to Action*, was a catalogue of horrors. I found it unbalanced, in every sense of the word.

His recent *book – Crouching Tiger: What China's Militarism Means for the World –* seemed far less the comic book, but offered the perspective of the prosecutor trying to assure the jury that his insistence on the death penalty for the defendant is solely in the interests of justice.

Navarro is far more likely to be feared by China than loved. While *Crouching Tiger* is well informed, it is also wrong-headed. Yet, it is also extremely easy to understand – and this is where his Trump-type talent comes in.

Most economists write with the delicate touch of crane operators and communicate with the verve of the comatose: by the time sentences come to their tortuous end, you want to bury the author, period.

Not so with Navarro, who is also a popular public speaker. He is exactly the sort who could grab control of the new American president's ear – and perhaps even the American peoples' – and not let go.

For China, this could present a tough dilemma. It could either try to utterly ignore the "trade tsar", or blast him with propaganda at its worst, while point by point trying to refute all his nattering negativity. Neither tactic holds promise.

Navarro is capable of making a grand run through the Washington TV talk show line like a practised chorus-line hoofer, aiming to dazzle the unknowing with verbal footwork; or even, to be fair, raising a point or two whose validity even China's behind-the-scenes policy wonks might privately acknowledge. The answer to the arguments of this new Trumpeter of Limited Trade, it seems to me, is simple but not likely.

Build fewer "hard-kill" missiles, "Mighty Dragon" fighters, warships, nuclear ballistic-missile and diesel subs, poorly disguised surveillance vessels and the rest of the expensive hard stuff. Accept that you've reached the upper limit of your island-hopping and sandy-shoal upgrading. Make friends and influence neighbours.

For China, the Trump epoch will prove an ordeal, especially if this first week of the new administration is anything to go by. React to every taunt and non-truth and bite at every baited hook, and before long your head will be spinning and your policy unhinged. Accept that this man is, pardon the very unoriginal phrase, a bull in the China shop. Stay on high ground and negotiate skilfully. Above all, improve your international profile with a thoroughly upgraded public diplomacy. Sack all your top propagandists; start from scratch; build on your cultural depth; be elegant, not grating. Help keep the world from war.

Sure, Trump doesn't consciously want war with China. But he operates with a very limited skill set, and he is predictably unpredictable.

More and more, the burden will seem to land on China to calm the superpower seas. Show the world you are up to it.

"Across the broad swathe of world history," notes Navarro in *Crouching Tiger*, "in fully 11 of the 15 times since 1500 that a rising power like China faced an established power like the United States, war resulted more than 70 per cent of the time."

Don't become history's next tragic statistic, Beijing. Return to "peaceful rising" and mean it. Over time, well-established US institutions, including the courts, media and even Congress, will gather themselves into a kind of multi-tasking containment policy to blunt the worst of Trump. Over time, things will get better. Don't overreact now.

P.S. The trade policy of President Trump, at this writing, appears to be somewhat different from that of Republican presidential candidate Trump. Professor Navarro may be finding that he was hired by one man, and has wound up serving a different one. Running for president is one thing; governing the country is another.

AND THEN THERE'S...

"Legend has it that the emperor Napoleon once said of China, 'there lies a sleeping giant. Let it sleep, for when it wakes it will shake the world.'"

— *China Watcher: Confessions of a Peking Tom,* by Richard Baum, University of Washington Press, 2010

46 | TRUMP NEEDS TO GET SMART AS NORTH KOREA KEEPS UP 'MISSILE DIPLOMACY'

SOUTH CHINA MORNING POST, MONDAY, 13 FEBRUARY 2017

Tom Plate says US policy on North Korea must stem from astute first-hand intelligence, lacking thus far, starting with recognising the country and setting up an embassy

RETROSPECTIVE:

If any recent American policy in Asia can be said to have misfired in a most ineffective and embarrassing way, it might have to be the one toward Pyongyang. The late Warren Christopher once confirmed to me that during his four-year stint as US secretary of state, North Korea was always on the Top Five hot list that he prepared for the president. But as aware of the boiling little trouble-making Kim Family Dynasty as it was, Washington could never put together an effective game plan for that small and wobbly half-nation of 25 million people and maybe 24 stockpiled nuclear weapons. This column was meant to suggest that the hard-line policy, while perhaps morally justifiable, has been a strategic failure. It might have been far more effective to have embraced this terrible regime – as the US has over the decades constructed close bilateral relations with many other mean and embarrassing regimes in so many parts of the world – and employed a more cunning policy of loving it to death.

Twitter and telephone diplomacy between America and Asia has become such a new normal since Inauguration Day that it was almost a relief to catch sight of an actual Asian leader in the White House.

That was Japanese Prime Minister Shinzo Abe, in non-virtual mode. This is good experience for Donald Trump, the world's most famous former real estate mogul. Maybe the new US president might do more of this – perhaps travel some – in order to avoid remaining the prisoner of his own thoughts, which do not always bear up under scrutiny, sometimes not even under his own.

Abe arrived just after Trump had reached out to touch someone else: President Xi Jinping. With that phone call, the US president later declaimed, the Sino-US "one-China" policy was solidified anew. Let us so hope.

The policy has arguably worked well, even, in part, for Taiwan – at least existentially.

Let us be real: America would more readily hand back Texas to Mexico than the mainland would without a fight permit Taiwan to distance itself further. Even so, in Taipei circles, this latest diplomatic call from Trump has to be viewed as much of a setback as the one in December was a triumph. That was when Taiwan's president, Tsai Ing-wen, called to congratulate Trump, and the unprepared then president-elect answered as if it were no more a big deal than taking a call from a golfing buddy.

But one such call does not constitute a policy shift. The danger right now is to overreact to any aspect of Trump's yo-yo diplomacy.

He is but learning the ropes of this difficult job, and at warp – or perhaps Twitter – speed.

In all fairness, the fact is that the US presidency is no easy position to field, whether it is an internationally savvy George H. W. Bush entering the White House in 1989 or a domestically savvy Bill Clinton in 1993.

On Sunday, North Korea threw up into the East Asian sky something like an intermediate-range missile, as if to set the stage for the launch of a longer-range incontinental ballistic missile (ICBM), able to reach the US. Yet another unwanted "incoming" for America's leading untried politician.

Yo-yo diplomacy is what we are going to get for the time being. In addition, you will see substantial displays of pullback syndrome, often termed "clarifications".

Trump's critics claim he shows all the hallmarks of a bully. If this is true, then confronted with superior bullying power, the standard bully can be predicted to back down rather than go to the wrestling mat. Personally, if his psychoanalysing critics have it right, I would be more comfortable with an American president who can take a punch without, say, always punching back and risking nuclear war.

Let's see what the reaction is to North Korea's latest attention getting "missile diplomacy". Washington had already been abuzz over some kind of upcoming reckoning. Trump had awarded his first "red line" to the possibility of a North Korean ICBM test. No doubt the Xi-Trump phone call touched on this, as did the long sessions with Abe.

The Chinese would be immeasurably discomforted by any pre-emptive action against its technical ally, Pyongyang. The Japanese might not be wildly thrilled about a blow-up in East Asia, either. Neither would treaty ally South Korea, with its capital Seoul but a short rocket hoist from the North's bunkers.

The inherent tension, and the nervousness it induces, is reminiscent of America and Iraq circa 2002. That ill-conceived invasion was based on an incorrect assessment ("bad regimes would topple like dominoes") and faulty intelligence (non-existent weapons of mass destruction). It was all baloney.

The seeming surety with which the US establishment is now

touting North Korea as the second coming of Iraq is unsettling. We do not know enough about it: the US has no embassy in the country, not even a half-baked mission. What little ground-based intelligence we have derives from secondary sources, or from political escapees whose emotionality mitigates proportionality. Californians who have travelled to North Korea are less convinced than Washington that proposing to topple a bad regime will prove any wiser in East Asia than it has in the Middle East.

Prominent California aeronautics businessman Spencer H. Kim, an advisory board member of the RAND Centre for Asia-Pacific Policy and a respected critic of military intervention, says: "We are encumbered with a full range of preconceptions and stereotypes constantly played back by both the media and propaganda to the point that reality has been distorted out of all proportion. And we are all, on all sides of this debate, unconsciously victims of the distortion." A possibly overconfident Trump believes the US can handle North Korea, but who knows? Certainly not the CIA. Perhaps Trump could put through another call to his friend Xi. The Chinese, who have scant economic interest in observing a nuclear weapon land on its biggest market, have been urging America to stay cool; perhaps they know something we don't.

Of course that would not be a brutally high standard, would it? Maybe the US should swallow its ideological pride, recognise North Korea (as the UN does), and get an actual working embassy up and running there – staffed with a sprinkling of especially competent, if poorly disguised, CIA agents with their ears to the ground to find out, in the immortal campaign phrase of Trump – "what the hell is going on".

North Korea is a country about which we know even less than we did about Iraq.

Donald Gregg, a former CIA station chief in Seoul and national security aide to President George H. W. Bush, quips (but with total sincerity): "North Korea is America's longest running intelligence failure". It's time to get smart.

P.S. President Donald Trump is noted for having said that the US "will deal with" the Democratic People's Republic of Korea if China can't or won't, or if it won't chip in and help. That's good tough John Wayne talk. But it is hard to see what he can do given the reality of the Peninsula's geopolitics and nuclear-weaponisation. What is his trump card? I prefer a policy of total engagement and gradual change, as mentioned in the Retrospective.

AND THEN THERE'S...

"[Secretary of State Colin] Powell gradually developed personal relations with Foreign Minister Tang Jiaxuan and his successor, Li Zhaoxing, which allowed Powell to discuss matters with them over the phone. On those occasions, Powell openly shared his expectations concerning China's exercise of its influence on North Korea. 'About one-half of China's foreign assistance goes to North Korea, and some 80 per cent of the energy and economic assistance that North Korea receives is provided by China,' he pointed out in an interview in February 2003. 'China has a role to play. I hope China plays this role.'"
— *The Peninsula Question: A Chronicle of the Second Korean Nuclear Crisis,* by Yoichi Funabashi, Brookings Institution Press, 2007

47

Why China should reach out to the US to counter Kim Jong-un

South China Morning Post, Monday, 27 February 2017

Tom Plate says Beijing should follow up its stunning move to suspend North Korean imports with an overture to Washington, given its high stakes in the stability of the Korean peninsula

RETROSPECTIVE:

Published in 2012, *Conversations with Ban Ki-moon* was the fourth volume in my "Giants of Asia" quartet, and maybe the most difficult to pull off. The poor, hard-working career Korean diplomat was being battered – or, worse yet, ignored – by the Western news media, and fought at almost every turn of reform by the well-entrenched, Machiavellian UN bureaucracy. He was re-appointed for a second term by the UN General Assembly, but after two full terms – 10 years in that high office – he was the first to confess, to himself as well as to me, of his extreme disappointment and personal sadness that the first Korean UNSG in history had been able to do so little to realise his dream – and that of many millions of Koreans worldwide – of a more normal Peninsula. Alas, reunification of some kind – however tentative and gradual – seemed longer off than ever. In the interviews for the book, which took place in 2010–2011, he declared flatly that lack of progress at the end of his 10 years would have to be chalked up as a personal failure. Perhaps that is a harsh self-judgement – what (at this writing) has Beijing really done to solve the problem, not to mention Washington? But the bitterness is deeply personal, and Ban, rightly or wrongly, points no fingers at anyone else. This is a noble man.

There is a time to be dainty and subtle, but this is not that time. There is a time to be blunt and brassy, and that time is now. The need for China and the United States to come together in a persistently adult geopolitical twosome has never been more urgent. Gamesmanship must be minimised. Statesmanship must be maximised.

Just ask career diplomat Ban Ki-moon. The other night in Los Angeles, he brought the point home well, as perhaps only someone who had scaled the heights to UN secretary general could. His venue was a hotel ballroom where the Pacific Century Institute, which works behind the scenes for peace and understanding between America and East Asia, presented Ban with its 2017 "Building Bridges" award, and Ban returned the compliment with a thoughtful discourse. Now in private life, this workaholic Korean, so respectful of the high office he was privileged to hold for a decade, was thus able to loosen up a bit on a subject dear to his heartburn: North Korea. And what the adoring audience got was a glimpse of Ban at his best.

By now, North Korea has ticked off almost everyone. That recent missile test-shot in the face of our new and unnervingly inexperienced US president unsettled many; the Kuala Lumpur airport assassination operation evidently orchestrated by Pyongyang turned stomachs all over the world. And so Ban laid it on the line: the young North Korean leader, Kim Jong-un, is pushing his luck big time.

This was not characteristic Ban, in public at least; and it had bite because the Korean diplomat, only the second UN secretary general from Asia, is known to know China and its leaders as well as anyone not Chinese. On the whole they like him, they respect him, and they supported him. For his part, Ban understands how they think and why they think it.

When poorly informed Western commentators and leaders unctuously pile on the cheap rhetoric and demand that "China do more", as if it could push over unloved but nuclear-armed Pyongyang with a pair of chopsticks, Ban rolls his eyes. But they went wide open when the Xi Jinping government announced the suspension of all North Korean imports, including even coal.

Something new may be up. Beijing looks down on Pyongyang, and the North Koreans have little use for China. But the Chinese Communist Party, not unlike (in the oddest way) our American Tea Party, fears change. Regime collapse on its borders conjures up nightmares of an implosion of Syrian proportions; or of an ominously united Korea (North and South) under a Western umbrella. The Chinese government is religious on the principle of inviolable sovereignty and beyond sceptical of forced regime change option.

Even so, some kind of thoroughly worked-out China-US approach to Pyongyang could not only promote future stability on the Korean peninsula; it could prove positively salient for the future Sino-US relationship.

China would deserve all the credit in the world if it made a move to close the gap further. The truth is that even when Beijing takes sensible positions, Beijing rarely gets respect. The worst is assumed even if the original intention might well have been otherwise.

Let me give this point a Hong Kong twist: take "one country, two systems". Many people imagine a late-night office somewhere in Zhongnanhai, lights burning long into the black night, an anti-autonomy squad creepily plotting the next evil move to erode

Hong Kong's identity.

After all, a multibillionaire businessman, recently snatched from his Hong Kong hotel by mainland agents, is taken somewhere – but where, who knows? Was this cliché movie scene no more than another chapter in the ongoing mainland power struggle? Or was the snatch-and-go operation a deliberate dagger into the heart and soul of "one country, two systems"?

Anything's possible; but note that the sensational trial of Donald Tsang Yam-kuen (who'd served as the special administrative region's chief executive for seven years with Beijing's overt blessing) proceeded apace within Hong Kong's indigenous legal system. No mainland intervention was reported. And it was a huge case. Tsang – one of the most intelligent leaders I have ever interviewed – has been jailed. That's a pity; but it's a high-profile example of the local Hong Kong justice system in action, not quashed by mainland intervention.

The SAR, like Singapore, worries about its survival as an autonomous entity precisely because it is so small. But from the mainland's point of view, something like half a dozen of its cities are even more populous than Hong Kong. So, as important as it is, Hong Kong is just one major problem on the big worry list for President Xi. Beijing simply does not have anywhere near as much time to focus as exclusively on Hong Kong as Hongkongers appear to have to focus on themselves.

Xi, it seems to me, could fairly complain that his job is tougher than President Donald Trump's. China's population, he could note, is something like 1.4 billion; America's is about 325 million. With four times as many people, Xi may say he has to endure four times as many headaches as Trump, who doesn't even have feisty, self-absorbed Hong Kong screaming in his face. But both do share the common headache of Pyongyang.

The US and China need to work on the problem together – better, closer, sooner. What Ban Ki-moon is trying to tell Kim Jong-un is that this looks set to become the next chapter in the Korean peninsula ordeal. His sense is that maybe the time has come to get real.

P.S. At this writing, another noble Korean gentleman (whose modesty dictates anonymity) is working to set up a Korean Peace Foundation, with the former UNSG at the helm. This is an idea of considerable merit and vision. I hope very much it comes to pass.

AND THEN THERE'S...

"... Once countries believe that Washington has locked them in their gunsights – particularly bankrupt, corrupt little dictatorships – no one should be surprised if they raced to get a nuclear weapon. This is the Cold War curse. Perhaps nothing could have deterred Kim Jong-il from finishing the project his father started.... Even the world's sole superpower does not control enough economic levers by itself to squeeze a tiny, destitute dictatorship."

– *The Inheritance: The World Obama Confronts and the Challenges to American Power*, by David E. Sanger, Harmony Books (Random House), 2009

48

THINK AGAIN, BEIJING: CARRIE LAM IS THE WRONG PERSON TO LEAD HONG KONG OUT OF THE POLITICAL STORM

SOUTH CHINA MORNING POST, MONDAY, 13 MARCH 2017

Tom Plate believes the central government should back John Tsang, the leader the people want, rather than unpopular Carrie Lam to be the SAR's next chief executive

RETROSPECTIVE:

I almost always stay away from the endorsement game; and surely an American columnist would be well advised to honour the people he writes for by leaving their election choices to themselves. But the 2017 semi-election to choose a new chief executive (governor) of Hong Kong was a special case. One worried about Hong Kong splitting into two, when the best way forward was to work as one. So I endorsed the underdog not favoured by Beijing.

Does the Chinese Communist Party possess the political wisdom and emotional range to handle the many difficult challenges that catch the world's eye?

Since the 1997 handover, the special administrative region of Hong Kong has been in the limelight. On the whole, its new life under Beijing's absolute sovereignty has not gone badly: People's Liberation

Army troops are not befouling the streets, as much of the Western media once all but predicted; the economy sails along, and this dandy gem remains one of the world's most iconic metropolises … up-and-coming Shanghai notwithstanding.

An election is coming at the end of this month that could put all this at serious risk. Indications are that the winner, and thus Hong Kong's next leader, will be Carrie Lam Cheng Yuet-ngor, the former chief secretary, because the Xi Jinping government prefers her, and because Beijing pulls enough weight within the city's Election Committee — the elite group of electors that chooses the chief executive — to get what it wants.

What evidently it doesn't want is former financial secretary John Tsang Chun-wah, or anyone capable of even semi-independent leadership. Like the former British colonial government, the Chinese like their Hong Kong leader tame and lame.

Yet, this capable and likeable civil servant is running strongest in the public opinion polls (by as much as 14 percentage points by one estimate). But Tsang will not be the next chief. This anomaly arises because Hong Kong's "election" method is not the basic one-person, one-vote deal; it's "democracy" of a filtered sort.

Hong Kong is not alone, by the way, in using a bizarre intermediary system that dilutes voters' sentiment. Mathematically simple, one-person, one-vote systems are not everyone's cup of tea.

Even the United States selects its No 1 via a patchwork quilt of 538 electors collected from its 50 states. Sadly enough, this crazy system has the talent to select as the winner a candidate who failed to win a majority of the overall votes. In 2000, George W. Bush was second to Al Gore by 543,895 votes. In 2016, Donald Trump was second to Hillary Clinton by 2,868,691 votes. Now the world, you see, will just have to learn to live with this "loser".

Is the Hong Kong system for selecting its leader so categorically different? By the end of the month, the 1,194-member Election Committee is to produce, by majority decision, the next chief. Mathematically, that is close to one elector per 6,000 people; by comparison, the US has one elector for every 600,000 people. Choose the system you like better.

Ten years ago, in Singapore, the late Lee Kuan Yew was wondering about Hillary Clinton, who at that time looked a slam dunk to become US president someday. How good was she? I shot a glance at the university colleague with me in Lee's office at the Istana, the government palace, and we agreed: she's good enough. Lee mulled that over: "Good enough? Well, good … Because anyone you elect president, we in Asia have to live with."

Similarly, anyone selected by Hong Kong as its next leader, the rest of us will have to live with. This means that if the leader is popular and can govern well and keep relations with Beijing steady, we are all winners. Then, Hong Kong stays the shining jewel and avoids turning into … a Taiwan in diapers.

But if the next leader is problematic – whether incompetent or in other ways – then it becomes an international problem and we are all losers, especially relations between China and the US, as American public opinion of China will very probably sour.

Let's look at Beijing's record in pulling the strings. The about-to-leave Leung Chun-ying, widely disliked, is publicly unimpressive but is almost a paradigm of the ideal for Beijing: an administrator who takes orders. His predecessor, Donald Tsang Yam-kuen, was a distinctly capable technocrat but, due to the recent conviction for malfeasance in office, finds himself in a jail cell in Stanley Prison, praying that his lawyers can come up with a miracle. The first post-handover chief executive, Tung Chee-hwa, was booted out by public pressure in

2005. Wile he remains civically active and in Beijing carries on as vice-chairman of the Chinese People's Political Consultative Conference, he was also far more of an administrator than a leader.

It's a near certainty that none of Hong Kong's first three chief executives will be crowned by history as great Chinese leaders, in the company of Zhu Rongji, Zhou Enlai and others.

Accordingly, Carrie Lam would seem to fit nicely into this unthreatening tradition of mediocrity – as John Tsang very well might not. "Don't rock the boat" is the course Beijing wants. But probably what it will get instead is the opposite: endlessly turbulent political waters that will sink a hapless Lam, as they have Leung and Tung.

Since taking over in 2012, the Xi government has made a number of commendable decisions. This is not one of them. Is it too late to switch Beijing's fateful finger of favouritism to Tsang? For, in pushing Lam over Tsang, Beijing is playing a losing game. You'd hate to see Beijing make a major blunder in its custody of Hong Kong. But such appears to be looming. Please think this one through again, Beijing.

P.S. Of course the favourite won. I wish her only success, as would every American concerned with the future of Hong Kong. I also wish Beijing would listen to me more often. A critic of my work once described me as "Beijing-friendly". This was not incorrect. But Beijing rarely listens to anyone when it feels an issue of sovereignty is involved. In this case it did; by contrast, what I thought was at stake was Beijing's ability to trust all the people of Hong Kong with an issue of such symbolic importance.

AND THEN THERE'S...

"The typical person worldwide, in their role in civil society or the market, has small effect on my life, but that effect is positive. I am better off with that person than without them. Unfortunately, politics tends to change that. Politics threatens an ideal of mutual respect and regard."
– *Against Democracy,* by Jason Brennan, Princeton University Press, 2016

49

How the Xi-Trump summit can rebuild Sino-US trust and bring stability to the Korean peninsula

South China Morning Post, Monday, 27 March 2017

Tom Plate says erosion of mutual trust is the biggest obstacle to China and America jointly reducing tensions in East Asia, but the Florida summit offers their leaders a chance for change

RETROSPECTIVE:

Summits can be over-rated but never ignored. Some work out better than others; all deserve their day in the sun. We journalists are always tempted to simplify complex issues of international relations into contests of wills and personalities. For one thing, such a structure is easier to write; for another, it is easier to read. There is even a touch of validity to the technique: some issues can only be decided with the leaders at the top agreeing in mutual decision. Underlings simply cannot get the rock up the hill by themselves. It needs a very big push (or pull) from the top when the issue is a big one.

In the second term of Bill Clinton's presidency, and the reign of Jiang Zemin and Zhu Rongji, when both sides put economic engagement over geopolitical jiujitsu, overall trust levels between the US and Chinese governments seemed to be on an uptick. When China entered the World Trade Organisation – in 2001, just months into the George

W. Bush administration – the Clintonites had reason to feel they had made a bit of history. Bilateral ties seemed to be heading in a pragmatic direction. There was, between the two, a quantum of solace.

Some degree of trust is essential if the relationship is not to become dysfunctional. In western social science, the power of transactional trust is seen as central to social stability and economic efficiency. The very routine of habitually working together well can create its own positivity, a sort of social currency or bonus human capital. Clinton's ace trade negotiator, Charlene Barshefsky, developed a close relationship with the exceptional Zhu, then China's premier, and she would fly to Beijing at his invitation to offer officials briefings on WTO intricacies. A bilateral bitcoin almost seemed in the minting.

These days, one key impediment in the all-important Sino-US relationship is the relative waning of mutual trust. After the US-ignited global meltdown of 2008–2009, Chinese reverence for the macro-economic wisdom, and probity, of Wall Street/Washington evaporated. And ever since the rise of President Xi Jinping and his pushy Pacific policy in the South China Sea, America's take on Beijing went from a little trust to lots of verify. Today, the bilateral bitcoin is battered.

Consider the divergence of viewpoints about the hot-headed, hot-wired and nuclearised North Korea. America's current policy thrust, says Foreign Minister Wang Yi, is nothing less than a "freight train" careering toward calamity. How alarmist? In Seoul , US Secretary of State Rex Tillerson issued threats: the military option is "on the table"; the US policy of "strategic patience" is history.

This was backed by his boss, who in a March 17 tweet trumpeted: "North Korea is behaving very badly. They have been 'playing' the United States for years. China has done little to help!" This is high school international relations.

Watch out: the Donald Trump administration might bluster into a 21st-century equivalent of the Cuban missile crisis. Beijing (and others across Asia) make a fair point when they wonder aloud why the US could live for decades with the capable Soviet nuclear threat, but can't tolerate North Korea's mini-arsenal. To be sure, everyone would be much less edgy if Pyongyang could be induced to downshift to non-nuclear; and surely only China working with the US, as well as with Seoul and Tokyo, can make the near-impossible happen.

But maybe it's too late for that – let's just blame China, right? Certainly one gets from US media scant sense that Xi might also have a point in his bitterness about the US anti-missile system being installed in South Korea. The THAAD (Terminal High-Altitude Area Defence) system is designed to knock down North Korean (or even, presumably, Chinese) missiles. The whole thing smells of US military-industrial complex run amok. The installation will render the Korean peninsula less stable (and perhaps inspire Beijing to counter with new systems of its own) – for the installation could theoretically create opportunity for the US to put a first-strike option "on the table": vaporise 90–95 per cent of North Korean missile sites and assume THAAD will corral the retaliatory rest.

The South's front-running presidential candidate Moon Jae-in, of the centre-left Minjoo Party, says hold off on missile-defence deployment for the moment. His South Korea benefits enormously from trade with the mainland.

Then again, if THAAD proves a dud (hardly inconceivable with these complex systems), then its installation would have done nothing at all to protect South Korea – except to further spook Pyongyang and Beijing, and ratchet up a missile arms race. Caught in this mess are US friends the South Koreans, now scampering to find a new president; and US friends the Japanese, who have everything they need

to become a nuclear power – except public support. Yet the hawkish administration of Prime Minister Shinzo Abe might get exactly that if the North Korean cowboys continue their missile-shot practice, their paranoia magnified by the macho US-South Korean ground exercises. Xi, who next month travels to Mar-a-Lago in Florida for a weekend summit with Trump, has a few cards he might play.

For starters, his government could call off the nationalists hounding South Korean businesses due to their government's US missile alliance. This infantile nonsense is beneath the dignity of China, a great and historic power, and does little to enhance trust in East Asia.

For its part, the US might say it views Beijing's overall presence in the South China Sea more like that of the US in the Caribbean than that of Russia in Crimea, and agree with Xi that a US signature on a non-aggression pact with Pyongyang would be much less harrowing than a nuclear missile crisis – as even Tokyo has been nervously muttering under its breath.

Xi could use some face to show North Korean leader Kim Jong-un that a nuclear freeze is a must if the regime-change option is to drop off the White House table. These gestures would help add to a sense of trust to US-China relations.

Even more detrimental than the imbalance of trade in the bilateral relationship is the imbalance of trust. It needs to be put right.

P.S: China doesn't want a unified Korea and the US, with 30,000 troops in the South, doesn't want a nuclearised North Korea. If the US unilaterally pulled its troops out of the South – but kept an aircraft carrier group bobbing in the seas nearby – might the Chinese re-calculate the equation and make a different decision in its national interest?

AND THEN THERE'S...

"Both Chinese and American contributors point to domestic factors as an important element in deepening mutual mistrust and suspicion and making it harder for leaders to forge common ground. They identify a number of factors that constrain the actions of leaders – including the nature of the decision-making processes in each country and the roles of interest groups and the military. These concerns should not lightly be dismissed. The past 20 years have seen disappointment in both countries that the relationship has not progressed to the level that many hoped. Despite the extraordinary intensity of the engagement between the two sides, both informed and casual observers see signs of trouble – a potential spiral (to use the process identified by both Wang Shuo and Christopher Twomey) that, if left untended, could see a deterioration in the relationship that might, in the worst case, actually lead to conflict. A relationship that started out on such an optimistic note on both sides at the beginning of the Obama administration has faced tensions on a myriad of issues ranging from Taiwan and Tibet to the Copenhagen climate change summit, North Korea, cyber-intrusions, and the proper role of multilateral institutions in the South China Sea."
– *Debating China: The U.S-China Relationship in Ten Conversations*,
   by Nina Hachigian, Oxford University Press, 2014

50 | WHY THE US NEEDS CHINA TO SUCCEED, AND VICE VERSA

SOUTH CHINA MORNING POST, MONDAY, 10 APRIL 2017

Tom Plate says whether to cooperate or not isn't really a choice when survival is at stake for the US, China and the rest of the world

RETROSPECTIVE:

Of all the many truly wise quotations in this book – and as you now see from the columns and the "And Then There's…" that we are blessed with many thoughtful scholars and journalists – it may be that Oscar Wilde might just win the Quotation Prize. As you will read below, in his book, *The Picture of Dorian Gray,* he writes: "The way of paradoxes is the way of truth. To test reality we must see it on the tightrope." The tightrope in our case – especially for those of us who care deeply about the relationship between China and the US – is the bilateral. No two countries needing each other to such a profound degree share such an intensity of tension that so easily could push the planet off of the tightrope of world order and down into apocalypse. This is the great paradox of our time.

Last week, the 45th president of the United States paid proper tribute to the People's Republic of China – which, by the way, would have been a whirlwind week for the Trump administration even without the big-deal dinner for leader Xi Jinping. And though the summit venue was the annoyingly opulent *tuhao*-class Mar-a-Lago resort in Florida, it was otherwise calming on the nerves to observe our often off-key Donald Trump saying and doing, for once, the right thing.

Trump was in celebrity toasting mode at the Mar-a-Lago show. With his wife Melania at his side, he rightly praised the "incredibly talented" Peng Liyuan, President Xi's wife, and steered clear of the phoney-baloney "free and frank exchange of views" verbiage to characterise his "long discussion" with Xi, from which talks, he quipped, "I have gotten nothing, absolutely nothing." For once, the joke was not on Trump, whether or not he was joking.

China, as even the disturbingly unschooled Trump understands, has arrived. To put the matter bluntly (and to put aside for now the US strike on Syria), China is no ordinary nation, and, with all due respect to Japan and its extraordinary place in the world, America's relationship with China is its single most important bilateral relationship.

But their histories are so different. "It is scarcely appreciated in the West today," writes journalist Howard French in his refreshing and utterly essential new book, *Everything Under the Heavens: How the Past Helps Shape China's Push for Global Power*, "that the 'international system' we so readily take for granted is actually a recent creation. It took shape between the middle of the nineteenth and the middle of the twentieth centuries, and started to be cobbled together at the precise moment that China was being subjugated by others and the world order it had sustained."

The new international system is now working its way into our lives, and change can be upsetting. Many Americans worry about China and some even insist war is inevitable. This is not going to happen. Neither China nor the US will ever invade the sovereign territory of the other. Such primitivism would be nonsensical. There is a no valid reason, neither ideological nor geopolitical, to justify war. It would be a stupidity – a plunge into a black hole of insanity. Both would be morally guilty of world endangerment, and both governments would reveal themselves as pathetically incompetent.

An enduring, high level of cooperation between the two giant powers is the only intelligent way forward if the species itself is not to be endangered by the lowest level of international non-cooperation: nuclear war.

Yet, I suppose anything is possible. For example (and I found this personally hard to stomach), some in the US media rushed to praise the US missile strike on a Syrian airfield with near-war lust – dropping their independent, critical role as if it were a false front all along. This cheerleading was so depressing – reminiscent of the media's go-go lust in 2003 for the Iraq invasion.

On live TV broadcasts, one media figure celebrated the Tomahawk launches as "beautiful pictures at night"; another gushed "there is much to applaud in President Trump's decision to attack the Assad regime…" The warmongering instinct of our media is not its finest trait and is sometimes frightening.

Many Chinese believe their nation is the new big thing and the United States is a big old thing. Some Americans agree – that the US is declining (in the phrase of Joseph Nye in his nifty book, *Is the American Century Over?*) while China (in the phrase of Joseph Nye in his nifty book, *Is the American Century Over?*) is "recovering". Both sides are only half right, and this is the paradox of today's emerging world order. To borrow from Oscar Wilde in his book, *The Picture of Dorian Gray*: "The way of paradoxes is the way of truth. To test reality we must see it on the tightrope."

In the present case, the tightrope is China and the US trying to stay on a balanced message. China is rising, obviously, but any serious loss in economic ground speed will cause the superliner to stall. Any crash would be devastating, and not just in Asia. And while America is not declining (in my opinion), it is in a kind of holding pattern – lumbering along in contrast to China's returning to its ancient vigour.

When, if ever, will China "overtake" the US? Certainly not tomorrow: China's population is ageing while America's is freshened by immigration.

The two political systems are deeply flawed: the former often moves too rigidly under central command; the latter will freeze up due to constitutional fragmentation and two-party uncivil war. Each in its own way is dysfunctional and semi-effective. The consequences of Chinese "stall" and American "stasis" would suck the life out of the global economic bloodstream. It is thus in the core national interests of both China and the US to help one another if others are to thrive as well.

This positivistic geopolitical proposition is not shared widely enough in either country. The opposite view is all too common. This would mean that both sides, in effect, should root for the other to fail. This could add up to a doomsday machine – triggering world collapse, maybe even a world war.

The Sino-US relationship hangs on the tightrope of a paradox. To keep from slipping off, each needs the other to succeed to maintain balance. Instead of leading to war, the challenge is to keep the geopolitical equipoise steady. Only a balance of mutual need can solidify the peace – and undergird a new world order.

P.S: I am happy that this 50th column in the great South China Morning Post newspaper comprises the final column in this book. Perhaps a second edition of **Yo-Yo Diplomacy** *will require a concluding chapter. But we have covered so much ground, touched on so many issues, that it is best for your author to say goodbye for now, and leave you with this special concluding column — and a pair of profound thoughts from two of the smartest thinkers in print. One is from Harvard, the other from Heaven. While there is a very vast difference between these two entities, to be sure, wisdom is wisdom, wherever it comes from.*

AND THEN THERE'S...

" ... Too much fear can be self-fulfilling. Whether the United States and China will manage their well is another question. Human error and miscalculation are always possible. But, with the right choices, a regional war is not inevitable, and the rise of China globally is a long process that is still far from signifying the end of the American century."
— *Is the American Century Over?*, by Joseph S. Nye Jr.,
  Polity Press, 2015

NOT TO MENTION:

"Ruin from Heaven
we can weather
Ruin from ourselves
We never survive"

– from the *'t'ai Chia'*, as quoted in *Mencius,* translated by David
   Hinton, Counterpoint (Perseus Books Group), 1998

BIBLIOGRAPHY

Bader, Jeffrey A. 2012. *Obama and China's Rise: An Insider's Account of America's Asia Policy*. The Brookings Institute, Washington, D.C.

Baum, Richard. 2010. *China Watcher: Confessions of a Peking Tom*. University of Washington Press.

Bremmer, Ian. 2015. *Superpower: Three Choices for America's Role in the World*. Penguin Publishing Group.

Brennan, Jason. 2016. *Against Democracy*. Princeton University Press.

Brown, Kerry. 2016. *CEO, China: The Rise of Xi Jinping*. I. B. Tauris Company.

Cha, Victor D. 2016. *POWERPLAY: The Origins of the American Alliance System in Asia*. Princeton University Press.

Cheng, Li. 2016. *Chinese Politics in the Xi Jinping Era: Reassessing Collective Leadership*. Brookings Institution Press.

Cohen, Warren I. 2000. *America's Response to China: A History of Sino-American Relations*. Columbia University Press.

Delury, John and Schell, Orville. 2013. *Wealth and Power: China's Long March to the Twenty-First Century*. The Random House Publishing Group.

Falk, Richard A., Juergensmeyer, Mark, and Popovski, Vesselin. 2012. *Legality and Legitimacy in Global Affairs*. Oxford University Press.

Funabashi, Yoichi. 2007. *The Peninsula Question: A Chronicle of the Second Korean Nuclear Crisis.* Brookings Institution Press.

Galen Carpenter, Ted and Dorn, James A. 2000. *China's Future: Constructive Partner or Emerging Threat?.* CATO Institute.

Hachigian, Nina. 2014. *Debating China: The US-China Relationship in Ten Conversations.* Oxford University Press.

Hayton, Bill. 2014. *The South China Sea: The Struggle for Power in Asia.* Yale University Press.

Hinton, David. 1998. *The 'I'ai Chia', as quoted in Mencius.* Counterpoint (Perseus Books Group).

Jacques, Martin. 2009. *When China Rules the World: The End of the Western World and The Birth of a New Global Order.* The Penguin Press.

Lampton, David M. 2001. *Same Bed, Different Dreams: Managing US-China Relations 1989–2000.* University of California Press.

Navarro, Peter. 2015. *Crouching Tiger: What China's Militarism Means for the World.* Prometheus Books.

Nye Jr., Joseph S. 2015. *Is the American Century Over?.* Polity Press.

Polumbaum, Judy with Xiong Lei. 2008. *China Ink: The Changing Face of Chinese Journalism.* Rowman & Littlefield Publishers.

Pomfret, John. 2016. *The Beautiful Country and the Middle Kingdom: America and China 1776 to the Present.* Henry Holt and Company.

Ringen, Stein. 2016. *The Perfect Dictatorship: China in the 21st Century.* Hong Kong University Press.

Sanger, David E. 2009. *The Inheritance: The World Obama Confronts and the Challenges to American Power.* Harmony Books (Random House).

Shambaugh, David. 2013. *China Goes Global: The Partial Power.* Oxford University Press.

Shambaugh, David. 2016. *China's Future*. Polity Press.

Shenkar, Oded. 2006. *The Chinese Century: The Rising Chinese Economy and Its Impact on the Global Economy, the Balance of Power, and Your Job*. Wharton School Publishing.

The writers, artists and editors of the South China Morning Post and edited by Sharp, Jonathan. 2013. *The China Renaissance: The Rise of Xi Jinping and the 18th Communist Party Congress*. World Scientific Publishing.

White, Hugh. 2013. *The China Choice: Why We Should Share Power*. Oxford University Press.

Wise, David. 2011. *Tiger Trap: America's Secret Spy War with China*. Houghton Mifflin Harcourt Publishing Company.

Wittenmyer, Terry D. 2015. *Fearing China, Asking the Question: Should We Fear China?*. Zebra CAT Publishing.

Xi, Jinping. 2014. *The Governance of China*. Foreign Languages Press.

Zhu, Rongji. 2011. *Zhu Rongji Meets the Press*. Oxford University Press.

INDEX

1644–1911 Qing Dynasty   160

1929–1939 Great Depression   262

2008–2009 Global depression   28, 211, 248, 282

1962 Cuban Missile Crisis   80

1982 Law of the Sea   191, 192

1989 Chinese Democracy movement   49

1989 Tiananmen Square   80, 151, 158, 246

1995–1996 Taiwan Strait Crisis   104

1996 Taiwan presidential election   104

1997 Asian financial crisis or "Asian Contagion"   59, 60, 247

1997 Hong Kong handover   100, 103, 128, 148, 180, 247, 276

2001 Hainan Island incident   214

2002 America & Iraq   268

2003 Iraq invasion   288

2008 Bush bubble   133

2000 Olympics   123

2009 Copenhagen Climate Summit   163

2009 Nobel Peace Award   124

2015 Paris Climate agreement   254

2016 Nobel Peace Prize   124

2016 United States presidential election   105

2017 Building Bridges   272

2017 Semi-election chief executive of Hong Kong   276

2017 World Economic Forum   251

A

ABC Radio   216

Academy of Military Science   154

Adam Smith   131

Admiral Harry B. Harry Jr.   242

Agence France-Press   252

Agent Orange   220

aggressive diplomacy   215

Air Force One   212, 252

Air-Sea Battle Concept   227

Al Gore   183, 277

Al-Qaeda   133

Alaska   79

Albert Camus   183

Albert Einstein   219, 229

Alibaba Group   14

All-China Journalists Association   119

America   75 (see also *United States*)

America First   257, 259

America Second   257

America's ignorance   113

American campaign   92

American consumer boycott   168

American democracy   29

American diplomacy   237, 238

American journalists   81, 85, 254

American politicians   203

American politics   258

American presidential campaign   108, 229

American public   60, 192

American Tea Party   273

American trade policy   262

Anatole Kaletsky   28

Andrew Nathan   122

Anti-American   178 , 223

Anti-China   70, 168, 196, 197, 238,

anti-China campaign rhetoric 89

anti-communism 25

anti-corruption campaign 70, 122, 123, 124, 159

anti-earth emissions 88

anti-Singapore 83

anti-social network of violence 152

Argentine Republic 169

Aristotle 235

Arkansas 67

art of the deal 88, 90, 97

Article 23, Basic Law 128

Article 3 63

Asia 74, 75, 78, 213, 218,

Asia Media International 155

Asia Pacific region 140, 201, 215

Asian arms race 178

Asian authoritarian 102

Asian currencies 132

Asian diplomacy 225

Asian financial crisis 93, 131, 133

Asian Infrastructure Investment 99

Asian multiculturalism 111

Assad regime 288

Association of Southeast Asian nations (ASEAN) 108, 111

Atlantic Ocean 215

atomic bombing 172

Australia, Commonwealth of 216, 242

Australia National University 74

authoritarianism 29, 82, 85, 158, 207

B

Balanchine ballet 60

Ban Ki-moon 78, 117, 163, 164, 172, 271, 272, 275

Bangkok 132

Bangladesh, People's Republic of 138

bank 99

Bank of China 74

Barack Obama 47, 48, 79, 87, 108, 109, 121, 137, 139, 140, 1 61, 167, 168, 171, 172, 201, 210, 212, 214, 219, 243, 258, 260

Barack Obama administration 104, 173, 190, 241, 285

Barry Eichengreen 93, 94

Barry Posen 109, 110

Basic Law 148

BBC 184

Beethoven 20

Beijing 14, 64, 67, 68, 69, 70, 75, 77, 78, 79, 87, 104, 105, 110, 129, 132, 141, 142, 149, 150, 154, 157, 166, 167, 169, 178, 181, 190, 196, 207, 210, 215, 223, 224, 240, 247, 251, 272, 276, 277

Beijing blueprint 30

Beijing celebration 78

Beijing Consensus 29, 30

Beijing financial authorities 131

Beijing-friendly 280

Beijing's Chaoyang District 163

Beijing's national security 142

Benigno Aquino 225, 226

Bernie Sanders 136, 137, 140

Beyonce 20

bilateral relations 111, 220, 228, 266,

bilateral tensions 178

Bill Clinton 49, 67, 90, 238, 240, 252, 267, 281

Bill Clinton administration 132, 178

Bill Hayton 155

binary conceit 28

binary thinking 2 9

Black prisons 147

blocking Internet 158

BMW 114

Bob Dylan 124

brain-washing 85

British 90, 201

British colonial government 277

British government 97, 100

British imperialists 154

British Museum, London 99

British pound 132

British-Chinese relations 99, 100

Brooks Brothers 251

Brunei, Nation of 152

Buckingham Palace 98

C

California 180, 269

California economy 202

Californians 269

Cambodia, Kingdom of 225

Cambodia bombing 138

capitalism 71, 185, 188, 187

Captain James Kirk 215

Caribbean 107, 215, 243, 284

Carnegie Endowment for International Peace 80

Carrie Lam Cheng Yuet-ngor 276, 277, 279

Catholic 142

Causeway Bay bookstore 127, 183

Central Party School 69, 168

Central People's Government 128

Centralized Southeast Asian government 82

Centre for Strategic and International Studies in Washington 242

Charlene Barshefsky 282

Charles Wolf Jr. 30, 248

Chelsea Clinton 252

Cheng Li 189

Cheong Yip Seng 84

China (see also *People's Republic of China*)

China Central Television 120

China Daily 210

China Global TV Network 249

China-North Korea relations 273

China Policy Programme 206

China Radio International 120

China-Russia relations 250

China's public diplomacy 211

Chinese civilization vs. the rest 154

Chinese Confucianism 123

Chinese diplomacy 62, 215, 226, 244,

Chinese domestic issues 130

Chinese dream 231

Chinese economy 60, 133, 134, 168, 181, 248, 250

Chinese elite 211, 220

Chinese exports 202

Chinese financial market 94

Chinese financial stock market 57, 126

Chinese foreign ministry 102

Chinese government 58, 59, 60, 192, 236, 245, 247, 253, 254

Chinese journalism 61

Chinese labour 202

Chinese leadership 71

Chinese mainland government 180

Chinese media 126

Chinese military 168

Chinese national mentality 257

Chinese nationalism 202

Chinese naval 64, 90

Chinese party 245

Chinese People's Political Consultative Conference 279

Chinese policymakers 93

Chinese political system 196

Chinese public relations 251

Chinese renminbi 70, 92, 94, 95, 132, 134, 183

Chinese socialism 186

communist China 151, 154

Communist Party of China 23, 65, 79, 97, 98, 150, 180, 185, 202, 205–207, 210, 211, 273, 276

China debate 68

China policy 69, 248, 260

China question 113, 114, 137

Chris Patten 182

Christopher Twomey 285

Chungsha Islands (Macclesfield Bank) 153

CIA 197, 225, 231, 269

CIA agents 269

clash of perspectives 151

Climate Change summit 285

climate deal 174

Clinton 72, 129, 168, 169, 221, 226, 252, 253

Clinton administration 90, 233

CNN 144

Cold War 15, 88, 111, 115, 138, 151, 171, 175, 223, 275

Columbia University 122

communism 122, 185

communist 24, 38, 71, 89, 142, 247

communist atheist 123

communist government 60

communists 114

Condoleezza Rice 161, 163, 164

Confucian 29, 124

Congress 264

Controlled media 179

Copenhagen 162, 285

Cornell Law School 237

Cornell-University 205

Corruption 29, 40, 70, 86, 187, 210

Corruption campaign 211

cosmopolitan 151, 254

cosmopolitan politics 208

Council on Foreign Relations 232

Courtis Global & Associates 143

Crimea 284

crisis 80

Cuban missile crisis 283

cult of Xi 158

Cultural Revolution 119

currency manipulation 96

currency speculation 132

cyber warfare agreement 88

cyber-intrusions 285

D

Dalai Lama 239

Dante's Inferno 109

David Beckham 98

David Cameron 201

David E. Sanger 275

David Hinton 290

David Laventhol 21

David M. Lampton 96

David Shambaugh 120, 125, 130, 140, 150,
   165, 206, 207

David Wise 170

Davos 134, 251, 252

deal diplomacy 244

Defence White Paper 64

Degas 234

Democratic nominee 108

Democratic Party 258

Democratic People's Republic of Korea (DPRK)
   85, 144, 157, 159, 232, 259, 266, 268, 269,
   270, 273, 284, 285

   ICBM 268

   nuclear buildup 215, 282

   imports 273

   missile 283

Democratic Progressive Party (DPP) 105

Deng Xiaoping 55, 80, 100, 122, 128, 149,
   158, 180, 181, 182, 183, 189, 202, 219

Deng Xiaoping Theory 51

Dennis Blair 214

deterrence argument 174

dictatorship 81, 275

diplomacy 65, 117, 142

Disneyland 87

dollars 94, 95

Domestic pressures 198

Donald Gregg 16, 269

Donald J. Trump 61, 67, 68, 72, 73, 96, 109,
   112, 113, 114, 134, 141, 156, 166, 167, 168,
   169, 170, 209, 220, 227, 233, 235, 236, 237,
   239, 241, 243, 249, 251, 252, 253, 258, 259,
   261, 264, 267, 284

Donald J. Trump administration 236, 262,
   283, 286

Donald Rumsfeld 262

Donald Tsang Yam-kuen 274, 278

Doomsday 171, 174

Dow Jones 73

Dr. Ben Carson 112

Dr. Charles Wolf Jr. 69, 70, 71

drones 147

Dutch 197

Dwight Eisenhower 238

E

E. B. White 36, 176

earth emissions 88

East & South China Seas 64

East Asia 53, 54, 55, 79, 144, 191, 226, 238,
   243, 268, 269, 272, 281, 284

East Asia and the West 78, 79

East China Sea 54, 89, 168

East West Centre of Honolulu 119

ecological protectionism 187

economic development 82

economic elite 123

economic failure 76

economic scientism 33

Election Committee 277, 278

electoral college vote 238

electoral democracy 218

elite group 187, 277
Eric Hobsbawn 26, 28
Ernest Bloch 40
ethical political journalism 42
Europe 197, 233
European journalists 252
Ezra F. Vogel 122

F

Facebook 151
Falklands 169
financial markets 94
Financial World 133
First Amendment 126
First World 44
First World War 20, 41
Five Principles of Peaceful Coexistence 150
Florida 284, 287
Florida summit 281
foreign aid 70
foreign exchange transactions 94
foreign policy 113, 138, 166, 167, 115, 218, 241
foreign relations 198
Fortune Magazine 182
Fr. Randy Roche 12, 13
French Republic 155
free market 59
free market economics 71
free speech 148
freedom 82
freedom of the press 184
Fu Cong 147, 149
Fudan University, Shanghai 155

G

G20 summit 212
gardening metaphor 221, 222
General Douglas MacArthur 144
Geneva 147, 190
geopolitics 70, 107, 193, 204, 218, 223, 225, 229, 230, 281
geopolitical regression 202
geopolitical solar system 34
geopolitical stability 90

George H. W. Bush Sr. 16, 67, 72, 88, 171, 244, 267, 270
George Orwell 42, 64
George Schultz 220, 221
George Soros 131, 132, 133, 134
George W. Bush 109, 183, 238, 262, 277
George W. Bush administration 282
George Washington University 206
George Yeo 34, 74
Georgetown's School of Foreign Service 214
Gerard Ford 139
Germany, Federal Republic of 179
global financial architecture 133
global governance 164
global greenhouse gas emissions 162
global media 236
gglobalisation 202, 251, 252, 253
Goh Chok Tong 205
Gordon Chang 205
government media relations 84
Graham Allison 143
Great Britain 98, 155
Great Depression 257
Great Wall of China 64, 98
Greg Autry 262
Gregorian calendar 246
Grenada 200
Guantanamo prison 147
gun violence 147

H

Hague court 192
Hague tribunal 242
Han society 186, 187
Hangzhou 212
Hanoi 103, 193
Hans Schattle 155
hard-line 266
Harold Macmillan 99
Harry Harris 214, 215
Harry S. Truman 48, 87, 172
Haruki Murakami 173, 174
Harvard Kennedy School 60, 214
Harvard University 22, 122, 137, 152, 188

Harvard's Belfer Center research   143

Hawaii   90

Henry Kissinger   80, 92, 136, 137, 138, 139

Hilary Putnam   152

Hillary Clinton   108, 113, 136, 137, 138, 139, 166, 177, 201, 219, 220, 224, 227, 233, 238, 277

Hiroshima   167, 171, 172, 173

history   213

Hitler   85

Hollywood   133, 240

Hong Kong   14, 59, 96, 123, 126, 129, 132, 146, 147, 149, 150, 187, 256, 273, 276

   election   277

   election proposal   84

   justice system   274

   legislature   50

   Hongkongers   77

   Hong Kong Bookseller Case   126, 180, 181 (see also *missing booksellers* and *Causeway Bay bookstore*)

   Hong Kong dollar 134

   Special Administrative Region   128

Hu Jintao   88, 105, 176, 177, 178, 179, 182

Hugh White   74, 175, 227

human rights   24, 67, 137, 148

humanitarian neo-socialism   187

Hunan   101

Hundred Years (War)   20

I

Ian Bremmer   116, 203, 208

immigration   289

inauguration of Donald J. Trump   238, 256, 258

Incontinental ballistic missile (ICBM)   268

India, Republic of   199

India's Nehru   181

inequalities   187

international relations   281

intellectual elite   123

international climate control   259

international court ruling   194

international currency system   95

international financial crisis   66

international ignorance   115

international law   191, 192, 194, 242

international markets   132

International Monetary Fund (IMF)   132

international politics   129, 190

international press   252

international rules   190

Iowa   249

Iran nukes   259

Iranian pact   253

Iraq, Republic of   192, 269

Ireland   83

Iron Lady   100

Isaiah Berlin   50, 219

Islamic State   220

Islamist extremism   113, 152

issue of sovereignty   280

Istana   278

J

J. William Fulbright   24, 198

Jacques Derrida   188

James A. Baker   88, 244

James A. Dorn   76

James Steinberg   238

Japan   78, 87, 107, 154, 160, 167, 168, 172, 179, 190, 243, 283

   Japan Self-Defence Forces   63

   Japanese, the   268

   Japanese aggression   154

   Japanese diplomacy   62

   Japanese economy   53, 94

   Japanese foreign policy   55

   Japanese yen   94

Jason Brennan   280

Jesuit   13

Jiang Zemin   98, 281

Joerg Rieger   188

John Delury   50, 86, 101

John F. Kennedy   80, 147, 203, 237, 238

John Hopkins University   240

John Pomfret   135

John Tsang Chun-wah   276, 277, 279

John Wayne   270

Joint Chiefs of Staff   80

Jonathan Schell 42
Joseph S. Nye Jr. 288, 290
Joseph Tsau 14
journalists 234, 261, 281
Judy Polumbaum 61, 106, 184
Junichiro Koizumi 54
Jürgen Habernas 117, 118

K

Kaiser Wilhem II 41
Karl Marx 59, 99, 251
Keith Harper 147
Kenneth Courtis 143
Kerry Brown 196, 222, 255, 260
kidnapping 147
Kim Jong-il 275
Kim Jong-un 156, 272, 275, 284
King's College, London 196
Kishore Mahbubani 34, 99, 259
Klingons 215
Kofi Annan 163
Korean Peace Foundation 275
Korean peninsula 157, 271, 273, 275, 281, 283
Korean War 144
kowtow diplomacy 141
Kuala Lumpur 86
Kuala Lumpur airport assassination 272
Kuok Group 14
Kurt Campbell 211, 220, 238
Kuwait 84

L

LA World Affairs Council 214
Lao People's Democratic Republic 225
Las Vegas 133
Latin America 138
Law of Unintended Consequences 227
Lee Hsein Loong 83, 205
Lee Kuan Yew 80, 81, 82, 83, 85, 124, 204, 205, 219, 278
Lee Kuan Yew School of Public Policy 34, 84, 259
Leung Chun-ying 278, 279
Lhasa 239

Li Keqiang 58, 91
Li Zhaoxing 161, 163, 164
liberal capitalism 24
liberal-democratic governance 188
LIFE magazine 21
Lin Gu 61, 106
Lincoln 235
London 103
Long Island newspaper 21
Lord Palmerston 100
Los Angeles 118, 127, 181, 232, 240, 256
Los Angeles Times 15, 21, 85
Lowy Institute 242
Loyola Marymount University 12
Lunar New Year 95

M

Ma Ying-jeou 104, 124
Macao Special Administrative Region of the People's Republic of China 79, 146, 148
Magna Carta 99, 128
Mahathir Mohamad 59
Mainland Consensus 243
Malaysia 85, 152, 168, 225
Manila 64, 193, 197, 223, 224
Manila's case 192
Manila's foreign policy 225
Mao era 14
Mao Zedong or Mao Tse-tung 48, 70, 80, 81, 101, 128, 158, 159, 207, 224, 230
Maoist dictatorship 81
Maoist left 81
Mar-a-Lago 239, 284, 287
Margaret Thatcher 100, 169
Mark Juergensmeyer 194
Mark Landler 168
Mark Zuckerberg 151
Martin Heidegger 32
Martin Jacques 250
Marxism 185, 186, 187, 188
Marxist fundamentalism 39
Max Weber 139
media 60, 156, 164, 201, 233, 264, 269
Melania Trump 287

Methodist theologian   188
Mexico (United Mexican States)   141, 267
Michael Pillsbury   68, 69
Michael Suaine   80
Middle America   257
Middle East   99, 109, 220, 269
Middle Kingdom   39
militarism   78
military   80, 212
military forces   260
military hardware   215
military security   166
Minjoo Party   283
Mischief Reef   109
missile diplomacy   266
missing booksellers   147–148
MIT   109, 214
Moldova, Republic of   146
Mongolian Lawmakers   91
Monroe Doctrine   107
Moon Jae-in   283
Moscow   166
Mother China   149, 182
multilateral institutions   285
multinational corporations   69, 84
mutual trust   179

N

Nagasaki   172
Najib Razak   86
nanny state   83
Nansha Islands (Spratly)   153
Napoleon   265
Nascar   258
national censorship   151
National Intelligence   214
national isolationism   258
nationalism   81, 197, 198, 202, 251, 253, 257, 284
Nato's future   259
Naval Academy   214
Neiman Foundation of Harvard University   22, 149
Nelson Mandela   124
Neo-Marshall Plan   99

Neo-Marxist   187
neoliberal market economics   186, 187
Netherlands   196
new authoritarianism   234
new Cold War   154
new world order   289
New York   94, 162, 163, 164, 209, 233
New York newspaper   21
New York Review of Books   158
New York Times   85, 168
New York Times Beijing   76
New Zealand   84, 146
Newsday newspaper   21
Niccolò Machiavelli   73, 271
nihilism   40
Nina Hachigian   285
Nobel Peace Prize   121, 124, 137, 143, 208
Nobusuke Kishi   63
Noel Annan   50
North America   60
North American   257
Norway   84, 146, 205
nuanced policy   243
nuclear   201, 227, 268, 273
nuclear arms   171, 173, 253, 275, 270
nuclear ballistic-missile   263
nuclear disarmament   174
nuclear issue   254
nuclear missile crisis   284
nuclear policy   253
nuclear power   179
nuclear proliferation   157, 167
nuclear war   172, 174, 288

O

Obamas   224
Oded Shenkar   71
Oklahoma   73, 74
One China   243, 251, 254, 267
One country, two systems   128, 129, 147, 148, 149, 150, 180, 181, 184, 273
one-party communism   100
open-globe trading   251
oriental economist   93

Orville Schell   50, 86, 158

Oscar Wilde   31, 117, 286

Oval Office   259

Oxford University   214

P

Pacific   75, 127, 202, 229, 240

Pacific Century Institute   16, 44, 272

Pacific Command   214

Pacific Council on International Policy   44

Pacific Lake   10

Pacific policy   282

pacifism   63, 78

Paris   162, 164

Paris Accord   162

Paris Climate Change Agreement   161, 164

Paris Climate Control Protocol   162

Patrick E. Tyler   76

Paul Keating   216

Paul Merage School of Business   261

peace   78

Peace Memorial Ceremony Hiroshima   172

peace-journalism   19

peaceful development   150

peaceful rising   174

peaceful rising diplomacy   62

Pearl Harbour   214

Peloponnesian War   20

Peng Liyuan   98, 103, 287

Peng Xunhou   154

Peninsula's geopolitics   270

Pentagon   70, 79, 168, 232, 248

People's Action Party (PAP)   83, 84, 205, 207

People's Daily   102, 120, 134

People's Liberation Army (PLA)   39, 48, 64, 79, 80, 154, 276,

People's Republic of China (PRC)   73, 75, 77, 78, 79, 81, 87, 96, 99, 114, 126, 146, 147, 185, 192, 213, 237, 242, 263, 286 (see also *China*)

Permanent Court of Arbitration   191, 196, 225

Peter Navarro   167, 194, 261, 263, 264

Philip Clayton   187

Philippines, Republic of the   64, 90, 152, 168, 190, 191, 192, 194, 198, 218, 223, 224, 225

philosophers   81

philosophy's hypothesis of the Twin Earth   152

PLA military   124

PLA navy   108, 109, 110, 247

Politburo Committee   80

Politburo Standing Committee   211

political incorrectness   254

political leadership   122

political storm   276

political system   207

Pol Pot   137

Pope Francis   141, 142, 144

Pope's kowtow diplomacy   142

popular vote   238

positive geopolitics vs. negative geopolitics   289

Post-Mao   38, 196

postmodern Marxism   187

power-sharing   216

PowerPoint   70

PRC Consulate   102

US presidential campaign   219

US presidential candidates   70, 103

Press Freedom Committee of the Foreign Correspondents 'Club of Hong Kong   148

Princeton University   189

propaganda   178, 263

protectionist   257, 262

provincial pedagogy   151

public diplomacy   197, 253

public opinion   19

public policy   177

public politics   177

Pyongyang   157, 215, 266, 268, 272, 273, 274, 283, 284

Q

Qian Qichen   88, 119, 244

quantum theory   229

Quemoy and Matsu (Kinmen)   105

R

Rachel Carlson   42

racism   147

RAND   26, 68, 69, 70, 248

RAND Centre for Asia-Pacific Policy   269

RAND Corporation   70, 71

Reform Party   85

reformer   81

renminbi bonds   99

Republican   109, 113, 167, 168, 169, 209, 249, 264

Republican Party   258

Rex Tillerson   282

Richard Bookstarber   33

Richard Dennis Baum   37, 265

Richard Falk   189, 194

Richard Nixon   80, 137, 138, 139

Rockefeller   237

Rodrigo Duterte   223, 224, 225, 226

role of government   262

Roman Church   144

Rome   141

Ronald Reagan   238, 254

Rupert Murdoch   14

Russia & US nuclear armament leaders   174

Russia economy   250

Russian Federation   29, 114, 209, 249, 259, 284

S

S. R. Nathan   205

Salami slicing metaphor   194

Sanctions   157

Santa Monica   103

Scandinavian   186

Scandinavian parliamentary democracy   82

Second Global War   143

Second World War   78

Security Council   144, 147, 254

Selena Gomez   133

self-brain wash   25

self-deception   40

Self-Strengthening Movement   160

Seoul   132, 268, 269, 283

Shanghai   74, 119, 277,

Sheila Smith   54

Shinzo Abe   54, 63, 64, 65, 78, 166, 170, 267, 284

Shisha Islands (Paracel)   153

shorting campaigns   132

Sichian Daily Group   120

Silicon Beach   44

Silicon Valley   44

Silk Road   119

Singapore, Republic of   9, 29, 31, 74, 77, 81, 82, 84, 103, 104, 124, 146, 187, 195, 204, 205, 206, 208, 219, 246, 254

elections   2015 82, 83, 84, 85

system   85

foreign policy   207

Sino-US relations   17, 31, 45, 68, 71, 73, 74, 75, 88, 105, 113, 117, 118, 138, 178, 207, 227, 230, 238, 240, 241, 243, 247, 252, 267, 273, 281, 284, 286, 289

Sino-British relations   99, 100

Sino-Japanese Relations   53, 54, 55, 56

Sino-US cooperation   144, 161, 164

Sino-US diplomacy   89

Sino-US market   73

Sino-US tensions   241

Sino-US trust   281

Six-Party Talks   157

smart diplomacy   141

social media   84, 244, 239

social science   69, 213

socialism   185

soft authoritarianism   29, 204

soft-power   19, 149, 193, 213

South China Morning Post   9, 14, 15, 290

South China Sea   36, 89, 107, 108, 110, 111, 143, 144, 151, 152, 153, 154, 158, 168, 169, 178, 190, 191, 196, 197, 203, 214, 226, 241, 242, 243, 247, 282, 284, 285

South China Sea ruling   214

South Korea   155, 163, 268, 283

Southeast Asia   205

sovereign currencies   131

sovereignty   197

Soviet Empire   171, 220

Soviet nuclear threat   283

Soviet Union   15, 38, 114

Special Administrative Region (SAR)   59, 274, 276

Spencer H. Kim   269

Stalin   79, 235

Stanley Prison   278

Starfort Investment Holdings   143

State Department   232

Stein Ringen   81, 199, 230, 231

stock market   72, 131

Strategic Economic Dialogue, Annapolis, Maryland   135

Subic Bay   90

Sun Tzu   55

sunspot cycles   33

superpower   217, 225, 275

superpower seas   264

Susan Shirk   178

suzerainty   36, 37, 40

Swiss Alps village, Davos   252

Swiss military 252

Switzerland   192, 246

Sydney   242

Syrian Arab Republic   273, 288

T

Taipei   104, 154, 267

Taiwan   96, 103, 124, 129, 184, 224, 237, 238, 243, 244, 245, 254, 267, 278, 285

   Taiwan issue   243, 247

   Taiwan phone call   236, 238

   Taiwan politics   104

   Taiwan question   105

   Taiwan Strait   240, 243

   Taiwanese diplomacy   237

   Taiwanese voters   104

talk diplomacy   117

Ted Galen Carpenter   76

Telephone diplomacy   267

Terminal High Altitude Area Defence   215

Terry Branstad   249

Terry D. Wittenmyer   91, 217, 231

Texas   180, 267

THAAD (see *Terminal High Altitude Area Defence*)

Thai baht   57, 247

Thailand, Kingdom of   84, 127

"the butchers of Beijing"   67

The Don   177, 179

The Economist   158

The Hague   64, 196, 197

Theodore Sorensen   237

theory of the two suns   34

Theresa May   201

think tanks   27, 103, 118, 196, 233

Thomas Fargo   214

threat of nuclear doomsday   175

threat of nuclear war   171

Tibet   285

Ting Chee-hwa   59

Tokyo   78, 90, 167, 283

Tony Blair   99

totalitarianism   77

trade policy   264

trade-relations   259

Trans-Atlantic relationship   99

Trans-Pacific Partnership (TPP)   201

transnational communication   151

Treaty of Nanjing   154

Trump transition   238

Trump trap   255

Trumpian rhetoric   254

Tsai Ing-wen   105, 236, 237, 240, 267

Tung Chee-hwa   182, 278, 279

Tungsha Islands (Pratas)   153

twilight zone   148, 149

Twin Earth metaphor   154

Twitter   239, 267

U

UCLA   37

UN/US Forces   144

Uncle Sam   167, 224

unemployment   200

United Arab Emirates University in Al Ain   155

United Media Group of Shanghai   120

United Nations (UN)   83, 144, 157, 161, 162, 163, 164, 254, 269, 272

   bureaucracy   271

   UN Convention   191

   UN Court   154

   Framework Convention on Climate Change   162

   headquarters   163

   Human Rights Council   147

   Law of the Seas   90

   Permanent Court of Arbitration   64

   Secretary General   78

Security Council 162, 163

women at the UN 163 University of
    California, Berkeley 93, 167, 178

University of Cambridge 188

University of Irvine 261

University of Oxford 230

Uruguay, Oriental Republic of 83

United States (US) 74, 75, 79 (see also *America*)

    anti-missile system 283

    bombing Chinese embassy 49

    Council on Foreign Relations 54

    diplomacy 104, 243

    economy 133

    election 167, 234

    exports 201

    Federal Reserve 73

    financial quake 133

    foreign policy 136, 237, 238, 242

    Fourth Fleet 243

    housing collapse 134

    State Department 226

    tariffs against China 190

    institutions 264

    invasion of Iraq 247

    media 85, 88, 120, 126, 204, 209, 210,
        258, 283, 288

    military 105, 110, 214, 283

    missile strike 288

    national election 229

    Navy 62, 242

    Pacific Command 79, 109, 242, 243

    presidential campaign 73, 113, 137

    presidential debates 219

    presidential election 67, 68, 166, 192, 248

    presidential race 67

    public 108

    think tanks 248

    trade 90

    Treasury 131, 203, 220

    troops in Iraq 192

    US-British alliance 99

    US-China Strategic & Economic Dialogue
        53

    US-Japanese relations 63

US-Korea relations 270

US-North Korea relations 282

US-South Korea relations 284

USS Zumwalt 215

utility 82

Uygur 123

V

Vanuatu, Republic of 146

Vatican City State 141, 142

Vermont 137

Vesselin Popovski 194

Victor D. Cha 111, 245

Vietnam, Socialist Republic of 65, 114, 152,
    168, 198, 223, 225

Vladimir Nabokov 233, 234, 235

Vladimir Putin 209, 210, 211, 249

Voice of America 184

W

Waldorf Astoria Hotel 163

Wall Street 28, 95, 211, 226, 282

Wang Daohan 119

Wang Gungwu 39

Wang Qishan 12

Wang Shuo 285

Wang Yi 240, 282

War of Resistance 154

War-journalism 19

Warren Buffett 188

Warren Christopher 67, 266

Warren I. Cohen 101, 145

Washington D.C 75, 78, 79, 80, 94, 98, 103,
    109, 110, 174, 178, 197, 207, 214, 224, 233,
    242, 252, 257, 258, 262, 263, 268, 269, 272,
    275, 282

Washington Consensus 28, 243

Watergate 128

Wen Jiabao 135, 210

West 151

Western arrogance 196

Western capitalism 185

Western commentary 234, 273

Western domination 259

Western elites 69

Western financial advice   131

Western financial media   59

Western human rights   207

Western journalists   81

Western leaders   273

Western media   57, 58, 59, 60, 70, 85, 88, 158, 163, 177, 182, 247, 271, 276

Western powers   160

Western primitivism   202

Western speculators   132

Western strategies   131

Western-style democratic governance   186

White House   49, 65, 87, 114, 139, 169, 170, 171, 177, 224, 232, 233, 249, 261, 267, 284

White House National Trade Council   262

William Stanley Jevons   33

William Jefferson Clinton   98

William Safire   85

Williams College   188

Winston Churchill   99, 208

Worker's Daily   120

world domination   38

World Economic Forum   135, 251, 252

world media   127

world order   194

World Trade Organisation (WTO)   49, 190, 191, 281, 282

writers, artists, editors of the South China Morning Post and edited by Jonathan Sharp   160, 179

Wu Shengli   107, 109

Wuhan   148

X

Xi Jinping   49, 51, 58, 64, 66, 77, 78, 79, 81, 88, 91, 98, 102, 103, 104, 105, 121, 127, 128, 139, 142, 156, 158, 159, 161, 171, 176, 183, 185, 209, 211, 212, 230, 234, 235, 249, 259, 284, 287

Xi Jinping administration   109, 128, 167, 201, 239, 273, 277, 279

Xinhua News Agency   120, 134

Xiong Lei   61, 106, 184,

Y

Yale University   22, 188

Yang Jisheng   22, 149

yo-yo diplomacy   45, 267, 268

yo-yo syndrome   15

Yogi Berra   156

Yoichi Funabashi   270

Yokosuka   214

Yonsei University in Seoul   155

Z

Zbigniew Brzezinski   92, 95

Zhongnanhai   236, 237, 238, 240, 273

Zhou Enlai   279

Zhu Rongji   47, 49, 50, 56, 59, 132, 158, 179, 182, 202, 210, 240, 279, 281, 282

Zurich   252

GIVING THANKS

We start by honouring the work of Ms Clementine Todorov, a distinguished graduate of Loyola Marymount University in Los Angeles, who did just about everything for this book except write it. She kept my spirits up with smart questions; she even took on the horror of preparing the complex Index.

Further at LMU/Los Angeles: I thank Dean Robbin Crabtree for understanding me, Associate Dean Richard Fox for caring about me, Department Chair Prof Robin Wang for inspiring me, Senior VP Dennis Slon for drinking with me, Prof Jennifer Ramos for collaborating with me, Prof Stella Oh for her innovative spirit, Prof Michael Genovese for strategizing with me, and President Timothy Law Snyder for occasionally laughing with me.

Internationally, I also cherish the constant input on the columns from Ms Xu Wei Wei, a PhD candidate in Chinese media at the University of Sydney, and Ms Alice Wu, a former student of mine and dedicated student editor of Asia Media when its home had been UCLA; she is now a well-known political commentator and political consultant in Hong Kong. In Los Angeles, Ren Jifang, the head of the political office of China's Los Angeles Consulate, for her office's readiness to work with me to advance mutual understanding and for tossing around ideas for substantive cooperation.

I also greatly value the encouragement and trust of the management of the South China Morning Post, one of the world's most valuable newspapers, including and especially its razor-sharp opinion editors – Robert Haddow and Chan Tse Chueen. In this context, Robin Hu and Cheong Yip Seng are always helpful in providing context, sophistication and dimension to my thinking. And Spencer Kim, the endlessly energetic creator of the Pacific Century Institute, with its focus on building personal and institutional bridges between Asia and America, has helped kept my column alive by insisting that I never ever give it up.

China is a very difficult subject to get one's arms and mind around. To the slight extent that I may have, I need to thank the unofficial tutoring of the late Lee Kuan Yew; his former foreign minister, the incisive George Yeo; George's former foreign-service colleague, the diplomat and transformational intellectual Kishore Mahbubani, now dean of the dynamic Lee Kuan Yew School of Public Policy; the late, great American policy intellectual at RAND, Charles Wolf Jr., whose penetrating intellect invariably sharpened any conversation; a healthily competitive crew of journalistic and academic colleagues (many of them you will see quoted in this book) who write about China and whom I greatly respect; and Richard Falk, now living in gorgeous Santa Barbara after four decades as one of the most intellectually provocative and exceptional members of the Princeton University faculty. He was my Woodrow Wilson School of Public and International Affairs graduate thesis advisor. I was lucky.

Finally, regarding my Publisher of the last 10 years or so, Marshall Cavendish: For this book, senior editor Rachel Heng, so precise and easy to work with; and of course Mei Lin Lee, the associate publisher, who has been central to all my books with Marshall Cavendish, a wonderful publishing house.

ABOUT THE AUTHOR

Photograph by Harvey Keys

Tom Plate is a university professor, a veteran columnist focused on Asia and America, and an educational innovator. A Los Angeles resident, this full-time Clinical Professor and Distinguished Scholar of Asian and Pacific Studies at Loyola Marymount University has orchestrated live interactive seminars with major universities across Asia, as part of LMU's path-finding Asia Media International. He teaches courses on Asia, the United Nations and US Foreign Policy; and is the author of 13 books, including the bestsellers *Confessions of an American Media Man* (2007) and the "Giants of Asia" series, published by Marshall Cavendish. Born in New York, he was educated at Amherst College, where he was Phi Beta Kappa, and Princeton University, where he was awarded his professional degree in public and international affairs. He has received a number of journalistic recognitions, including from the American Society of Newspaper Editors, its Deadline Writing Award. For more details, please see: https://en.wikipedia.org/wiki/Thomas_Plate

ALSO BY TOM PLATE

The "Giants of Asia" series:

Conversations with Lee Kuan Yew

Conversations with Thaksin

Conversations with Mahathir Mohamad

Conversations with Ban Ki-moon

Other titles:

Confessions of an American Media Man:
What you find out after journalism school

The Fine Art of the Political Interview:
And the inside stories about behind the "Giants of Asia" conversations

In the Middle of China's Future:
What two decades of worldwide newspaper columns prefigure
about the future of the China-US relationship

In the Middle of the Future:
Contemporary history through a newspaper column